Power
&
manoeuvrability

Edited by Tony Carty and
Alexander McCall Smith

PRESS
EDINBURGH

Published by Q *Press Ltd*
58 Queen Street
Edinburgh EH2 3NS
Scotland

ISBN 0 905470 04 4

E 6551 1 2

Designed by Ruari McLean
Printed and bound by T & A Constable Ltd, Edinburgh
Set in Linotron Plantin

Contents

Editors and contributors

Tony Carty lectures on international law and relations at the University of Glasgow. He was formerly a lecturer in law at the University of Paris and an Alexander von Humboldt Fellow at the Max Planck Institute, Heidelberg. His articles and reviews on international relations have been published in various books and journals. He is also currently Foreign Law Adviser to the Highlands and Islands Development Board.

John Ferguson is a lecturer in Sociology at the University of Strathclyde and a free-lance journalist. He is author if a number of articles on the land question and is Consultant to the Highland Regional Authority.

Stephen Maxwell is a former fellow of the Royal Institute of International Affairs, London and for three years worked at the University of Edinburgh. He has lectured widely on politics and international affairs and is one of Scotland's best known political writers.

Dermot McAleese, after lecturing at the University of Ghana and Johns Hopkins University, returned to Ireland where he is now Dean of Graduate Studies at Trinity College, Dublin. Author of numerous monographs and articles on international trade, he has also published papers on industrial specialisation in small open economies.

Alexander McCall Smith lectures on comparative law at the University of Edinburgh, having formerly been a lecturer in Law and Jurisprudence at the Queen's University of Belfast. He is author of numerous articles in legal and philosophical journals, as well as in the press. In 1977 he was awarded a Chambers Literary Prize.

John Purvis, after graduating at St Andrews University, worked for ten years in international banking in New York, Milan, London and Edinburgh. He now runs his own consultancy firm based in St Andrews, specialising in advice on, *inter alia*, banking, foreign exchange and money markets.

Preface

The editors and contributors wish to record their gratitude to a number of people who have contributed to this book either with suggestions or valuable assistance on certain points, principally to Peter Cameron, who gave most valuable assistance in researching the history of the Labour Government's renegotiation after 1974 of the oil licences; to Alan Millar, who advised on the financial links between US oil majors, banks, and insurance companies; and, amongst others, to Grant Baird, Michael Counahan, Gavin Kennedy, Jim McGilvray, Donald MacKay, Tom Nairn, and Michael Spens. The Highlands and Islands Development Board enabled Dr Carty to visit nine Western European countries to discuss with them their rural land acquisition controls. Finally, invaluable help was given at all stages in the writing of this book by our publisher, Peter Chiene, who also generously hosted the conference of contributors.

Introduction

Tony Carty and Alexander McCall Smith

Today's small state is in some senses stronger than it has ever been and in some senses much weaker. It is stronger in the sense that a complex set of international norms has been developed to protect state sovereignty and an international forum is available to protect them. It is weaker in the sense that the domination of the world economy by interests largely beyond the reach of state control has led to a sustained threat to national sovereignty. Possibly it is also weaker because of the move towards multinationalism and larger political and military units, a move which is sometimes seen as justification for the questioning of the future existence of small, 'awkward' states.

Yet although the last century has seen a seemingly inexorable tendency towards political consolidation at the expense of the smaller political units, the remaining years of this century are likely to witness the widespread questioning of the rationale for large, multinational states, and a possible call for the small, culturally homogeneous state. Already this process has begun. In Europe and North America, resurgent nationalist movements aiming at the fragmentation of modern states, have posed considerable problems for the assumptions of national unity previously enjoyed by the states in question. Reaction to these movements has ranged from outright rejection to enthusiastic acceptance. In many cases their political opponents have labelled them as reactionary and simplistic manifestations of political discontent. Portrayed as chauvinistic and hostile to the ideal of international co-operation, these movements have been forced to contend with widespread misrepresentation. Yet any but the most cursory study of their political aetiology and complexion tends to reveal the inadequacy of such analyses. In most cases deeply democratic, the modern nationalist movements represent the aspirations of the small or the 'submerged' nations to establish their own political cultures. They have little in common with the aggressive nationalism which is rightly seen as a threat to peace.

This shallowness of much of the political reaction to the modern nationalist movements is fortunately in part countered by the efforts of serious scholarship to understand what lies behind the phenomenon of national resurgence. Numerous theories have been advanced. For some, like Patricia Mayo in *Roots of Identity*, a study of Breton, Basque and Welsh movements, modern nationalism is best understood as a response to the impersonality of modern centralist states and the failure of these states to provide the institutional means for the expression of identity.[1] Mayo writes from the point of view of the social scientist alarmed at the level of contemporary 'anomie', Hugh Seton-Watson in his Survey *Nations and States* takes the historian's view.[2] Yet he too hints at the same interpretation of the contemporary threat to the larger state. Modern controversies about the obsolescence of the 'nation state', he points out, usually assume that the weakening of current national loyalties will lead to the replacing of such loyalties by loyalties to larger units. The opposite phenomenon, however, may be regarded as equally credible — their replacement by narrower loyalties. This in many cases is what appears to be happening. The abandonment of a United Kingdom focus, for example, need not be replaced in the public mind by a European one; a regional loyalty is an equally feasible alternative. For Tom Nairn, who attempts to provide a Marxist analysis of nationalism in Scotland, Wales, and Northern Ireland, these national movements are best understood as the inevitable concomitant of the overdue demise of the British state.[3] Crucial to Nairn's thesis is the role of the unequal development of the peripheral regions of the United Kingdom, an idea which was also explored by Michael Hechter in his *Internal Colonialism*.[4]

The possibility of Scottish independence is today a very real one, largely dominating recent political debate in Scotland and precipitating the Westminster government into fairly radical constitutional concessions. The issue of Scottish independence is not a particularly novel one. The debate on Scotland's relations with England has been a continuing one since well before the Act of Union in the eighteenth century. The Union did not put the issue to silence, although Scotland participated with some enthusiasm in political union with the pre-eminent colonial power. There were, of course, signs of dissent and indications that the loss of national independence was resented. Walter Scott, for example, writes in his *Provincial Antiquities* that 'at the period of the Union every reader must remember the strong agitation which pervaded the minds of the Scottish nation, who could not, for many years, be persuaded to consider this incorporating treaty in any other view than as a wanton surrender of their national independence'. In the English view, the Union created an indissoluble political bond. England wanted, and seemed to achieve, one 'inseparable state governed by one and the same sovereign' (to use the words of the constitutional writers, Dicey and Rait).

From 1945 the assumptions of British political unity came under increasing challenge. Between 1967 and 1969, the Scottish National Party, the only major Scottish political party advocating independence, enjoyed a growing popularity, claiming in 1968 the largest party membership of any political party in Scotland. Electoral victories followed, as the party claimed the votes of an increasing number of disillusioned supporters of the pro-Union parties. The nature of this support was complex, and it is clear that not all of these voters supported independence, but its political significance was, and remains, considerable. Scottish independence, like its Quebec counterpart, is no longer a romantic notion widely considered irredentist; it is a distinct possibility calling for serious study.

The Scottish independence question is also of considerably wider significance and interest than the other current issues of domestic United Kingdom politics. The independence movements in Canada, Spain and Scotland all appreciate that in spite of their considerable differences they are part of the same overall phenomenon. In common they face the same fundamental questions: can a small state successfully detach itself from a larger unit and establish its independence? What will be the nature of this independence? Will it be illusory, as many former colonial countries feel their independence is, or will it be a real independence? In answering these questions there are no useful precedents. There is no case of a part of a large Western state with a highly developed economy seceding from a metropolitan region. The only guidance is that which can be had from an examination of the possibilities and an assessment of the dangers. That is what this book is about. The answers it attempts to provide are of relevance for cases other than that of Scotland, although Scotland is the principal case study.

The most obvious concern of those attempting to create small independent states is the problem of vulnerability. This question is already a feature of the Scottish debate and figures prominently in the arguments of the opponents of Scottish independence. According to this argument, even if Scotland were to attain its independence, its future would be largely determined in London. This is because the Scottish economy would continue to be intimately bound up in the economy of the remaining United Kingdom and decisions taken about the United Kingdom economy would therefore still affect Scotland. The metaphor which Pierre Trudeau used to describe what it is like to be the United States' weaker neighbour ('It's like sleeping with an elephant — every little twitch tends to be felt') is perhaps appropriate here. According to the pro-Union argument, there would be no real independence and Scotland would indeed be in a worse position in that it would not be able to participate directly in the decisions which would affect it. The economic side of this argument tends to stress the reliance of Scottish industry on United Kingdom orders and the dependence of Scottish financial institutions on English markets.

In these terms, the task of justifying Scottish independence is seen as falling on those who argue that a small Scottish state would not be measurably worse off than a Scotland which is part of the United Kingdom. Similarly, in Quebec the national movement must convince supporters of confederation that a Quebec detached from the rest of Canada would not be economically and politically vulnerable, an ideal candidate for United States satellite status. The questions of internal viability have, in Scotland's case, been widely canvassed, particularly in Professor Donald MacKay's *Scotland 1980.*[5] This book was concerned with the economic problems which an independent Scotland would face, with issues of industrial policy and restructuring. Our concern in this study is with the comparatively neglected issue of international relations, with the posing of the question of how Scotland would deal with the particular problems of international relations which would be expected to confront a small state in its position.

Obviously the direction taken by an independent Scotland in its relations with other states would depend to a large extent on the political complexion of the emerging state. Its willingness to combat external control, its attitude towards other Western European states — indeed its entire foreign policy stand will be determined by the perception of Scotland's international position of the new Scottish political establishment. The importance of foreign policy will, however, soon be brought home to Scottish politicians. As Tom Nairn points out, 'for small, struggling nationalities foreign relationships are always vital, and often decisive. Existence inside a decaying empire has blunted our sensibilities in this respect.'

For the purposes of this analysis we assume that any likely Scottish government will follow one of the patterns of existing Western European governments, and will fall somewhere along the spectrum between a socialist government with a pro-Third World stance (the Swedish model) and a cautious government of the democratic Right. In the absence of stronger evidence, Scotland's current political ethos and experience indicate an option somewhat closer to the former possibility than the latter. In British terms, such a government would be comparatively radical.

The form in which an independent Scotland emerged would no doubt influence the degree of radicalism it evinced. If the dissolution of the United Kingdom state is strident and contested, and an independent Scotland emerges in circumstances of discord, any comfortable predictions about the 'mixture as before' are likely to be proved wrong and the chances of a radical government are heightened. On the other hand, a smooth transition, negotiated and met with no great resistance, would diminish the degree of difference between the foreign policy standpoint of the new state and its predecessor. For our purposes, we have not chosen one specific option. We are concerned more with showing some of the options which could present themselves, and particularly how a radical Scottish government would find its freedom of action limited by international constraints.

The theme of manoeuvrability is thus central, as it is here that the reality or illusory nature of Scottish independence will be tested. Initially, the problem of manoeuvrability presents itself in relation to the political process of establishing the new state. How will such a state be greeted in Europe and North America? It is sometimes naïvely assumed that an independent Scotland would find willing allies in establishing its independence. As Stephen Maxwell points out (*Politics*), this is unlikely to be the case. Gloomy predictions of external intervention are improbable, but political support from within the EEC and from other independence movements will not necessarily be forthcoming. In the former case, the conflict of interest is obvious; in the latter, the identity of interest is not as strong as is sometimes supposed.

In establishing its independence, a process which Stephen Maxwell explores in detail, it is possible that exponents of Scottish independence will have recourse to a claim for Scottish 'self-determination'. The right of self-determination is a controversial one, particularly when applied to secession, and it is dubious whether the right as it is currently defined in international law could be claimed with much authority by Scottish politicians seeking to establish independence in the face of international opposition. Here the distinction between the position of a new Scottish state and that of the typical newly independent state would be quite apparent; the right of self-determination clearly applies in the case of the state seeking decolonisation.

Like the newly independent states of the Third World, though, Scotland would face problems of state succession which would significantly restrict its room for manoeuvre. Although the law in this area is currently undergoing revision, international law would define reasonably clearly certain limitations on the new state's freedom in respect of treaty obligations, membership of international organisations, property rights, debts and contractual obligations. Independence would not mean a completely clean slate in relation to Scotland's dealings with other states.

Following the emergence of the state and the ascertaining of the 'point of departure' which international law allows it, we examine four issues which allow for the exploration of the themes of power and manoeuvrability. One of the major pre-occupations of the small state is likely to be its natural resources, and we have chosen to examine two of these, land and oil, to illustrate how the small state can act to establish its independence of external control in the face of considerable pressure. Fisheries might have been as appropriate a choice in Scotland's case because of the obvious importance of fishing in the Scottish economy. Certainly the fisheries question poses major questions of manoeuvrability in international relations, particularly in respect of the conflict between claims to greatly increased zones and the principle of access favoured by the EEC. There have, however, been numerous studies of the fisheries problem and very many fewer of land. Consequently, as control of land purchase and usage has a very clear international dimension and raises questions of accepted standards of international behaviour, land is used to illustrate the process whereby the small state may act effectively to protect its more vulnerable interests. Assessing the current discouraging picture of land control in Scotland, the conclusion is reached that action can be taken which need not compromise Scotland's international position (*Carty and Ferguson*).

Less freedom of action is available in respect of oil. Here we are not concerned with how much oil there is or what could be done with the revenues. Nor are we concerned with deciding how much oil would go to Scotland or, for that matter, to Shetland. Instead this study is a case study of multinationals and the small state. The ground rules are uncertain; the OPEC revolution is not complete and nobody, even those in the oil industry, knows what the current standards are. If an independent Scotland decided to take a radical course (and there are reasons why it should want to do this), it would be challenging the oil majors in a way in which Norway did not. No Western government has to date faced the problem of bringing its oil regime into line with OPEC standards (*pace* Carter's attempted energy policy), and a Scottish government which sought to do so would need all its diplomatic skills to handle the large number of actors involved in such a task. The fact that it has been suggested that the oil companies themselves have yet to make up their minds on what to do if faced with such a threat adds another element of uncertainty in the complex equation of power.

Trade and money are the final matters to be considered (*McAleese and Purvis*, respectively). A small state acutely dependent on international trade, particularly with one trading partner, is extremely vulnerable. To what extent are such devices as protective tariffs, control over foreign investment, and the use of exchange controls possible instruments of an independent economic policy? Alternatively, would it be possible to suppose that economic nationalism would not be a central part of an independence platform and ask whether a continuity through independence could secure a relatively easy adherence to existing trading partners.

Monetary policy is a special item in Scotland's case, owing to the fact that a monetary surplus would develop in Scotland which would be out of proportion to the country's real G.N.P. and international trading significance, and excessive reserves would inevitably lead to a revaluation of the currency. There is also the threat of long-term inflows of capital attracted by the strength of the Scottish currency and possible outflows disruptive of production and trade patterns. To what extent can a small state attempt to control or direct an international monetary circle of which it is such a small part? Is there a wider community which it can join, and can it have any confidence in the private flow of capital?

Although the common theme is manoeuvrability, in another, more practical sense, the common thread running through the book is the importance of all the issues discussed for Scottish public opinion. These are all issues which are of crucial significance in the political debate in Scotland, and the treatment of each topic takes this fact into account. The mechanics of independence are dealt with in a way which demonstrates considerable caution — Scottish independence will meet with little enthusiasm internationally but will also not face insuperable diplomatic or legal obstacles. In contrast, monetary and oil policies are investigated in a way which could place great demands upon the governing skills of a new Scottish state, if not amounting in themselves to an invitation for a 'baptism of fire'. Again, in the land and trade chapters, the emphasis is on the analysis of the implications of attempts to minimise external control or dependence.

If one conclusion can be drawn from the entire study it is that there is no reason why the small, newly independent state should not take its place in the world community. Its room for manoeuvre will be strictly limited by the realities of its comparative powerlessness, but this does not mean that it will be devoid of possibilities for action in those areas which it may regard as of particular importance for its real interests. In the case of land control and oil, for example, it is *only* by exercising sovereignty that Scotland could hope to protect its national interests. The taking of the cautious view of what the small state can achieve, moreover, need not limit our view of the significance for international law and relations of the emergence of independent states in Scotland, Quebec, and elsewhere. These states will have to be taken seriously by the West if they come into existence, and it is conceivable that they may lead to the penetration of the West itself by some of the ideas and pressures emanating from the Third World since 1945. Such a process would in itself be of lasting importance for the final years of the twentieth century.

I
Politics

Stephen Maxwell

SOVEREIGNTY AND INTERDEPENDENCE

The future welfare of Scotland requires that Scotland be able to take her own decisions in international affairs. She will be able to do that only if she recovers full rights of a national sovereignty. This claim will be denounced by the conventionally wise, in the Scottish National Party as in other quarters of political opinion, as rank heresy. The received wisdom holds that the growth of international interdependence has made the concept of national sovereignty redundant, if not positively dangerous. The prosperity, perhaps the very survival, of mankind in the modern world requires that states surrender their sovereignty to supranational institutions as part of a process of political integration.

In fact outside the communist world, only one significant essay in political integration has been undertaken since 1945 — the European Economic Community. Outside Western Europe the movement has been overwhelmingly in the opposite direction. The increase in the membership of the United Nations from 51 at its foundation to over 140 today testifies to the fact that political *dis*integration has been the international norm in the post-war world. To manage the problems of interdependence in this decentralised international society, there has developed in the place of the supranational institutions of the integrationist model a host of functionally specialised agencies of intergovernmental co-operation. The loss of political impetus within the EEC, the probable centrifugal effects of a further enlargement of its membership and the final achievement in June 1977 of industrial free trade between EFTA and the EEC suggest that the EEC itself is more accurately interpreted as a defensive reaction by declining imperial powers than as a positive response to international interdependence.

Once the obsession with integration has been discarded, the paradox of the parallel growth of international interdependence and political decentralisation begins to dissolve. The same economic and technological forces which are weaving the web of global interdependence pose extraordinary dangers for politically exposed societies. The multinational corporation can ravage a community's resources on land or in the sea with a thoroughness beyond the capacity of a natural disaster: internationally mobile capital can strip a society of the control of its industrial and natural resources: mass population movements made possible by new transport technologies can threaten fragile cultures with extinction: in an age of intercontinental nuclear missiles a community can find itself pinpointed as a nuclear target as the result of a decision by a metropolitan authority to site a nuclear weapons' base on its territory: even the expansion of international trade has increased the vulnerability of local economies to decisions on tariffs or currency exchange rates taken in distant centres. The possession of sovereign rights of state action represents for most societies their best hope of defending themselves against the dangers international interdependence presents while sharing in the benefits it offers.

Scotland's recent experience within the United Kingdom provides local evidence of the way in which the growth of international interdependence can encourage political disintegration.

In no area is international interdependence so obvious as in military affairs. By chain reaction a decision by one state can visit nuclear catastrophe on the world. The scientific and technological developments which have created this precarious unity for mankind have had particular political consequences for Scotland. Scotland's geographical location and lack of a political voice qualified her in the 1960's to serve as a forward base both for the United States' missile submarines on which the stability of the nuclear balance depended and the United Kingdom missile submarines which the London Government saw as its entry fee to the nuclear club. While the increased range of both missiles and submarines has made Scotland's base facilities superfluous in strictly military terms, Scotland continues to play a vital role in the Western alliance system as a base for submarine communications, radar warning installations and air reconnaissance over the northern seas as well as occupying a key role on the southern flank of the Greenland–Iceland–United Kingdom gap through which the expanded Soviet Northern Fleet must pass to gain access to the oceans of the world.

As a small country Scotland has long been dependent on trading opportunities outside her own frontiers. It was to secure trade outlets to England and to England's colonial markets that Scotland sacrificed her Parliament in 1707, while the eighteenth-century tobacco trade with the Americas provided the capital which financed Scotland's pioneering efforts in the industrial revolution. In the twentieth century the high unemployment which Scotland suffered as a result of the protectionism generated by the inter-war depression demonstrated the extent to which the Scottish economy's dependence on trade had grown in the era of Scotland's industrial leadership. The further growth of world trade since the Second World War has contributed to a position in which some 40%[1] of Scotland's gross domestic product is today dependent on trade.

The political implications of economic interdependence are thrown into high — indeed exaggerated — relief by the key role oil now plays in international politics.

The oil reserves in the seabed between Scotland and Norway constitute only a fraction of known global reserves — about 2% according to most estimates. But located as they are on the edge of Western Europe, the world's largest energy importer, they represent an enormous economic and political asset. To the Scottish Nationalists they represent the means of turning the tables on unionist opponents who argue that Scotland cannot afford independence. To the London Government they offer a chance — perhaps the last chance — of reversing the United Kingdom's relative economic decline. To the multinational companies they represent a supply of a high price commodity on the very doorstep of their largest customer in one of the politically most stable areas of the world. To industrialised Western Europe they represent an indigenous source of energy with which to reduce their excessive dependence on external supplies. To the West as a whole they represent an emergency strategic reserve against the contingency of politically motivated interruptions of supply.

Some economic catalyst or other was probably necessary to transform the defensive sense of Scottish nationality into an electorally aggressive Nationalism. The fact that it was oil which provided the catalyst has served to emphasise that Scotland, lacking her own political institutions and instruments of economic control, is a province not merely of the United Kingdom but of a wider Western economic and political system.

The dominant role foreign, particularly United States', capital played in the development of Scotland's oil resources has drawn Scottish attention to the extent of Scotland's dependence on foreign capital in other areas of her economy. Leaving aside the United States' investment in Scottish oil, Scotland has the highest level of *per capita* $ investment in the world after Canada. When other external ownership is taken into account 59%[2] of Scotland's manufacturing labour force is discovered to be employed in concerns controlled from outwith Scotland.

Among its many other effects, the world oil crisis of 1973 helped to generate a new awareness of the extent to which even the most highly industrialised economy depends on natural resources. This awareness found Scotland, situated on the edge of a highly industrialised area which lacks internal supplies of many basic resources, herself well endowed not only with energy in both renewable and non-renewable forms, but also with food, timber, fresh water, deep-water access and, not least, land itself. Continuing international disputes over fishing limits and the conservation of fish stocks around Scotland's coasts provide a topical illustration of the dangers to which Scotland's resource wealth exposes her.

As a response to the pressures bearing on Scotland's territory, population and resources in the new international conditions, the rise of Scottish Nationalism reflects a divergence between Scottish and United Kingdom interests on a number of key policy issues.

Since the Campaign for Nuclear Disarmament first publicised in the 1950's the dangers of living in a nuclear world, sections of Scottish political opinion have brooded over the prospect of annihilation without international representation. It is probable that an independent Scotland would consider that a balance of Scottish interests required her to continue her present communications' and reconnaissance roles in the Western defence system. However, the presence on Scottish territory of United States' and UK nuclear submarine bases enhances Scotland's importance as a nuclear target without serving any Scottish interest. While the closure of the submarine bases would not upset the strategic balance, it would upset the balance of advantage for the United Kingdom in maintaining a nuclear deterrent. By locating her operational nuclear submarine base in Scotland, the London Government has been able to purchase its membership of the nuclear club at a lower price in United Kingdom terms than she would have paid had the base had to be located closer to the United Kingdom's English heartland. There can be no cause for surprise if Scottish opinion does not share London's view of the current price as a bargain.

Scotland's high level of dependence on international trade gives her a close interest in the United Kingdom's commercial policy. Within the post-war framework of a steady liberalisation of world trade under the General Agreement on Trade and Tariffs (GATT), there has been no irreconcilable conflicts of interest between Scotland and the United Kingdom commercial strategy. There have, however, been differences of emphasis as on the issue of UK membership of the EEC. Scotland's high export dependence as a small economy and the geographically diverse pattern of her exports (in 1973 only 23% of Scottish exports went to the original six members of the EEC compared with 35% of UK exports.)[3] give her reason to fear a protectionist reaction from her main trading partners — particularly the United States — to such protectionist aspects of the EEC as the Common Agricultural Policy. For the future the strength of the capital goods sector of Scottish industry means that Scotland's export opportunities will lie as much in the developing countries, particularly the rapidly expanding markets of the oil producers, as in the EEC. It must also be expected that at a time of increasing protectionist pressure Scottish opinion will become impatient to have the commercial bargaining potential of Scotland's oil deployed in defence of Scottish exports such as whisky which have to face widespread discrimination in foreign markets with inadequate support from the UK Government.

Scottish and UK interests diverge significantly over the management of Scotland's natural resources. England's interest as a net importer of resources is reflected in UK policies which undervalue resources either by depleting them too quickly to meet a short-term need, denying them adequate investment or, in the case of resources which are the object of international negotiations, treating them as a disposable bargaining asset.

Oil produces the most dramatic illustration of the conflict of interests. The Scottish economy's limited capacity to absorb new financial resources gives Scotland an interest in a rate of depletion of the oil reserves which would allow the financial benefits to be phased over several decades. By contrast the pressing short-term needs of a United Kingdom economy ten times the size of the Scottish economy, impel the UK Government to pursue a depletion rate far above the Scottish optimum.

Scottish and UK interests clash even more directly over the use of oil revenues. The revenues are most valuable to Scotland as a capital fund from which to finance a fundamental, long-term restructuring of the Scottish economy. An allocation of the oil revenues according to current UK policy guidelines — or to any guidelines which would win acceptance within the UK — would fall far short of Scotland's needs. If one thing is clear in the confusion of claim and counter-claim, it is that UK control of Scotland's oil resources will deny Scotland the relative economic advantage from oil which she derived from her coal and iron ore deposits in the eighteenth and nineteenth centuries.

As a politically sensitive issue of resource management oil is closely followed by fishing. Scottish waters contribute 40% of total UK fish stocks and nearly 30% of EEC stocks. But the international pressure on fishing stocks is now such that non-Scottish fleets can enjoy access to Scottish waters only if Scottish fleets accept restrictions on their activities in their home waters. In both the initial negotiations for UK entry to the EEC by the Conservative Government of 1970 and the renegotiations of the terms of membership by the Labour Government of 1974, Scottish fishing interests were sacrificed to the United Kingdom's assumed need for EEC membership. That record augurs badly for the prospects of Scottish industry now that the UK is firmly committed to the complex 'trade-off' process by which the EEC takes its decisions.

Scottish forestry provides an example of a Scottish resource mismanaged by omission rather by commission. In spite of the fact that the UK imports £2000m of timber and timber products each year and that within the EEC the demand for timber is expected to grow at least at a rate half as fast again as the anticipated rise in production, the potential in Scotland for doubling the area under afforestation without impinging on good agricultural land is neglected. The fact that the growth rate of timber in Scotland is one and a half times the EEC average while costs are approximately two-thirds the average, makes the neglect all the more remarkable.[5]

The neglect of Scotland's forestry potential is due partly to a failure to ensure the efficient use of the most basic of all resources — land. The reasons for that failure are less relevant here than the fact that the development potential of land in many previously neglected areas of Scotland is now being recognised. The growth of tourism and recreation has highlighted the value of the Highlands as one of Western Europe's few remaining 'wilderness' areas. Oil developments have created a demand for sites for rig construction, on-shore installations, and downstream processing facilities. Improvements in marine transport technology have enhanced the value of Scotland's deep-water access and of her location off the European continent. The prospect of scarcities of natural resources, including timber, has encouraged a reappraisal of the development potential of the land hitherto regarded as economically marginal or sterile. This new interest in Scotland's land as an economic resource is reflected in the growing volume of speculative purchases and institutional investment which it now attracts.

In the absence of protective measures, Scotland faces the prospect of an accelerating take-over of her natural assets by external capital, parallel with the continuing take-over of her industrial assets. There is little hope of a UK Government taking the necessary protective measures. As a net importer of most of the resources with which Scotland is endowed, the United Kingdom's interest is in controlling her sources of supply as far as she is able. Furthermore, London's role as an international financial centre makes the UK reluctant to restrict the freedom of action of financial interests. A merely 'regional' Scottish interest in restricting ownership of natural resources and in limiting the freedom of action of capital will never carry the sufficient political weight within the UK to command a serious response.

The salience of such policy issues renders the traditional terms of the Scottish debate superfluous. Defence policy, fishing limits, commercial policy and the strategy of resource development are all the prerogative of sovereign authorities and well outwith the powers of both devolved assemblies and provincial assemblies within a federation. Even those forms of federalism which allow scope for a determined provincial assembly to exercise some control over ownership of land and industrial asset would find it difficult to accommodate so direct a clash of interests as exists between Scotland and England in these areas. By reinforcing the external pressures bearing on Scotland's territory, resources and population, the growth of international interdependence has helped to establish the primacy of the case for sovereign independence.

INTERNATIONAL REACTIONS

Scotland's foreign policy options will obviously be powerfully determined by the circumstances of her constitutional separation from England. Unionists and Nationalists each have their favoured scenario. The SNP pretends to believe that throughout the process of separation English opinion will be true to its democratic and constitutionalist faith. The process of separation will be initiated by the winning by the SNP of a majority of Scotland's 71 seats at Westminster, with or without a majority share of the Scottish vote. As the majority Scottish representation in the House of Commons the SNP MP's would then claim to possess, by the criteria Westminster itself uses to identify a Parliamentary mandate, a mandate for Scottish independence. They would, therefore, demand to meet with representatives of the governing Party or coalition at Westminster to discuss a timetable for the repealing of the Act of Union and beyond that for the transfer of specific powers from Westminster and Whitehall to a Scottish Parliament and administration.

The Nationalists are not so unrealistic as to assume that Westminster will accede to these demands in a mood of cheerful resignation. Westminster is expected (at the very least) to wage a campaign of prevarication and delay in order to secure for the English economy unfettered access to the benefits of Scotland's oil for as long as possible. More likely, Westminster will not be at all inclined to accept the inevitability of the end of the Union and the consequent loss of her control over Scotland's oil. In the likely event that the SNP majority of seats had been elected by a *minority* of the Scottish vote, Westminster would hope to isolate the SNP from popular support either by an offer of radical devolution within the United Kingdom, perhaps followed by a referendum on devolution or independence, or even by an immediate referendum on a choice between independence and union. SNP would risk the loss of public sympathy in Scotland if it rejected either of these counter-offers by Westminster out of hand. SNP's own absolute commitment to constitutional action reflects a strong constitutionalist ethos in Scottish politics which SNP would defy only at its peril. While reserving for itself an option on independence as the ultimate goal, Scottish opinion would almost certainly prefer to explore whatever options short of independence were offered to it by Westminster rather than face a major constitutional crisis created by unilateral action by a SNP majority of Scottish MP's.

The SNP itself would probably be in a sufficiently 'bullish' mood to believe that it could turn either of Westminster's options to the advantage of the independence cause. It is a firm article of Nationalist belief that a strong Scottish Assembly would feed Scotland's appetite for power. Alternatively, a referendum on independence or union would provide the Nationalists with a strategic compensation for the tactical defeat that might be inflicted on the cause of independence in the first ballot. By approving the referendum as means of settling the constitutional relationship between England and Scotland, Westminster would be throwing away what some Unionists — and some Nationalists too — believe may be her strongest defence against independence — the fear in the minds of many Scots that Scottish independence could be gained only at the cost of a major constitutional confrontation with Westminster and the risk of violence. Nationalists would quickly seize the fact that Westminster herself was initiating a referendum as a weapon to dispel that fear. They would argue that by initiating a referendum Westminster was committing herself, implicitly and morally if not explicitly, to the appropriate legislative and political action in the event of a vote in favour of independence; and whatever the result of the first referendum a precedent and principle would have been established.

Such are the sanguine calculations of the Nationalists. Hard-line Unionists recommend an altogether different response by Westminster to the first demand for Scottish independence by a SNP majority of Scottish MP's — a flat 'No' not only to independence but to any concession what-

soever. They calculate that the Nationalists would be strait-jacketed between Westminister's refusal to make any concessions and the SNP's own
rejection of all forms of non-constitutional action. In this scenario unilateral withdrawal from Westminster by the SNP majority of Scottish MP's
is excluded not only by SNP's categorical commitment to constitutional
action but because it would be assessed by the SNP itself as unacceptable
to Scottish opinion. The Nationalist balloon, puffed up by Westminister's
past eagerness to conciliate Nationalist opinion, would finally collapse.

This Unionist scenario underestimates the inherent dynamic of the
situation that would be created by Westminster's blank 'No'. Whatever the
technical, legal definition of what constitutes constitutional action, Westminster, in refusing any concession to a Nationalist majority in Scotland,
would be widely held to have acted in an undemocratic and arbitrary manner in conflict with the principles of self-determination and of the representative majority on which its own claim to legitimacy ultimately rests.
This abandonment of democratic 'fair play' by English Parliamentarians
would put Scottish organisations of the British parties on the defensive and
would provide a justification for those Scottish Nationalists who would
reject the English definition of constitutional action in terms of Parliamentary sovereignty in favour of the allegedly native doctrine of 'popular' sovereignty. Having adopted the hard-line strategy as a way of preserv-
ing the Union, Westminster might find that it had succeeded only in
accelerating the erosion of unionism in Scotland.

It is possible that the combined pressure of these responses within the
United Kingdom would induce Westminster to modify its comprehensive
rejection of Scottish demands. Its incentive to do so would undoubtedly be
increased if the Nationalists were able to inject into the situation a sense of
crisis powerful enough to register with international opinion.

It is clear from public statements that Nationalists place great importance on the part international opinion could play in influencing Westminster's response to a demand for Scottish independence. Having
achieved an effective mandate for independence from the Scottish electorate, it seems that the Nationalists' aim would be to persuade English
political leaders that their choice lay between on the one hand accepting
the Scots' right to self-determination with the prospect of a subsequent
Anglo-Scottish agreement on the sharing of the benefits of Scotland's oil,
and on the other a major political and constitutional crisis with the attendant risk of the collapse of international confidence in the United Kingdom. In clarifying for international opinion the nature of the choice facing
Westminster the Nationalists would insist that the fundamental point at
issue was Scotland's right to self-determination — that is her right to seek
full and sovereign membership of the international community with all the
duties and rights of such membership.

In developing this appeal to acknowledged principles of international
rights, they would declare their readiness to have Scotland's will for inde-

pendence tested in a referendum held under international supervision. They would emphasise that Scotland's legal rights over the oil, as concomitants of sovereignty, were non-negotiable and that any disputes about the boundaries of the English and Scottish sectors of the North Sea would require to be submitted to the judgment of the appropriate international legal authorities.

Once those rights and procedures had been agreed, but not before, discussions could begin on the measures a future Scottish Goverment might take to ensure that the transfer of the legal rights over North Sea oil to Scotland did not mean that England was denied access to the economic benefits of the oil. The Nationalists would not expect Westminster to accept simply on trust the readiness of a future Scottish Government to share the benefits of the oil with England. Lacking the power to commit a future Scottish Government, the Scottish negotiators would emphasise that the close interdependence of the English and Scottish economies made a sharing of the oil benefits a matter of vital self-interest to Scotland. They would emphasise that England is by far Scotland's largest single export market, taking well over 50% of Scottish exports, and that it would be folly for Scotland to cause a serious deterioration in the English economy, let alone its total collapse, by denying it access to the benefits of the oil.

The means of ensuring continued access for England to the oil benefits present few technical problems. They might include an agreement by Scotland to earmark a proportion of her foreign currency earnings for a foreign currency pool with England on which England could draw to finance her deficit on her ex-UK trade in exchange for making sterling assets at a guaranteed parity available to Scotland for the financing of Scotland's non-oil trade deficit with England. On the basis of her oil wealth Scotland might directly guarantee international loans to England to allow her more time to adapt to her new circumstances. Or she might pursue a deliberate policy of buying back into Scottish control English owned assets in Scotland, or use some of her surplus oil revenues for the purchase of assets in England.[6]

The sharing of oil benefits would, however, be only one of the items in the independence 'package' which Nationalists would offer to English and to international opinion. They would signal their acknowledgement of the wider interdependence between Scotland and England by urging the case for an Association of states of the British Isles, based on the example of the Nordic Council, as a framework for co-operation between the two countries, and by stressing their desire to remain a member of NATO albeit on a non-nuclear basis.[7] What response could the different international interests making up international opinion be expected to make to this presentation of the Scottish case?

The governments with the greatest potential influence on the outcome would be the North American and the Common Market governments. Although the Scottish Nationalists would seek to enlist the sympathy of the American public, partly no doubt by reminding it of the United States' own origins, there is no effective constituency of Scots-Americans as there is of Irish-, Jewish- or Ukrainian-Americans. Indeed the ease with which Scots emigrants have integrated not only socially and economically but also politically with their adopted countries is one of the features of Scotland's experience as a 'submerged' nation. In any case whatever influence highly placed individual sympathisers with the Nationalist cause might be able to exert would almost certainly be outweighed, if not by Anglophile sentiment, by the propaganda efforts of spokesmen for the Westminster Government and for commercial interests.

There is indeed a school of Left-wing thought in Scotland that believes that Scotland will win her independence — if at all — only in the teeth of active opposition from neo-colonialist forces in the United States and the United Kingdom. In its most melodramatic version this thesis depicts Scotland as a potential Vietnam.[8] In a more considered version Scotland is classified as a member of an international 'awkward squad' consisting, in Tom Nairn's words, mainly of 'small nations, relatively developed, and either dominated or heavily overborne by larger, more backward nations — damned for being too small in population yet too big for their boots, damned for getting in the way of greater powers and stubbornly insisting on their rights, damned for being in the wrong place and being too advanced and too conceited to lie down and be walked over like provincials'. As fellow-members of this misfits' club Nairn lists Czechoslovakia, Catalonia, the Basque country, Croatia, Ulster and Cyprus.[9]

In a certain ideological perspective Scotland does indeed appear a likely victim of British and American neo-imperialism. We have already noted the extent of Scotland's dependence on US and English capital, the importance of Scotland's oil in the political economy of the West and Scotland's important role in the Western alliance system.

The differences between Scotland's position and the position of the other members of Nairn's awkward squad are too many and too complex to discuss here. The general weakness of the Left-wing thesis lies in the obvious fact that the presence in a country of some of the features of neo-colonialist dependence does not necessarily lead to intervention by the colonial state against a Nationalist movement. Two logically quite separate factors must also be present — a sufficient will to intervene and an effective opportunity to do so. Neither the will nor the opportunity are likely to exist in Scotland's case.

The attitude of the United States' Administration itself would be subject to conflicting considerations. It would no doubt prefer the safety of the UK *status quo* to the uncertainties of Scottish independence, but it is difficult to identify any crucial US interest which would be endangered by Scottish independence. A Scottish Government could certainly be expected to pursue a more restrictive policy towards US investment in Scotland, but it would hardly be more restrictive than Norwegian policy, for example, and it might even be welcomed by Labour interests in the US concerned about the 'export' of American jobs by US investment overseas. The foreign and security policy options of an independent Scotland are discussed below. At this stage it is enough to note that the immediate objectives of an independent Scotland as outlined by the SNP — non-nuclear membership of NATO, an Association of States of the British Isles, and a renegotiation of the terms of EEC membership prior to a referendum — fall well within the range of policies followed by other Western European democracies. It may be assumed that Scottish opinion would not wish to add to the uncertainties inseparable from the achievement of independence itself the further uncertainties which would accompany any immediate post-independence *démarche* in external affairs. Once the existence of a major political crisis in the United Kingdom had been clearly established, the first priority of the US Government, for a variety of political and strategic reasons, would be to see it quickly resolved one way or the other — provided always the solution lay within an acceptable range of political outcomes.

Even if a US Administration, influenced perhaps by alarmist advice from a maverick intelligence source, were to conclude that an independent Scotland would be politically unreliable in a way serious enough to warrant US response, it is not easy to see what it could actually do to obstruct the progress of the independence movement or, independence once achieved, to coerce a Scottish Government.

The credibility of threats of direct economic sanctions against an independent Scotland — threats which the US Administration has refrained at least since the days of Dr Kissinger from using against the prospect of 'Union of the Left' governments in France and Italy — would be difficult to establish. Thanks to her strong resource base an independent Scotland will enjoy a high credit rating in international financial markets. In the medium-term, indeed, Scotland will herself be a large contributor to international capital markets while in the short-term she would be able to seek financial support from the governments of fellow oil producing states in the event of more traditional sources of credit being cut off. In any case she will not have to carry the mountain of debt which preceding state administrations in Quebec bequeathed to the incoming Parti Québécois Administration in 1977.

Like the United States Government, US industrial and financial interests would no doubt prefer to continue dealing with an amenable and familiar government in Westminster rather than a prickly and inexperienced Nationalist Administration in Scotland. US companies have, however, become used to adapting their operations to political changes where these appear inevitable, and the adaptations they would expect to have to make as a result of Scottish independence would appear modest by comparison with others they have been obliged to make. Even if they did determine on active opposition the means to do so would be hard to find. The credibility of threats of economic sanctions would, again, be difficult to establish. A shortage of investment capital is one problem with which an independent Scotland will not have to contend. Quite apart from the attraction for private investors of what will be one of the world's fastest growing economies, a surplus of investment capital will be available to Scottish public authorities in the form of oil revenues. Furthermore the development of Scotland's other natural resources should prove increasingly attractive to long-term investors.

There would, no doubt, be threats by foreign companies or even Scottish companies to transfer their Scottish operations outside Scotland, in emulation of the campaign being waged by some large employers in Quebec. Scotland's position is, however, far stronger than Quebec's. Large businesses in Scotland will not be able to give their threats a gloss of justification by pleading the harmful effects of discriminatory language legislation. Furthermore, any attempt by a Westminster Government to support a campaign by large employers in Scotland by threatening to refuse a commercial agreement with an independent Scotland, in the way that the Canadian Federal and provincial governments have supported Quebec employers, would quickly be assessed as a bluff. The balance of economic and commercial bargaining power lies decisively with Scotland. Not only is Scotland England's biggest single export market, but England could expect the surplus she currently enjoys on her Scottish trade to grow even larger during the post-independence restructuring of the Scottish economy. Deprived of the support of the foreign currency earnings of Scottish oil, the state of the English balance of payments would be such that no English Government could seriously contemplate the loss of that surplus. Leaving aside the bargaining power Scotland would possess by virtue of her energy reserves and other natural resources, it is difficult to imagine any of Scotland's other trading partners rushing in where England feared to tread.

While military intervention against Scottish independence — the possibility that intrigues Scotland's apocalyptic Left — can be ruled out on general political grounds, other forms of intervention might be contemplated. It is unlikely that overt political intervention would go beyond the issuing, or more probably leaking, of Administration warnings about the dangers of 'extremist' forms of independence. As such they would be part of a wider propaganda battle in which the Nationalists would be facing a range of opponents.

It is the possibility of covert intervention that most stirs the Scottish imagination. In the circumstances envisaged here, Scottish opinion will presumably be thoroughly altered to the possibility of direct action by *agents provocateurs* designed to discredit Nationalism. Indirect action to support the 'internal enemies' of the new Scottish state might, therefore, appear a more promising strategy. A sizeable minority of the present population of Scotland will probably never be reconciled to independence. It does not follow, however, that members of that minority will be willing to collaborate with external agencies to secure the overthrow of the new Scottish state by undemocratic and possibly violent means. It is impossible to identify any section of Scottish society which would feel so threatened by independence that it would resort to illegal means of opposition. The dire forecasts of visiting English Liberals notwithstanding,[10] there is no analogy between Scotland and Ulster. Where the Catholic minority in Ulster has been deliberately excluded from political power, Scottish Catholics have in the past enjoyed access to political power through the Labour Party and are today well represented in a National Party which is officially committed to the disestablishment of the Presbyterian Church. In social and economic terms, although the Catholic community still contributes a disproportionate share of Scotland's deprived, more and more Catholics are escaping from the social ghettos to which they were largely confined in the nineteenth and early twentieth centuries. Nor, unlike their Ulster cousins, have Scottish Protestants any reason to identify Nationalism with an alien Church, although the more perceptive might recognise it as an agent of secularisation. Independence will certainly offend the sentiments and injure the ideological *amour propre* of that minority of the Scottish public which is hard-line British unionist but, again in contrast to Ulster, it will not present the sort of threat to the social or economic interests of any section of that minority which would provoke extremist resistance.

In any case, it can surely be assumed that US policy makers in considering their response to Nationalism would recognise that Scotland, with its long democratic traditions and its highly developed political and social institutions, is far different from the banana republics in which the US has traditionally deployed its skills in covert intervention and 'destabilisation'.

As a last resort an external agency determined to intervene against Nationalism might give support to extremist English or British Nationalists in England. Yet every advance by neo-Fascist movements in British politics strengthens the hands of the Scottish Nationalists by polarising English politics and undermining international confidence in the United Kingdom.

Finally, predictions of US intervention against Scottish Nationalism should be discounted against recent international experience. It is not clear why a country which over the past five years has accepted decisions inconvenient to its own interests by oil producing states, including Norway, should feel impelled to adopt a course of action against Scotland which would earn it massive opprobrium if not from Westminster or Brussels certainly from much of the rest of international opinion. Moreover, it must be apparent to all but the most bigoted of US analysts and politicians that US intervention would risk reinforcing whatever anti-American tendencies already existed in Scotland, to the detriment of the United States' continuing economic and political interests there.

If the probability of United States opposition to Scottish independence is exaggerated among the unionist Left, the prospect of Canadian support is often sadly misjudged by sections of the Nationalist movement. Canadian opinion would be far too sensitive to its own nationalist problem in Quebec to lend any significant support to Scottish Nationalism. Their very prominence in the Canadian Anglophone Establishment will make the most influential among the Scots Canadians the least willing to express support for Scottish Nationalism for fear of compromising their opposition to Quebec separatism. Indeed, if any politically significant expressions of support come out of Canada they are more likely to come from the Parti Québécois Administration in Quebec than from descendants of the Scottish diaspora.

The instinctive response of the Common Market, both in Brussels and in the national capitals, would be one of hostility. As the guardian of the idea of a greater united Europe the Brussels establishment would see in Scottish Nationalism both a general political danger and specific economic dangers. The demand for Scottish independence as articulated by the SNP will strike the ears of the committed European federalist as the voice of the old unregenerate Adam of European nationalism and would surely shatter the last illusion of those advocates of a Federal Europe who have persisted in seeing Scottish Nationalism as the most advanced example of a European regionalism whose historic function is to undermine the established states of Europe from below as integration within the Common Market constrains them from above.

Even the more pragmatic Marketeer would regret the emergence on the European scene of a state headed by a political party committed to policies on fishing, oil development and foreign investment for example, in direct conflict with the principles of the Treaty of Rome, and to an oil depletion policy deterimental to the Community's interest as a massive oil importer. Scotland's withdrawal from the market as a result of an adverse decision in a referendum on renegotiated terms would be a serious political blow to the Market while her presence in the market would powerfully reinforce that organisation's already well developed centrifugal tendencies. Official expressions of hostility to Scottish independence would no doubt be restrained by a politic fear of providing Scottish anti-Marketeers with a Brussels bogeyman with which to frighten Scottish opinion, but it is certain that Scottish Nationalists could not hope for support from Brussels.

Even the degree of support which Scottish nationalists might expect from European regionalist or autonomist movements is doubtful. The majority of them are committed to some form of Federalist solution, based on the Common Market, which would deny the states of Europe the sovereign independence claimed for Scotland by the Nationalists. The admiration which some supporters of regionalist movements currently evince for Scottish Nationalism might not survive concrete political evidence of Nationalist determination to enlist Scotland in the ranks of the nation-states of Europe. In any event no country with the exception of Belgium has a regionalist or autonomist movement strong enough to exert an important influence on its metropolitan government.

The national capitals of the EEC would hardly be less hostile than the central institutions to Scottish demands. Short of an improbable Gallic plot to revive the 'Auld Alliance' in the interests of embarrassing the historic common enemy, the French response would be determined by their dislike of Nationalist policies on oil depletion, fishing limits and reform of the common agricultural policy, and by a fear on the part of official *étatiste* opinion that any expression of sympathy for the aims of the Scottish Nationalists would be eagerly turned against the French state by autonomist movements within France. Given the present trends within the EEC, it is improbable that these fears would be counter-balanced by any need for Scottish help in ensuring the victory of the Gaullist concept of *l'Europe des patries.*

West Germany's response would be powerfully influenced by the fear that the emergence of an independent Scotland would, by accelerating the disintegration of the Common Market, weaken what opinion in the Federal Republic regards as an essential support of her post-war reintegration with the Western world. Furthermore, as the biggest energy importer in Western Europe, West Germany has a larger interest than any other state in establishing North Sea oil as a strategic energy reserve for Western Europe by bringing it under a common energy policy within the Common Market.

The Nationalists could hardly expect any more support from the Benelux countries. Any sympathy which the Belgians and Dutch might feel as small nations for the ambitions of the Scottish Nationalists would be outweighed by their disappointment as pioneers of the EEC at Nationalist hostility to European integration. Like the other founder members of the EEC both Belgium and the Netherlands would stand to lose from Nationalist policies on fishing, oil depletion, foreign investment and reform of the common agricultural policy. The only possible source of official support within the Benelux countries would be Volksunie members of a Belgian Government. Among EEC members, Denmark and Ireland would have the least reason to oppose the emergence of an independent Scotland. Irish opinion would no doubt be tempted to interpret Scotland's secession from the United Kingdom as the final act of the Decline and Fall of the British Empire. On a more mundane level an Irish Government might hope that the renegotiation of the terms of Scottish membership of the EEC would succeed in establishing the principle of exclusive national fishing limits of fifty miles or more, and that the superfluity of oil which an independent Scotland would possess would encourage a Scottish Government to adopt a more relaxed attitude in disputes over median lines in the Irish Sea and around Rockall than a Westminster Government has yet been willing to do. On the other hand in proportion to her gross domestic product Ireland has more to lose financially from the dilution of the common agricultural policy — one of the chief Nationalist aims — than any other EEC member. What is more, the EEC offers Ireland a way of diversifying her political as well as her economic links away from excessive dependence on the United Kingdom. In so far as Irish opinion saw an independent Scotland as adding to centrifugal forces in the Common Market it would tend to be hostile. Irish opinion might also be worried that political upheaval in the United Kingdom would weaken the United Kingdom's hold on Ulster sufficiently to allow that province's evil genie to spread its lethal mischief throughout the island.

Denmark shares Ireland's interest in the common agricultural policy but, in marked contrast to the position in Ireland, Danish popular opinion is generally hostile to the Market while Danish official opinion is opposed to greater political integration within the EEC. The predominant, anti-EEC section of Danish opinion might welcome the emergence of an independent Scotland for the same reasons that opinion in the founding members of the EEC would regret it. If Scotland were to join Denmark's fellow members of the Nordic Council outside the EEC the anti-Marketeers in Denmark would feel encouraged to intensify their campaign for Denmark's withdrawal. However, as a member of the EEC Scotland's value to official opinion as an ally in the campaign against political integration might, in view of the way things are developing anyway, be outweighed by the threat Scottish policies on fishing limits, oil, depletion, and reform of the agricultural policy present to Danish interests.

If the majority of Common Market governments will be disposed on grounds of national interest to regard the demand for Scottish independence unfavourably they will nevertheless have reason to exercise discretion in pursuing that opposition. Although interested governments could seek to influence opinion in Scotland and England by making known their attitudes to anticipated Nationalist demands for renegotiated terms for Scotland's membership of the EEC or for a free trade agreement between Scotland and the EEC, they would presumably have some regard for the principle of non-interference in the affairs of another state. Like the Commission itself the governments of the EEC countries would wish to avoid so alienating Scottish opinion that in the event of independence being achieved Scotland rejected EEC membership out of hand. With her fishing, energy and other natural resources Scotland would command respect as a free trade partner of the EEC as much as she would be valued a member. The Danish and Irish Governments would of course feel similarly inhibited from expressing any sympathy they might feel for Scottish ambitions by their need, whatever the outcome of the contest between Westminister and the Nationalists, to continue to cultivate good relations with the London Government.

It would be melodramatic to say that the Scottish Nationalists will find the hands of their North American and West European neighbours turned against them in their moment of crisis, but it is clear they certainly cannot expect them to be extended in eager support.

The response of two further groups of countries needs to be considered — the Nordic countries and the Organisation of Petroleum Exporting Countries. The Nordic countries are regarded by many Scottish Nationalists as their natural allies. Geographical proximity and historical connections are only two of the bonds which Nationalists claim.

Norway and Iceland are valued as examples of two countries which themselves gained complete independence only in the twentieth century and did so moreover without using violence. These two countries also share with Scotland the need to defend national fishing grounds against the pressure of fishing fleets from much larger states. Norway shares Scotland's interests and her problems as an economically developed oil exporting country situated on the northern edge of the world's largest oil importing area. Scotland's security interests are inextricably interwoven with the web of military and political relationships known as the 'Nordic balance'. Norway and Sweden face problems of regional development in their northern areas comparable to those Scotland faces in the Highlands and on the West coast. The constitutional relationship between Denmark and the Faroes is considered by some Nationalists to be a possible model for the relationship between Shetland, and possibly the other island groups of Scotland and the central Scottish Government. In an era in which the economic advantage may be swinging to countries which possess a favourable balance between population and resources, Scotland shares with the Nordic countries as a whole a relatively privileged position among the industrialised countries of Western Europe. Scottish Nationalists like to believe that the Nordic connection is cemented by a shared exemplary commitment to democratic values. The Nordic countries, including Denmark as the only EEC member, might indeed welcome the widening of the breach in the commercial and institutional solidarity of the Common Market which Scottish independence would seem to portend. Norway and Iceland would no doubt also welcome the additional support an independent Scotland would give to their policies of extended 200-mile fishing limits. Norway would see a further advantage in having the UK sector of the North Sea oil province transferred to the control of a Government committed to a depletion rate policy and other policies similar to her own. Public sympathy in Iceland and Norway and to a lesser degree in the other Nordic countries would undoubtedly be with the Scottish Nationalists rather than the Westminster Government.

On the other hand political opinion in Norway would share with official opinion in the other Nordic countries a fear that the emergence of an independent Scotland would introduce a new and perhaps unpredictable actor into a highly sensitive theatre of international politics. The continuing political importance of London even as capital of a truncated United Kingdom and the continuing economic importance of England as a market for Nordic exports would reinforce Nordic caution in responding to Scottish claims. There is little reason to believe claims by some Nationalists that the Nordic countries would be willing to identify with the Scottish cause to the extent of introducing the issue at the United Nations, unless it was to be Iceland with its fondness for acting the political maverick.

The Organisation of Petroleum Exporting Countries includes the only countries outside North America and Europe which would be expected to have a serious interest in the outcome of the contest between Scottish Nationalists and the London Government. Although OPEC itself has a general interest in controlling the rate of global oil production, Scotland's contribution could never be significant enough to give OPEC as such a serious economic interest in the outcome. Norwegian and Scottish oil reserves are of interest to the OPEC producers only by virtue of their possible role as a short-term strategic reserve for Western Europe in the event of a repetition of the 1973 oil embargo. The exceptional position of Norway (and by extension Scotland) as a developed Western European oil producer, is reflected in the fact that Norway has not joined OPEC. It is conceivable that the Middle East oil producing countries would be willing to use their financial strength to exert pressure in favour of the Nationalists in the interests of securing the transfer of control over Scottish oil from a United Kingdom Government firmly within both the International Energy Agency and the EEC to a Scottish Government likely to align itself with Norway outside the IEA and possibly outside the EEC. However, as the benefits to the Middle East oil producers of such a transfer would be no more than marginal (not to say speculative) any concerted action is improbable. If any support was forthcoming from among the ranks of Arab oil producers it would more likely be from a maverick such as Libya, acting from sheer ideological braggadocio, and for that reason be unacceptable to Scottish opinion.

Nationalists are then being unrealistic if they expect international opinion to rally to their support. As we have seen the most important Governmental and economic interests will have reason to be cautious, if not hostile, towards Nationalist claims. What official support is forthcoming will be either from small or maverick states with little influence, or from states with an interest in fomenting a crisis in a leading member of the Western alliance, in which case their support will tend to discredit the Scottish cause in the eyes of both international and United Kingdom opinion.

The Nationalists can, of course, hope that whatever their views on the merits of independence itself the United Kingdom's friends and allies would feel impelled to warn Westminster that it could not rely on their support for a policy of dogmatic immobilism which threatened to add a major political and constitutional crisis to the other problems which the UK faced, and that if it could not stare down Nationalism it had better reach a compromise even if it proved temporary. The impact of this message on Westminster would depend on the economic and political circumstances of the United Kingdom. If as a result of Scotland's oil the United Kingdom balance of payments was in a healthy surplus and sterling was strong, Westminster would probably feel able to ignore external pressure for a conciliatory policy. If on the other hand sterling was weak or the economy was facing industrial strife, or political stability was threatened by a polarisation on the Left and the Right, financial pressure through the IMF or other financial institutions or direct political pressure from allies, might have some impact.

In the former case the outcome of the contest between the Nationalists and Westminster would depend on the balance of political forces within the United Kingdom. The advantage would lie with the Nationalists. They would be sustained by a sense of nationality aroused by Westminster's denial of the principle of self-determination and no doubt strengthened in self-righteousness by the generosity of the Scottish offer to share the benefits of the oil with Westminster. Their opponents in contrast would be weakened by divisions within their English ranks over both the principles and the tactics of Westminster's response, by the fragmentation of their Scottish ranks under the impact of the surge of Scottishness, and by the fear of forging a final, perhaps indissoluble, identification of the 'Scottish cause' with Nationalism which would transform Scottish independence from merely one of a range of possible outcomes to the historically inevitable one. The dynamic of this situation would push Westminster towards a strategy of political manoeuvre designed at best to isolate the Nationalists and at worst to prolong Westminster's unfettered enjoyment of the benefits of Scotland's oil.

As part of its strategy of political manoeuvre Westminster will seize whatever opportunities are offered of making political mischief. Chief among these is the Shetland issue. By encouraging talk of a Shetland break-away from Scotland, Westminster would hope to undermine Scottish confidence that the oil wealth provided a guarantee of future prosperity. About two-thirds of the United Kingdom's known oil reserves lie in what would be Shetland's waters were Shetland a sovereign state. As an aspirant to full sovereign status Shetland would, however, almost certainly find international opinion reluctant to concede that she should have the same rights over marine and seabed resources as established states. To allow such rights to a community one-twentieth the size even of Iceland would be to open a Pandora's box of spurious claims by client micro-states at a time when the international community is engaged in trying to work out an international regime for the seabed.

Shetland's position as a far northern appendage of England would be equally problematic. As the case of the Channel Islands has shown international law allows such 'enclaves' an economic zone of only twelve miles. In Shetland's case this would place not only the oil reserves but also Shetland's traditional fishing grounds outside Westminster's jurisdiction. Considerable as the legal and constitutional barriers to Shetland opting out of an independent Scotland to unite with England are, they are less formidable than the political barriers the Shetlanders would themselves interpose as the full implications became apparent.

If following Scottish independence international law were to accept Shetland as simply an extension of the English mainland the position of the Shetlanders would become even more perilous than it is today. The whole burden of supporting England's economic recovery would then fall on the oil reserves off Shetland's coasts, leading inevitably to a rate of depletion even more wildly in excess of the optimal rate for Shetland than the rate projected by the present Westminster Government. Furthermore, having lost the fishing ground off mainland Scotland, Westminster would be under strong pressure to use Shetland's fishing grounds either as a bargaining counter to win concessions for the distant water fishing fleets of Hull and Grimsby in their traditional grounds or simply as a substitute for those grounds — if indeed she had not been forced under the common fisheries' policy of the EEC to surrender control to the Council of Ministers and Brussels. As a part of England Shetland would of course continue to depend on mainland Scotland for most of her communications, hospital facilities and a host of other services. In legislative terms she would depend on a remote legislature in which she would be alone in requiring special legislation to accommodate her legacy of Scottish statute and in which, presumably, she would have but a single representative.

However, the fact that a Nationalist Scotland would be far more likely than any Westminster administration to pursue oil and fishing policies sympathetic to Shetland's interests might not satisfy Shetland's new assertiveness. A case can be made for a constitutional realignment of Shetland not towards a Westminster Government with antipathetic interests in the far south but towards North Atlantic communities like Faroe and Greenland sharing some of the same problems. In this perspective Shetlanders should seek a constitutional relationship with Scotland comparable to the Faroe-Denmark relationship — that is a large measure of internal autonomy with special powers over fishing limits, guaranteed representation in the Nordic Council in the event of Scottish membership of that body and the right to develop her own links with members of the Nordic and North Atlantic community should Scotland not join the Nordic Council. Shetland's realignment to the North would complement the increased emphasis a Scottish Government would wish for its own reasons to place on its North Atlantic and Nordic links. However provocative the tactics adopted by Westminster in its dealings with Shetland, Scotland's best interests will be served if Scottish Nationalists restrict themselves to ensuring that Shetlanders are informed of SNP's consistently held policies on oil depletion, fishing limits and the decentralisation of power, as of the range of possible constitutional relationships between Shetland and an independent Scotland.

To sum up this section: Scotland will emerge on the international scene after a conflict of political wills with Westminster perhaps extending over a period of several years. The contest will have been conducted according to the imprecise and flexible rules of democratic competition. The resentment and hurt pride which Scotland's secession will undoubtedly have caused the English and the suspicion and frustrations which Westminster's prevarication and hard bargaining will have produced in Scotland will be controlled in the interests of organising the new relationship in a way that minimises disruption in the two countries.

Scotland's emergence will be regretted by the majority of those established Governments with which an independent Scotland will desire to have close relations. Those Governments will, however, have given only discreet expression to their opposition and, independence achieved, will be anticipating friendly relations with a new state committed to Western democracy and eager for membership of the range of international political, financial and commercial institutions which have developed since the Second World War.

Multinational corporations led by United States' companies with interests in Scotland will have resigned themselves to the need to adapt to what will appear in the light of their international experience to be only modest changes in their operating conditions. If any companies do withdraw from Scotland as a result of independence they are likely to be English or Scottish owned companies acting not from a rational assessment of their economic prospects but from the political prejudices of their Boards of Directors. The foreign policy options open to a Scottish Government will therefore be determined not by the intervention in Scottish politics of external interests but by the same complex range of factors which determine the foreign policies of most of the other small, developed states of North-Western Europe.

EXTERNAL RELATIONS

Every generalisation about the role of small states in international affairs generates its own counter-examples. The following generalisations therefore make no claim to be exhaustive. They merely indicate the constraints under which most small states must operate but from which some are able to escape by reason of their particular political and economic circumstances.

It is a cliché that in the modern world all states are interdependent. In fact at the one end of the spectrum of power there may be found states so deficient in the sources of power that while no other state is dependent on them they are dependent on, if only in the sense of being defenceless against, virtually every other country with which they have contact. At the other end of the spectrum the nuclear power is dependent for its very survival on the rational forebearance of its fellow nuclear powers. Small states are doubly dependent in security terms — dependent for their survival on the forebearance of nuclear states and for their general security on an international distribution of power which they are able to influence if at all only at the margins.

In economic affairs the difference between the super-powers and the small state is equally striking. With their vast natural resources and large home markets, the super-powers are in a position to sustain a high degree of self-sufficiency. Only some 5% of the gross domestic product of the United States, for example, comes from foreign trade. The smaller the country the greater, as a rule, is its dependence on trade. Japan with a population of 100 million derives about 10% of its g.d.p., from trade. The United Kingdom (pop. 55 million) 21%; Sweden (8 million) 23%; Norway (4 million) 40%.

The ratio of size to dependence on trade is, of course, neither invariable nor exactly proportionate. By virtue of their location or the structure of their economies, some countries may be exceptionally dependent. The Netherlands, for example, with a population of 13 million, is no less than 46% dependent on trade.[11]

The dependent position of small states in international affairs means that they have a general interest in upholding the rule of law in international affairs, for in law they enjoy equal status with larger and more powerful states. They have the same interest in supporting international organisations, for although in their internal structure international organisations usually make generous concessions to the hard facts of power politics, as in the veto power reserved to the Big Five in the United Nations' Security Council, they seldom discard altogether the principle of international equality. Hence the enthusiasm of the smaller members of the international community for institutions like the League of Nations and the United Nations. A small country may, of course, feel impelled to defy international law and the opinion of international bodies in defence of a vital national interest, as Iceland's unilateral extensions of fishing limits illustrate; but whatever its decision in such cases the small country will feel constrained to give greater weight than the large to supporting the principle of the rule of law.

Given its high level of dependence on trade the small country has a parallel commercial interest in the development of a network of international agreements securing wide access and stable conditions for its exports and imports. Here, too, unilateral action which might provoke retaliation from larger trading partners must be reserved by the small country as a course of last resort.

Given the uncertain prospects for effective international organisation and liberal commercial arrangements on a world scale, small countries may hope to secure them instead on a regional scale, perhaps in co-operation with larger countries. The European Economic Community and the European Free Trade Area represent alternative ways of organising international interdependence on a regional basis.

The political and legal structure of EFTA reflects the limited functional aim of the free trade area. The Stockholm Convention required of its signatories no more than the limited and specific surrender of sovereignty involved in any international agreement between states. It left them free to pursue divergent policies towards third countries. It established no supranational institutions. The task of enforcing the rules of the Convention lay with the member governments themselves acting through the Council of the Association. It was built, in short, on the belief that the economic interdependence of its members could be efficiently managed within a framework of political decentralisation.

The founding articles of the European Economic Community — the Treaty of Rome signed in 1957 by France, West Germany, Italy and the Benelux countries — represent an altogether different response to the needs of international interdependence. The free trade area emphasis on the exchange of goods as the dominant mode of economic interdependence is replaced by an ambition to achieve economic integration in the form of a single market in which all the factors of production, as well as the means of commercial exchange, will be subject to uniform conditions. The freedom of action of member governments is constrained by comprehensive rules forbidding discrimination against the economic activities of nationals of member states. Most important, the removal of obstacles to the free movement of the factors of production is seen as merely the first step towards political union.

The aim of political union was foreshadowed in the institutional provisions of the Treaty of Rome. The Treaty established an excutive body in the shape of the Commission with the power to issue directives legally binding on member states. To enforce the rules of the market it established a European Court with the power to direct and fine member governments. For the efficient government of the market the Treaty provided for the introduction of binding majority voting in its supreme policy making body, the Council of Ministers, and for the direct election of members to a European Parliament. In short, where the free trade concept assumes a politically decentralised international society organising its interdependence through a network of functionally specialised agencies, the common market concept aims to solve the problems created by the interdependence of its members by in effect *dissolving* them in an economic and political union.

The suitability for each small country of these alternative ways of managing international interdependence will be determined by its particular circumstances. A country whose policy interests on balance converge with the policy interests of its most dominant neighbours will be predisposed towards the centralised, integrationist model of international organisation represented by the EEC. The country with policy interests which diverge from those of its leading neighbours will tend to favour the decentralised model represented by EFTA. Only in Western Europe have small countries been presented with a real choice between the two models. The contrasting examples of the Benelux countries and Norway illustrate the range of factors which have determined their response.

The geographical position of the Benelux countries between France and Germany meant that the security interests of the Benelux countries argued strongly for an integrationist solution embracing those two traditional European rivals. The form of integration outlined in the Treaty of Rome — in the shaping of which the Benelux countries themselves played an important role — not only promised to bind France and Germany indissolubly together but also offered the Benelux countries a guaranteed role in collective decision taking. The pattern of the Benelux countries' foreign trade reinforced the case for integration. With over 70% of Benelux exports going to the markets of the original EEC members the advantage of securing guaranteed access to those markets outweighed the disadvantage of the immediate loss of freedom of commercial policy in respect of third countries and even the prospective loss of their freedom of economic manoeuvrability in respect of many aspects of their domestic economies. Integration certainly posed a threat of economic domination by their larger neighbours but during the imperial era both Belgium and the Netherlands had developed international financial and industrial organisations of a size to enable them to compete for the benefits of the extended home market created by integration with their counterparts from France and Germany. For the Benelux countries the balance of economic and political advantage was overwhelmingly in favour of regional integration.

For Norway the choice was more complex. With 50% of her exports going to the EEC countries she had strong commercial reasons to favour membership. On the other hand some economic interests in Norway — notably her agricultural and fishing industries — stood to be seriously damaged by the common policies favoured by the EEC members. What was more the small Norwegian economy had bred no multinational companies or financial institutions comparable in size to the largest German and French or even Dutch and Belgian organisations.

Integration would, therefore, present a particularly grave danger of economic domination by external interests. It would also progressively diminish that economic manoeuvrability on which Norway, like the other Scandinavian countries, had depended in the international economic crisis of the 1920's and 30's. Further, unlike the Benelux countries, Norway possesses valuable natural resources — in oil, fishing, forestry, hydroelectricity — which the application of the EEC's rules of non-discrimination would expose to exploitation by the superior capital and technological resources of other EEC members. Finally Norway's location in an area where divergent international influences — from the United States and the Soviet Union, from the Common Market and the Nordic countries — interact, make it important for her, for security and political reasons, to maintain a freedom of diplomatic manoeuvre which integration within the EEC would progressively deny her.

The cornerstone of Scotland's foreign policy must be a close working relationship with England. Scottish Nationalists often underestimate the practical problems of establishing such a relationship. History yields no example of two societies as closely integrated and as interdependent as England and Scotland are within the United Kingdom, reorganising their relations from positions of sovereign independence.

Nationalists, it is true, like to point to the situation of the Scandinavian countries following the achievement of Norway's complete independence from Sweden in 1905. Through many false starts the Scandinavian countries finally evolved the characteristic form of inter-state co-operation exemplified today in the Nordic Council and its associated institutions. Yet the problems of co-operation facing the states of the British Isles after Scottish independence will be of a quite different order of complexity from those that faced the Scandinavian countries at the turn of the century, or indeed, from those that face them today. Norway gained her complete independence after nearly a century of some form or other of internal self-government dating from the Eidsvoll Constitution of 1812. It must be assumed that Scotland will have had at most a few years' experience even of devolved government, and it cannot be excluded that she will have to face the problems of sharing in the management of her complex relationship with England without even that limited experience. The problems of separating the Swedish and Norwegian administrations in those limited areas of governmental action where they were united in 1905 in an era of minimal government, bear no relation to the problems of separating the institutions of a developed, interventionist welfare state in the last quarter of the twentieth century even when part of the framework for separate administrations already exists. Furthermore, where the Scandinavian countries were able to develop their common institutions as part of a gradual and deliberate growth of co-operation in politically non-contentious areas — cultural affairs, harmonisation of labour and welfare legislation, a common labour market — England and Scotland will from the outset need an institutional structure capable of absorbing the tensions created by the introduction of separate monetary, industrial and investment policies, for example — some of which may discriminate against the other partner — while continuing the detailed co-operation required for the efficient functioning of two partly integrated, closely interdependent economies. The structure will, in short, have to be resilient enough and flexible enough to act at the same time as an instrument of *dis*integration in some areas and of continuing *in*tegration, in many others.

Against the background of these problems SNP proposals for an Association of states of the British Isles modelled on the Nordic Council can be treated as no more than a starting point. Although much of the detailed co-operation at administrative level between the Nordic countries barely touches the formal structure of the Council, the exceptional density of the co-operation which will be required between England and Scotland will need to be provided for in the structure of the Association of British states. A standing mixed Commission of specially designated Ministers and supporting officials might go some of the way to meeting the need. At the very least a stronger and more cohesive secretariat than exists in the Nordic Council would be necessary. While the agreement of the Nordic countries in 1971 to add a Council of Ministers to the Council's institutions facilitated the extension of co-operation into new fields such as energy policy and resource management, areas of vital day-to-day importance to the Anglo-Scottish relationship such as monetary policy and demand management penetrate the Nordic Council structure only in set speeches by Parliamentarians and Ministers at formal Council meetings. Of greatest relevance to this discussion, however, is the fact that because of the wide divergences of policy the Nordic countries do not use the Council as an instrument of foreign policy co-ordination. In this area an Association of states of the British Isles would be subject to particularly severe strains.

Scotland's secession from the United Kingdom would, of course, by itself diminish the international status of the United Kingdom's successor state, whether it take the form of a continued union of England, Wales and Northern Ireland or an independent England *tout seul.* The loss of Scotland and of Scotland's conspicuous wealth would inevitably provoke suggestions that UK–England had finally forfeited its claim to be one of the world's leading powers. Conceivably UK–England's claim to continued permanent membership of the United Nations' Security Council could come under challenge, perhaps no bad thing if it prompted a re-examination of the fossilised structure of that organisation. Demotion in the hierarchy of international financial institutions would seem probable. Scotland's secession would also encourage the UK's critics in the EEC, foremost among them France, to bracket England with Italy, leaving EEC leadership to be disputed between West Germany and France. It would certainly further diminish England's standing with the small members of the EEC, once the UK's doughtiest champions within the organisation.

The strains will be further increased by Scotland's desire to reduce her dependence on England. Scotland will be as sensitive as any small state to the danger of being so dependent on a large neighbour that she forfeits freedom of political and economic manoeuvre. In spite of her wealth of resources Scotland will start life as an independent state uncomfortably dependent on the English market for her exports and on English capital for investment. England's poor economic record in terms of both market growth and of investment since the war will reinforce Scotland's political reasons for seeking to reduce her dependence. Some of the means of reducing economic dependence would no doubt have been included among the clauses of the post-independence economic settlement, including agreements by a Scottish Government to buy out English controlled companies in Scotland and perhaps to restrict English investment in Scotland. A Scottish Government could further be expected to pursue a vigorous policy of diversifying Scottish exports away from England to more buoyant markets in West Germany, the Nordic countries, North America and the Middle East.

In addition to the friction caused by Scotland's pursuit of policies deliberately designed to reduce England's economic dominance a Scottish Government would almost certainly find herself in dispute with an English Government over a number of issues of economic policy. Fishing limits is an obvious example. As 200-mile limits become the international norm, pressure from English and Common Market fishing industries for access to the 30% of EEC fishing stocks falling within a notional 200-mile Scottish limit would inevitably increase. A Scottish Government could choose in the interests of good Anglo-Scottish relations to give generous preference to English interests but it might be tempted to use its asset as a bargaining counter to win commercial concessions from other states, perhaps with the objective of lessening Scotland's export dependence on England.

Oil provides another example. Even if the rate of extraction and the marketing of the oil were included as part of the post-independence economic settlement there would remain endless scope for disagreement over the interpretation of particular clauses in the settlement. In any event, in the same spirit in which Norway has declined membership of the International Energy Agency, a Scottish Government would wish to avoid any legally binding commitment to surrender to England any part of its control over the oil in the event of a repetition of the 1973 oil embargo.

The most direct way of countering England's political influence would be deliberately to call in outside influence to redress the balance of Anglo-Saxon dominated British Isles. As we have noted Scotland stands like Norway at a point where diverse and often divergent interests interact. Not all the interested states are suitable as counterweights to English influence. The Soviet Union is obviously excluded on general political grounds. While the United States offers itself as an obvious area for export diversification, the very scale of US power and the pervasive nature of US interests would tend to reduce Scotland to the status of a client. A Scottish Government will moreover have to be prepared to risk offending the US Government and US multinationals in pursuit of its oil policies and the latter, if not the former, by its policy of limiting further inroads on the Scottish economy by the US capital.

In many ways Canada is better qualified than the United States to serve as a *point d'appui* for Scotland. Scotland's strong social and historic links with Canada are complemented by the fellow-feeling of the two countries each of which shares a land frontier with a disproportionately large and powerful neighbour. The Scottish and Canadian economies are both dominated to an exceptional degree by external capital. They face the same problem of defending their natural wealth against external exploitation in order to use it as the basis for developing a more autonomous, self-renewing industrial economy. As countries with long coastlines they share a common interest at a time of growing awareness of the economic possibilities of marine and seabed resources, in an international regime embodying the principle of extensive 'exclusive economic zones' for littoral states. They both have peripheral communities dependent on fishing at a time of growing international pressure on fishing stocks. They are both energy exporting countries under strong pressure to develop their energy reserves at a rate more suited to the needs of powerful neighbours than to their own. They both occupy key positions in the security dispositions of the world's greatest military power.

And yet, notwithstanding these common interests, the Canadian response to overtures from Scotland will be cautious. Even if the Quebec problem had been solved by the establishment of an independent state of Quebec, the effect of the resulting shock waves on the relations between the other states of the confederation from the Maritimes to British Columbia would continue to make Ottawa wary of too intimate a relationship with a newly independent state which might appear to some restless state politicians to offer a more or less respectable English speaking model of separatism in place of the proscribed French-Canadian one. Quite independently of the Quebec issue, the very extent of the US' economic domination of Canada might inhibit too close an association with a state born partly from an ambition to regain a measure of economic independence from those same interests.

Perhaps the ideal transatlantic partner for Scotland would be an independent Quebec itself. Like Scotland Quebec will have experienced all the problems of wresting independence from a resistant metropolitan authority. Like Scotland she will be in the process of discovering where the limits to the operation of independent economic policies lie in an economy still closely integrated with the economies of her former Federal partners. Both countries will possess a valuable natural resource base allied to an inherited lack of the native capital, technological skills and business infrastructure to develop it to their own long-term advantage. As North Atlantic littoral states both countries are equipped to play key roles in the development of marine policy. It is likely that at least the early administrations of both countries will be controlled by representatives of Nationalist movements which are secularist, bourgeois and reformist. Scottish politicians eager to diversify Scotland's international contacts might even consider Quebec's links with France as a diplomatic asset.

Scotland could seek a special relationship in two other directions — the Common Market countries and the Nordic Council countries. We have noted that the Common Market holds special attractions for a number of the small countries of Western Europe. But we have also identified probable conflicts of interest between Scotland and the majority of the Common Market countries in a number of key areas — oil development, fishing limits, the free movement of capital, common agricultural policy. While such conflicts of interest do not preclude Scotland's membership of the EEC, as a new member Scotland would find her fellow members aligned with England on most of the disputed issues. Scotland would, therefore, have took elsewhere for a reliable, long-term counter-weight to the preponderant English influence.

There remain the Nordic countries. The alleged Nordic obsession of Scottish Nationalists has provided the material for some mild controversy on the edges of the Scottish debate.[12] It must be admitted that Nationalists have sometimes claimed closer parallels between Scotland and the Nordic countries than do in fact exist. We have already questioned the relevance to the Scottish case of Norway's experience of the road to independence and the adequacy of the Nordic Council as a model for the management of post-independence Anglo-Scottish relations. Nationalists are perhaps most open to criticism when they suggest that independence would miraculously rid Scotland of the social and economic legacy of her industrial revolution transforming her overnight into a model Scandinavian welfare state. Nevertheless, the Nordic countries' record of innovation in social and economic affairs and of hard-headed competence in the management of their external affairs provides Nationalists with an effective answer to *a priori* arguments about the lack of viability of small states in the modern world. And a firm basis for projecting a special relationship between an independent Scotland and the Nordic countries lies in the complex of shared and interrelated interests in their external affairs.

To take the economic issues first. As oil exporters Scotland and Norway share the interest of other oil producing countries in supporting a high world price for oil. As oil producers who happen to be located on the northern periphery of the world's largest oil importing area — industrialised Western Europe — they are both subject to pressure to surrender control of their oil to organisations such as the IEA and the EEC representing the interests of oil importing countries. At the same time, as industrialised countries themselves, they have reason to be particularly sensitive to the effect of oil price increases on the economic buoyancy of their industrialised trading partners. In their search for ways of transforming their oil wealth into economic assets which will outlast the oil itself both are likely to identify the development of their own abundant natural resources as prime targets for investment. As small economies they will face the same need to defend their new investments from the colonial ambitions of multinational companies.

The two countries will be distinguished from most of their free world associates by the steadily expanding role which the public sector, financed from the oil wealth accruing to the state in the form of oil revenues, seems destined to play in their economies. Due to the limited capacity of their economies to absorb new wealth both countries will also face the need to dispose of large surpluses of oil generated capital on the international market.

Fishing provides another Scottish-Nordic link. Like Norway and Iceland, Scotland's fishing interests lie chiefly in off-shore — as opposed to distant — water fishing. By following Norway and Iceland in declaring a 200-mile limit Scotland could establish a base from which to negotiate reciprocal quotas with these and other North Atlantic fishing nations such as the Faroe or in collaboration with them to extract commercial concessions from trading partners lacking extensive fishing zones of their own. Oil development and the conservation of fish stocks are just two issues in the growing international debate about resource management. Although Western Europe as a whole is a net importer of raw materials there are important differences between the countries of Western Europe. The Common Market countries, for example, have a massive deficit on their trade in raw materials. Among the basic commodities only food yields an exportable surplus for the Common Market countries. At the other end of the commodity spectrum, the Common Market is 60% dependent on imports for her energy and virtually 100% dependent in oil.

By comparison with the Common Market countries the Nordic countries have a favourable balance of population and resources. Norway is a net importer of agricultural products but an exporter of fish products, energy and timber products. Sweden is an importer of energy but an exporter of timber products, iron ore and uranium. Iceland is an exporter of fish and more modestly of agricultural products and a potential exporter of energy. The commodity exports of metropolitan Denmark, the least well endowed of the Nordic countries, are restricted to a range of agricultural products, and on a more modest scale fish products. All the Nordic countries are generously endowed with resources of land and water while the location and geographical characteristics of Iceland, Norway, Faroe and Greenland mean that the Nordic community as a whole is exceptionally well placed to benefit from the growing interest in the development of marine and seabed resources. Scotland shares the Nordic countries' favourable balance of population and resources. Only in respect of agricultural goods does she suffer by comparison with the Common Market countries and even on food she is much nearer to self-sufficiency than England. Indeed, she achieves self-sufficiency in food in trading terms if her trade in fish and fish products is aggregated with her agricultural trade. Unlike England and the Common Market countries Scotland is a net exporter of energy in the form of oil. She has, in addition, substantial reserves of coal and is exceptionally well placed to develop alternative forms of energy such as wave power and wind power. She has a favourable land/population ratio, excellent deep-water access, abundant fresh water and a vast forestry potential. She also has significantly sized reserves of a number of scarce minerals the development of which could become commercially attractive (if politically controversial) if world prices were to rise dramatically. Not least, her location of the north-western flank of the continental land mass puts her, like the Nordic countries, in a good position to benefit from marine and seabed development.

The resource wealth of Scotland and the Nordic countries gives them an obvious interest in co-operating to try to maintain favourable terms of trade for their resource based exports. Given favourable terms, it also represents a source of bargaining power which they can use to advance their commercial interests as industrialised nations. The largest markets for Scottish and Nordic resource based exports — their exports of energy, fish and timber for example — are found in those industrialised countries of Western Europe which also provide the major markets for Scottish and Nordic manufactured exports. The long-term price trend in favour of commodity exports provides Scotland and the Nordic countries with a valuable counterweight to the commercial power which their trading partners enjoy by virtue of their sheer market size and of the fact that they have organised themselves into a Common Market armed with a common commercial policy. Scotland and the Nordic countries will derive further bargaining power from the attraction their natural resources will have for investors in their rich trading partners. Moreover if the capital wealth accruing to Scotland and Norway in the form of surplus oil revenues is made available to other members of the Scottish-Nordic community through such institutions as the Nordic Investment Bank it will serve to encourage a discriminating response to offers of capital from elsewhere.

Each of the common Scottish-Nordic interests which we have so far identified has been partly defined in contradistinction to a Common Market interest. This is no accident. The Nordic countries' relationship with the Common Market bears some resemblance to Scotland's relationship with England — a measure of economic integration and close commercial and political interdependence coexisting with conflicts of interest in key areas and a consequent need for political decentralisation. It follows that the Nordic countries have a close interest in the future development of the Common Market. We have seen how changes in the terms of trade may provide the Nordic countries with a defence against some of the dangers created by the economic integration of the Common Market countries. If, however, political union were to follow economic integration as envisaged by the founding fathers of the EEC, the consequent political dangers to the Nordic countries might not be easily averted. A united Europe would not be master of its own future if it lacked a common foreign policy. A common foreign policy presupposes a common defence force — and in the league of international states in which Europe would wish to be classified — a common defence force would have to include a nuclear capacity. The emergence of such a Europe would be incompatible with a continued US military presence in Europe. United States' withdrawal would not only undermine the foundations of détente, but also leave the Nordic countries in a hopelessly exposed position on Europe's northern flank forcing them to choose eventually between a Finnish-style neutrality dependent on the Soviet Union or absorption into the Common Market on whatever terms the Common Market cared to set. Sharing the exposed strategic position of the Nordic countries, an independent Scotland would share their choice.

It follows that the Nordic countries would take a close interest in the impact of an independent Scotland on the development of the Common Market. However, it cannot be assumed that the Nordic countries would prefer Scotland to withdraw from the Market. They would recognise that a Common Market which was willing to accommodate a country committed to an exclusive fishing zone, a right of control over foreign investment, a power of veto over a common energy policy and dilution, if not abolition, of the common agricultural policy would be a Market that had abandoned the idea of political and economic union. They might even calculate that centrifugal pressure from the north by Scotland, if exerted simultaneously with similar pressure from the south by the new Mediterranean members of Spain, Portugal and Greece, would transform the EEC into the extended free trade area which was the Nordic countries' aim when they participated in the formation of the European Free Trade Area in 1961. The fact is that the stubborn refusal of the EEC to develop towards economic and political union, the prospect of enlargement and the completion last year (1977) of the transitional steps to complete free trade in industrial goods between EFTA and the EEC have reduced both the economic and political significance of the EEC for the foreseeable future — a development which both Scotland and the Nordic countries have reason to welcome.

Scotland's maritime position will provide a further link with Nordic states. Like the two leading Nordic maritime states — Norway and Iceland — Scotland will lack the organisational means in the shape of multinational oil companies to compete successfully in an international free-for-all to develop marine and seabed resources. She will, therefore, share their interest in supporting an international regime for the seabed based on limited coastal zones under national control in conjunction with international regulation by an International Seabed Authority of areas outwith national limits.

If there is ample scope for Scottish-Nordic co-operation, the institutional form which the co-operation might take remains to be determined. The Nordic Council — the formal framework for inter-Nordic co-operation — has hitherto been directed at the harmonisation of social and labour legislation and cultural exchange. It has only recently even begun to approach some of the policy areas identified here, as in the formation of the Nordic Investment Bank (1976), plans for a Nordic energy network, and the preparation of a report on the Nordic countries' resource base. Inhibited by the differences between the security policies of its members and by Finland's special relationship with the Soviet Union, the Nordic Council has traditionally eschewed foreign policy matters. It restricted itself to only the most guarded expression of support for Iceland in that country's most recent dispute with the United Kingdom following her unilateral extension of fishing limits. The co-ordination of the Nordic countries' policy positions in GATT negotiations and in the United Nations has taken place outwith the Nordic Council framework.

Scotland's intimate relationship with England will impose its own restraints on Scottish-Nordic co-operation. Scotland's interest in close social and economic co-operation with England within the framework of a common market or free trade agreement, a common labour market and an agreement on the free movement of individuals and personal goods would complicate if not exclude Scotland's participation in the harmonisation of social and labour legislation which remains the chief concern of the Nordic Council. (It was presumably the dawning appreciation of this fact that caused the SNP in 1977 to replace its earlier commitment in 1969 to seek full Scottish membership of the Nordic Council with a commitment simply to 'explore the possibility of Scotland's membership of the Nordic Council'). If the Nordic countries were to admit Scotland to membership of the Council they would in effect be inviting a more abrupt extension of the Council's field of operation than they are yet prepared to accept. A further and perhaps even more decisive obstacle to Scotland's membership of the Council would be the fear of the current members that the admission of a country outwith the historic Nordic community would provoke the Soviet Union into resurrecting, through Finland, her earlier demand for Soviet membership.

DEFENCE AND DIPLOMACY

The probability therefore is that the Nordic countries would prefer to pursue co-operation with Scotland outside the Nordic Council. By reason of her geographical location alone Scotland is implicated in the military balance of East and West. Nevertheless, her overall strategic importance is somewhat less today than it was ten or fifteen years ago. The greatly increased range of the present generation of Soviet submarine missiles allows Soviet submarines to cover their targets in the United States from stations in the Arctic Ocean or even in the Barents Sea and other waters off the Soviet Union's Northern coast, where previously they could do so only from positions off the North American coast. In the Soviet Union's coastal waters Soviet submarines enjoy the security of operating from a 'rear' area into which US hunter-killers can penetrate only at considerable danger to themselves, while in the Arctic improvements in techniques of navigating under pack-ice allow Soviet submarines the advantages of improved concealment in its wide waters. The result is that the submarine-borne element of the Soviet Union's strategic deterrent no longer has to run the gauntlet of the Greenland-Iceland-Shetland gap.

Scotland's strategic importance to the West has declined in other aspects also. The extension in the range of Soviet missiles and submarines was preceded by extensions in the range of US submarines and missiles. When missile range and submarine endurance were limited it was important for the US to have access to forward operational bases such as the Holy Loch base in Scotland for her missile carrying submarines. Today US missile submarines can operate from bases on the North American coast without any significant loss of operational effectiveness. If the United States continues to value her base facilities at Holy Loch it is more for political than for military reasons.

Scotland's value as a base for radar early warning facilities for the Western Alliance has also diminished. The diversification of the United States' strategic deterrent away from dependence on aircraft and 'soft' land-based missiles into submarines and 'hard' land-based missiles, has reduced the importance of short-warning times in the event of a pre-emptive attack by the Soviet Union. In any case new techniques of surveillance and reconnaissance, including satellite reconnaissance, offer the prospect of far longer warning times than any land-based system can provide.

The decline in the importance of Scotland's contribution to maintaining the West's strategic deterrent should reduce the political opposition an independent Scottish Government would face from the United States in pursuing its policy of banning nuclear bases from Scotland. That policy will, in fact, prove more embarrassing to England than to the United States. Where the United States has no lack of alternative sites for operational bases on her extensive coastline, England must expect considerable political opposition to resiting her Faslane base facilities on the relatively congested English coastline, and having retreated from Scotland, could hardly use a location in Wales. But however resentful the two countries may be they will not wish to jeopardise Scotland's continuing contribution to Western security by provoking a confrontation over what will be an issue of only marginal importance in terms of the West's global security needs.

In spite of these developments, Scotland's military value to the West will still be substantial. The modern Soviet navy is equipped with both an impressive submarine hunter-killer capacity, for use against the US submarine deterrent, and an equally impressive 'interdict' capacity in the form of her surface fleet, for use against the sea communications between the United States and her European allies. The Greenland-Iceland-Shetland gap remains vital to the Soviet Union as an exit to the North Atlantic for both these elements. In sub-nuclear conflict between the Western allies and the Soviet Union control of the gap would be hotly contested by naval and air forces. The Soviet Union would wish to maintain the maximum ease of egress for her forces to the North Atlantic while the United States would be equally eager to block the gap. Indeed, the strategic importance of the gap is such that there would be a distinct danger of pre-emptive action by one side or the other, first in the form of a 'surge' deployment of forces into the gap, later in the form of escalation from one level of violence to the next, in order to win control. The West's early warning facilities and air-bases in Greenland, Iceland and Scotland would play a key role in the struggle.

Scotland's strategic role in the North Sea and the Norwegian Sea is, again, as a base for early warning reconnaissance and for defensive air capacity. However, this area will be exceptionally vulnerable to the Soviet Union. The build up of Soviet strength in the Kola peninsula means that Soviet military power now overshadows Norway and the Norwegian Sea. Indeed, many Norwegian military analysts consider that for all practical purposes Norway is already behind the Soviet Union's naval front line. Certainly in this area the Western allies will not be able to support their naval forces with air superiority as in the battle for the Greenland-Iceland-UK gap. Indeed the exact strategic value of the northern North Sea of Scotland's north eastern coast and Norwegian Sea and the West's military prospects there are alike problematical. It may be possible to defend North Sea oil installations from hi-jack attempts or other attacks at a very low level of violence, but it will certainly be impossible to protect them in a major conflict. At the same time these seas are unattractive to strategic submarine forces which can be more effectively and safely deployed in less constricted waters. Certainly Scotland has a role as a base for the reinforce-ment of Norway by air — if the local superiority which the Soviet Union enjoys both in the air and on the ground does not render Norway impos-sible to defend. Scotland's military value in respect of this area appears then to rest principally on her reconnaissance and warning role. Scotland's diminished strategic role and her exposed military position inevitably raise the question of her future relations with the Western Alliance. Even as part of the United Kingdom Scotland is a factor in that complex of political and military relationships known as the Nordic balance. Scotland's emergence as an independent centre of political and military decision-taking will further define a 'Nordic' dimension to the West's security problem.

The combination of Nordic countries' experience in the Second World War and the emergence of the Soviet Union as a military super-power drove the Nordic countries to re-examine their traditional policy of neutrality. Sweden chose to remain neutral while dramatically increasing her level of military preparedness. Norway and Denmark opted for NATO member-ship, but on a qualified basis which excluded the stationing of nuclear bases on their territory. Finland accepted a 'special relationship' with the Soviet Union which in effect, though not in the letter, bound her not to increase her military strength beyond certain very modest limits. As the phrase the 'Nordic balance' implies, the defence posture of each state depends on that of its fellows and a change of policy by one would have repercussions for each of the others.

The degree to which an independent Scotland will be constrained by the needs of the Nordic balance can be illustrated by examining the repercus-sions of a decision by Scotland to withdraw from NATO into neutrality.

Scotland's withdrawal would, first of all, have important consequences for the military balance in the North Atlantic. While it would not directly threaten the security of the American continent it would, by eliminating the alliance's air base and warning facilities in northern Scotland push Western surveillance back onto its Greenland and Iceland bases. It is likely that the Soviet Union would try to exploit the situation to extend its forward defensive line into the Greenland-Iceland-UK gap. In addition to strengthening the Soviet Union's naval defences, an intensification of Soviet activity in the area would also provide increased scope for the forward deployment of the Soviet 'interdict' capacity. As a result the security of sea communications between the United States and her European allies would be rendered even more uncertain than it is already. The political consequences of a Scottish neutrality would be more dramatic. Scottish neutrality, even on the Swedish model of armed neutrality, would not only leave NATO's northern flank militarily more exposed than at present; politically it would blow it wide open. Scottish withdrawal would almost certainly drive Norwegian opinion, already sensitive to the fact that Norway has been militarily outflanked by the build-up of Soviet military strength in the Kola peninsula, to the conclusion that Norway's continued membership of NATO simply exposed her to immediate attack from the Soviet Union in the event of conflict without the least chance of an effective NATO response. Two courses of action would then be open to Norway. The first would be to adopt Sweden's policy of armed neutrality. However, in pursuing this policy Norway would face handicaps from which Sweden is free. Her extensive frontiers with the Soviet Union and her long coastline dominated by Soviet naval power would pose an insuperable defence problem. In the changed circumstances following Scotland's adoption of neutrality, Norway would also lack the strategic asset Sweden enjoys in the form of a militarily committed rear area provided by Norway and other North European members of NATO. Furthermore, the very asset which could finance a policy of armed neutrality — Norway's oil assets — also represent a strategic liability in the event of conflict.

If armed neutrality on an individual basis is impractical a defensive alliance embracing the Nordic states as a whole, perhaps with Scottish membership, is no more realistic. The cost of such an 'armed neutrality' would be daunting even to countries as wealthy as Norway, Sweden and Scotland. Denmark would be likely to react to these changes in the Nordic balance by disengaging from her Nordic colleagues in favour of closer integration with the EEC. While the Soviet Union has periodically encouraged Finnish initiatives aimed at neutralising her frontiers with fellow Nordic members through the creation of 'demilitarised' frontier zones, certainly oppose Finnish membership using the Finnish-Soviet Treaty of Mutual Assistance to do so. Finally, NATO could hardly survive the withdrawal of Scotland and Norway into neutrality. Transatlantic pressure for a withdrawal of the United States' military presence in Europe would be matched in the EEC countries by increased support for a common European defence policy which would have to be based on a European nuclear force. The consequent polarisation of European politics between the Soviet Union and a nuclear armed Western Europe led by West Germany would shatter détente.

No countries would stand to suffer so much from these developments as the small countries on Europe's exposed northern flank. Their choice would then lie effectively between rejoining a continental alliance system even less capable than the present Atlantic system of providing for their security needs and certainly more perilous in political terms, or accepting a Finnish style relationship with the Soviet Union. It would, therefore, be in the interests of a Scottish Government to recognise that the structure of collective security which has evolved since the end of the Cold War provides an essential framework for the management of détente on which Scotland's prospects for gaining greater manoeuvrability in security policy ultimately depends. The question is then: what initiatives might an independent Scotland take to advance détente within the political parameters of the existing security alliances?

As one small member of the North Atlantic Alliance Scotland's power of effective initiative is, of course, strictly limited. Scope for a Scottish initiative is restricted to the North Sea. Having adopted a policy of refusing nuclear bases on Scottish territory a Scottish Government could collaborate with its fellow non-nuclear member of NATO, Norway, to seek an agreement with the super-powers on de-nuclearising the North Sea between Scotland and the Norwegian Sea between agreed latitudes. Under such an agreement the nuclear powers would undertake to keep nuclear warships out of the designated area. Such an agreement would cost the nuclear powers little. As we have seen the North Sea has few attractions for nuclear submarine forces of either East or West. The density of oil development, fishing and commercial marine activities makes concealment difficult. For the same reason, verification of an agreement would present few problems. An agreement to exclude nuclear warships from Scottish and Norwegian sectors of the North Sea, largely symbolic though it would be, would probably be as far as the interested states would be willing to go towards demilitarisation of the area. Norway and the United States would fear that restrictions on conventional surface fleets would erode NATO's capacity to give support to Norway in the event of a crisis. The existence of an agreement at all would give the Soviet Union an opportunity for diplomatic intervention in an area which, whatever its real military value, is of considerable economic and political importance to the future of NATO. (The fear of formalising Soviet interference in the North Sea would probably prove a decisive obstacle to Norwegian, let alone US, acceptance of SNP proposals for a Civil Maritime Control Agency composed of North Sea littoral states and the larger user states, including the Soviet Union, to supervise the complex of civil activities in the North Sea.)

An independent Scotland could, of course, take diplomatic initiatives along the more ambitious lines suggested in the SNP's foreign policy proposals, but as those proposals themselves acknowledge, progress would depend on multilateral negotiations in which Scotland's role could only be marginal.

Self-determination and state succession

Alexander McCall Smith

As Stephen Maxwell has shown, the political hurdles facing any attempt to assert Scottish independence could be daunting. But assuming that these hurdles were surmounted and the matter reached the conference table, what role would international law play in the process of bringing the new state into existence? There are two particularly important aspects of international law which might be expected to arise. The first — the question of the right of self-determination — would occur during the stage at which the right to independence was being asserted, both in the international context and within the United Kingdom. The second — the law of state succession — would be of crucial importance during the negotiations preceding independence. Both of these questions involve complex legal issues, but both are highly controversial and have a prominent political dimension.

SCOTLAND AND SELF-DETERMINATION

Commenting in 1921 on the use of the term 'self-determination', the American writer, Robert Lansing, expressed the view that 'it is an evil thing to permit the phrase to continue to dwell in the minds of men as expressing a principle having the apparent sanction of the civilised world, when it has been in fact thoroughly discredited and will always be cast aside whenever it comes in conflict with national safety, with historic political rights, or with economic interests affecting the prospects of a nation.'[1] Today, as in 1921, self-determination, like many other terms of political and legal discourse, is still a much abused expression. In few political and constitutional conflicts of a national character does it not form the staple of much assertion and counter-assertion. In the handful of remaining colonial conflicts, self-determination provides the theoretical basis for the claims of the colonised; in the larger number of struggles against political repression of minorities, the term is likewise extensively used; and in the more complex non-colonial secessionist movements, self-determination becomes the core of the secessionist rationale. In Scotland's case the expression has not been much employed by the proponents of independence possibly because the current political debate has focused on more pragmatic issues, and possibly because Scotland's right to decide its own future has not (until recently) been seriously questioned.[2] Once the issue progressed, however, to the point of constitutional crisis or political confrontation, the question of self-determination could become commoner currency in the Scottish debate.

If the meaning and content of the term self-determination is obscure in political discussion, its status in international law is hardly less problematical. It is now widely accepted that international law recognises the right of peoples to self-determination, but it is difficult to ascertain the legal content of any principle expressed in such broad terms. As Sir Ivor Jennings pointed out, the people cannot decide until somebody decides who are the people. So who can exercise the right and in what circumstances should the legal right be recognised? What, particularly, is the status of secessionist movements in terms of the right?

As the term was used by Woodrow Wilson after the First World War, the right of self-determination was intended to refer to the right of certain European states to determine their own political future.[3] The Wilsonian concept was no broader than that, and was certainly not intended to recognise a similar right vested in the peoples subject to European colonialism. In later usage, its application was extended, and during the United Nations era it was specifically applied to the colonial peoples in their struggle for independence. The right of self-determination now came to mean the right of the African and Asian nations (defined according to colonially drawn boundaries) to establish themselves as sovereign states. The preoccupation of the United Nations with colonial questions during the 1960s resulted in the lengthy elucidation of the principle of self-determination in this context; it was clearly conceived of as the right of the colonised to reject the political authority of the colonial powers.[4] Grounds for its assertion as a fundamental aim of the United Nations are to be found in Article 55 of the UN Charter itself, where self-determination is identified with the equal rights of peoples as the basis for the promotion of UN social and economic objectives. Yet it is clear that the UN did not intend to condone and encourage secession. The committee which discussed the concept of self-determination emphasised that it did not regard secession as being encompassed by the term, as its report indicates:

'Conceding the principle of self-determination it was strongly emphasised on the one side that this principle corresponded closely to the will and the desires of peoples everywhere and should be clearly enunciated in the Charter; on the other side, it was stated that the principle conformed to the purposes of the Charter only in so far as it implied the right of self-government of peoples and not the right of secession.'[5]

The right of self-determination served colonial nations well in their assertion of national sovereignty, but was to return to haunt a number of them in an unwelcome fashion. The attainment of independence in many cases has not solved chronic problems caused by arbitrarily drawn boundaries. The difficulties experienced by new states whose political boundaries do not accord with tribal or national boundaries gave rise to the emergence of numerous secessionist movements. This problem confronted both democratic and non-democratic states; even a relatively stable democracy such as India experienced secessionist pressure in Kashmir and

Nagaland. Amongst the African states, the prospect of chaotic Balkanisation was seen by the OAU as a fundamental threat to African unity and provoked a harsh and intransigent response.[6]

Outside the former colonial world, use of the self-determination argument has been made by the various secessionist movements which have sprung from the centrifugal pressure operating in previously secure multinational states. The fragility of multi-nationalism has been demonstrated by the past failure of many multi-national states either to assimilate or pacify national minorities, a failure which has been demonstrated both in Eastern and Western Europe.[7] With the emergence of secessionist movements in, amongst others, Canada and France, the principle of self-determination has been invoked as justification for challenging the constitutional *status quo*. Acceptance of the right of self-determination for subject peoples elsewhere was comparatively easy, but became more threatening when the same principle was used to suggest fragmentation of one's own territory. France, for instance, showed in 1977 in her reaction to the Parti Québécois that she tacitly supported self-determination for Quebec, but has not been consistent in extending the courtesy to secessionist causes within her own frontiers.

To determine how a Scottish claim to self-determination would stand in international law involves asking whether the new Scottish state would be considered a secessionist state, or whether it would be regarded as a state emerging as the result of the dissolution of a union. If the latter view were widely accepted, then there would be no problem in establishing a right of self-determination. Member states of a union or a federation may leave the union or federation without any international soul-searching on the effects of this on the right of self-determination. The literature on self-determination does not pay much attention to the fairly numerous cases of the dissolution of unions or federations (the dissolution of the Norway-Sweden Union and the withdrawal of Singapore from the Federation of Malaysia being two examples). In the case of unions and federations, it is assumed that the parties retain the right to withdraw, and such withdrawals have not raised controversial issues for the concept of national self-determination. In certain circumstances, however, for a variety of reasons the withdrawal of one of the parties may be regarded as more akin to secession of the sort attempted in Katanga, Biafra and East Pakistan. Since it is argued below[8] that an attempt by Scotland to leave the United Kingdom would fall into this category of secession, the status of secessionist movements in respect of the right of self-determination becomes relevant.

The practice of the United Nations and the experience of individual nations indicate that it is extremely difficult for a secessionist movement to rely on any recognition in its case of the right of national self-determination, though there are grounds for arguing that the right should apply in some of these cases. Ultimately, of course, the definition of the right assumes a revolutionary nature: if a sufficient number of secessionist movements successfully establish their independence, then the right may be established in their case. Before that stage, however, the existence of the right is more tenuous.

The attitude of the UN and its predecessor towards secessionist movements has been consistently hostile, reflecting the antagonism felt by established states towards the concept of secession. In 1921 a Committee of Inquiry of the League of Nations, commenting on the Åaland Islands case, stated in answer to the question of whether a minority can secede:

'The answer can only be in the negative. To concede to minorities either of language or religion, or to any fraction of a population, the right of withdrawing from the community to which they belong because it is their wish for their good pleasure, would be to destroy order and stability within states and to inaugurate anarchy in international life; it would be to uphold a theory incompatible with the very idea of the state as a territorial and political unity.'[9]

More recently, U Thant, as Secretary General of the UN, made clear his opposition to recognising a secessionist right of self-determination. Dealing with the attitude of the Nigerian Government towards Biafra, the Secretary-General remarked:

'. . . As far as the question of secession of a particular section of a Member State is concerned, the United Nations' attitude is unequivocal. As an international organisation, the United Nations has never accepted and does not accept and I do not believe it will ever accept the principle of the secession of a part of its Member State.'[10]

Again on the Biafran issue, U Thant argued that 'regarding the question of self-determination, I think this concept is not properly understood in many parts of the world. Self-determination of the peoples does not imply self-determination of a section of a population of a particular Member State. If the principle of self-determination is applied to ten different areas of a Member State, or five different areas of a Member State, or twenty different areas of a Member State, then I am afraid there will be no end to the problems.'[11] Although the Secretary-General's attitude appeared to become less rigid when he was faced with the East Pakistan crisis, his defence of the territorial integrity of existing states represents what has traditionally been the international consensus on the question.

Signs of a less restrictive interpretation of the right are to be found in the 1970 Declaration on the Principles of International Law concerning Friendly Relations. On self-determination, the Declaration qualifies its support of the principle in terms which do not totally exclude a right of secession:

'Nothing in the foregoing paragraphs shall be construed as authorising or encouraging any action which would dismember or impair, totally or in part, the territorial integrity or political unity of sovereign and independent States conducting themselves in compliance with the principle of equal rights and self-determination of peoples as described above and thus possessed of a government representing the whole people belonging to the territory without distinction as to race, creed or colour.'[12]

The significance of this is that in certain circumstances, where an unrepresentative government dominates and does not grant equal rights to a national group within its population, the right of self-determination on the part of a seceding group will not be treated as being totally subject to the principle of territorial integrity.

The opinions of doctrinal writers have reflected greater flexibility than the views expressed by states and international organisations. At the one extreme there has been unyielding hostility to the extension of the right to include secession. One American international lawyer, Rupert Emerson, has spoken of the general right in scathing terms:

' "All people have the right to self-determination." Since "peoples" is one of the loosest of terms, having no fixed and definable content, this assertion verges on being meaningless, or, alternatively, in the highly unlikely event of it being taken seriously, it is a declaration of an extreme libertarian or even anarchistic variety, authorising any group which designates itself as a people to disrupt the existing polity to set up a new one which meets their desires.'[13] In Emerson's view, it is a *reductio ad absurdum* of the principle to allow, amongst others, the French Canadians, the Welsh or the Sikhs the right to establish their own political structures.

The majority of other contemporary writers adopt a markedly less conservative attitude. The right of self-determination is seen in many cases as being one to which secessionist movements may have a claim. Though conscious of the difficulties of defining the circumstances in which the right may be exercised, its exercise in the context of secession is by no means excluded.[14] The recognition of the fragility of many multi-national states has led to a re-appraisal of the extent to which a complete rejection of the right of self-determination in all but colonial cases serves the cause of international stability. To exclude the right in some cases will not strengthen territorial integrity but compromise it.[15]

The successful secession of Bangladesh from Pakistan has recently provoked re-examination of the merits of the narrow definition of the right in international law. In the Nigerian case, only five states recognised Biafra's claim to independence,[16] and indeed the fate of Biafra did little for the extension of the right. Bangladesh was more successful and is now taken as a reason for asserting that the right of self-determination can now exist in non-colonial circumstances. Six special features of Bangladesh's situation can be taken to establish a right of self-determination in its case: physical separation from West Pakistan; the existence of linguistic, cultural and ethnic differences; regional disparity in economic growth; an electoral mandate for independence; brutal suppression by the West Pakistan armed forces; and the failure of East Pakistan to present a threat to stability in Asia if it were to become independent.[17] These criteria are a combination of some of the traditional criteria for the existence of a right of self-determination (language, ethnic identity), and some of the more modern criteria envisaged by the 1970 Declaration (suppression, economic neglect).

It will be obvious that although some opinion is moving towards an extension of the right of self-determination to include secessionist claims, it is necessary for some justification to be shown for secession other than the mere expression of political will to separate. In Scotland's case there is clearly no infringement by the United Kingdom of the principles proclaimed in the 1970 Declaration, and in these terms it might be difficult to establish a right of self-determination on Scotland's part. But would it be totally impossible on other grounds? In a comprehensive examination of the constitutional and legal implications of the accession to sovereignty of an independent Quebec, Professor Jacques Brossard has argued for the recognition of a right to self-determination on the part of Quebec. His argument is of significance to Scotland in that the parallel between the positions of the national movements in Scotland and Quebec is obvious. Both are part of a broadly similar political phenomenon, although there are differences in the constitutional background of Scotland and Quebec.[18]

For Brossard, the people of Quebec are clearly a people in terms of the United Nations recognition of the self-determination principle. The justifications produced for this are based on objective and subjective elements. Objective elements include the historical continuity of the Quebec people, the possession of a language distinct from that of the majority of Canadians, identification with a common religion, the possession of certain common socio-cultural values and association with a clearly identifiable territory. The subjective criterion for the identification of the French Canadians as a people is what Brossard describes as the *vouloir vivre collectif*, the desire to exist as a people which he argues has been present in Quebec since the widespread emergence of national consciousness in the nineteenth century. Brossard argues that the people of Quebec are a people in a sense in which Albertans are not. In Alberta's case, the population consists of people who consider themselves part of, and are in fact part of, a larger Anglo-Canadian identity, thus leading the Albertan identity to be characterised as regional. Having satisfied himself that a Quebec people exists for the purposes of the international law definition, Brossard argues that international law gives them a right to self-determination on a number of grounds. Quebec possesses the elements of a state structure (except for sovereignty); it possesses the requisite territory; and it would constitute a viable state enhanced with major natural resources.

Some of the arguments which Brossard adduces to support a right of self-determination for Quebec can be used to infer a similar right in Scotland. There is the obvious language difference between the two cases, in that the language element would not be a plank in any Scottish case, but the importance of this factor is, in any event, questionable.[19] On the question of the socio-cultural values criterion which Brossard considers, there is room for endless and ultimately unprofitable argument. Many would be inclined to the view that there exists very considerable cultural homogeneity between Scotland and the rest of the United Kingdom, and that on these grounds it would be difficult to establish the existence of a distinctive Scottish Community. Others would argue vigorously to the opposite effect, taking the view that a Scottish national identity has survived the Union and continues to resist assimilation. More powerfully, it might be argued that Scotland did once exist as an independent nation, and that once this fact is established, the right of self-determination is satisfactorily founded. This argument might serve to distinguish those cases with some record and memory of independent nationhood from other cases in which no such background exists. In the latter, a claim for self-determination appears more truly revolutionary, and therefore may be said to be less convincing.

Given, too, the difficulty of limiting claims to self-determination which could, as U Thant warned, lead to a deluge of claims that would play havoc with international stability, the criterion of historical identity does seem an attractive, if arbitrary, way of limiting the right. Yet even here there are difficulties. Is there to be a *numerus clausus* of historical nations, and what would be the cut-off point? This standard would assume that nations exist in the same form over centuries, something which is patently untrue. Identity is not static; new identities do overwhelm older ones and historical existence as a nation may have no bearing on a modern focus of identity.

Possibly the most satisfactory way of dealing with the question of the application of the right of self-determination in the case of Scotland and other small states seeking to emerge from existing multi-national states is to apply the criteria of viability, stability and participation. If a new state would pose an obvious threat to the stability of the region in which it finds itself, then there should be powerful reasons for not allowing it to secede from the existing state. If, as a state, it is not viable, having none of the administrative structures normally associated with statehood and no real chance of developing them, then it should likewise be denied the right of self-determination. Finally, if it is in no sense prevented from full, equal and real participation in the multi-national state, then this factor should diminish the force of a claim to self-determination made on any other grounds. The interpretation of this last criterion will be difficult, as there may be circumstances in which officially encouraged and facilitated political and cultural participation will only hasten the demise of values which a small and vulnerable people may wish to preserve. Applying these criteria to the Scottish case would be a difficult and controversial task. One point which might be made, though, is that the stability criterion could well be interpreted against any Scottish claim if an emerging Scottish state were to attempt to deprive the United Kingdom of access to essential natural resources. The prospect of the economy of a major European state being thrown into disarray by a secessionist movement would hardly be regarded as anything but a threat to regional stability.

The need to introduce into the debate the international law right of self-determination would only arise if there were to be determined opposition on the part of the United Kingdom Government or, in Quebec's case, the Canadian Government, to the granting of independence to their respective minorities after a clear mandate has been given for secession. The prospect of the two governments ignoring such mandates is difficult to assess. As Stephen Maxwell suggests, the United Kingdom would probably prevaricate, but would hardly contemplate repressive action. The Canadian response is perhaps more questionable; on the basis of certain statements made by the current Canadian Prime Minister, direct conflict does not seem inconceivable. The attitude of both these governments, however, will be influenced to some extent by international law arguments.

STATE SUCCESSION

If the problem of the right of self-determination seems a largely theoretical one, this is not the case with the law on state succession. There are in this area a host of practical problems including the question of succession to treaties, succession to membership of international organisations, succession to state property and debt, and succession to obligations entered into between the predecessor state and foreign investors. Ultimately, of course, many state succession questions will be decided by negotiation between the predecessor and the new state, negotiations in which hard bargaining is the rule. In this process of bargaining, however, international law forms the framework of the discussion. From this point of view, the Scottish case should be looked at in the light of the international law on state succession as it exists at present and as it is developing as a result of the lengthy consideration it has received from the International Law Commission of the UN. It is a complex and controversial area of international law, one in which there is a monumental literature and one which fully justifies Lord McNair's remark: 'He is a bold man, who dogmatises on the effect of state succession . . .'.

State succession can occur in a number of ways. A state may lose territory to another, requiring the acquiring state to inherit certain obligations attached to the territory concerned. Alternatively, a portion of a state's territory may secede to form a new state with its own international personality, or a state may emerge through the process of decolonisation. Unions may be formed out of a number of previously distinct states and, of course, may later dissolve. In all these cases, the rules of state succession may be applied to determine what in international law are the consequences of the changes that have taken place.

Since the end of the Second World War state succession has assumed a new importance. With the rapid process of decolonisation, numerous new states have emerged to independent statehood, ranging from the micro-states of the Pacific to large and influential African states such as Nigeria. This development has had the effect of giving rise to many practical problems of state succession and has posed a challenge to many of the ideological assumptions which had previously dominated international law. A period in which state succession has been of considerable practical importance has thus also been a period during which many of its fundamental principles have been coming under searching examination.

If most of the cases of state succession since the War have involved decolonisation, this is unlikely to be so in the future. With the exception of a handful of awkward colonial outposts, there are few remaining cases of traditional 'salt-water' colonialism. Any new states then are likely to be created in a different fashion, namely as a result of internal changes within independent states resulting from a desire to secede from existing political units. To date there have been few of these cases, but the possibility of future secessions exists. The rules of state succession might consequently be invoked in such previously secure states as the United Kingdom, Spain and Canada.

The collective attitude taken by the recently emerged states towards the question of state succession has been critical of the rules of international law.[20] Unwilling to be bound by rules of an international legal order which they did not participate in creating, the new states have called for the radical re-examination of many aspects of state succession. In this respect they have been motivated by a desire to avoid being unduly hampered by obligations contracted on their part during the era of colonialism. This has meant that in many cases they have been slow in indicating their attitude towards treaty obligations and have argued theoretically against the principle of succession to certain other obligations, such as concessions. In international affairs generally, these states are frequently described as the 'new states', a description which has been used by writers on international affairs to identify a group of states who appear to have certain common interests and certain common views. Some commentators apply the term to those states which have emerged from colonial status during the recent era of decolonisation; others, adopting a broader interpretation, characterise as new states all those states associated with the Third World and, in economic terms, relatively undeveloped.[21] Scotland and Quebec are not dependencies in the conventional sense of the term, but in certain respects their position as newly emerged states would not be entirely dissimilar to that of the other 'new states'. It is doubtful whether they would be widely classified as 'newly independent states' in the sense in which that expression is used, for example, by the International Law Commission in its discussion of state succession, but it is possible that they may see themselves as such and adopt a sympathetic approach to the 'new states' proper. The identification of a radical element within the independence movements in both Scotland and Quebec provides some evidence for such a possibility, but how far it would be translated into practice is difficult to assess. In Scotland's case, it is likely that a new Scottish state would wish to approach the problem of state succession in a cautious and relatively conservative way. If pushed into a corner, though, a more radical stance might be taken and claims might be made for 'newly independent' status. This, as will be explained below, would have certain implications for state succession problems.

Emergence and identity

Would an independent Scotland be a secessionist state or would there merely be a dissolution of a union? Since international law applies different rules in respect of some aspects of succession to obligations in the case of secession and in the case of the dissolution of a union, deciding the status of a new Scottish state is of more than mere theoretical interest. Any clear distinction between the two cases is initially confused by terminological problems. A state leaving a union can be said to be seceding from it, yet it is clearly a different process to the departure from an existing single political unit of, for instance, the population of a region. The latter is secession as it is understood in the debate of self-determination and in the law of state succession. The complexity of the distinction is increased by the problems associated with the concept of union. Unions can exist for various purposes and can involve the uniting of different functions of state. In some unions, the individual states may enter the arrangement with the intention of retaining a high degree of autonomy within the framework of certain common institutions; in others, the intention of the states at the outset may be the complete uniting of the organs of the state with a view to the full merging of political and institutional identity.[22] These may be described as unions, and this would be technically correct, but they are in essence fusions of states. Fusion may be distinguished from union by the fact of retention in the latter case of certain political institutions. Alternatively, adopting a functional approach, the absence of domination by one party might be a valuable criterion for distinguishing union from fusion. If there is successful fusion, leading to the incorporation of a smaller state within a larger, then an attempt by the smaller party to leave the enlarged state may reasonably be described as secession. Where there has been a freely negotiated union maintaining some aspects of the institutional personality of both parties, the leaving of the union by one state is a clear case of dissolution.

Applying these criteria to the Union between England and Scotland, we see that in many ways it seems more of a fusion or an incorporation of Scotland within the English state. The circumstances surrounding the union are the subject of heated debate, yet there does appear to be adequate evidence to justify the conclusion that the Union was not well received in Scotland and that even amongst those who accepted it, it was an acceptance *faute de mieux*.[23] Scottish opinion, indeed, favoured a federalist arrangement, but was denied this. After the Union had come into existence, attempts were made to sever it, but they failed, the Parliamentary attempt of 1711 being a particularly significant failure. The interpretation of the articles of the Treaty of Union in a way which was not contemplated by the Scots also illustrates the way in which a constitutional arrangement that had been intended, on one side at least, to be a partnership came to be viewed as an incorporation of the weaker state within an expanding partner which made no significant adjustments in its own institutional structure.[24] The effective incorporation of Scotland within the United Kingdom state and the Scottish failure to react against this development led to the almost total disappearance of a Scottish political system. Certain institutional structures survived (the Church, the legal and educational systems) but this did not amount to the continued existence of a Scottish state within the Union. For these reasons, an attempt by Scotland to leave the Union amounts more to a secession than to a dissolution. As one legal writer has put it, the Treaty of Union may have become of little more than mere historical interest.[25]

Identity

It is widely assumed in both political and some legal argument that if Scotland were to leave the United Kingdom, two new states would come into existence, a Scottish state (the old pre-1707 state) and an English state (incorporating Wales and Northern Ireland). This assumption was made by certain politicians in the recent debate over Scottish membership of the EEC. In the terms of this argument, as two new states would be created and as the United Kingdom would cease to exist, both the Scottish Government and the English Government would have to re-apply for membership of the EEC. This is not the case. If Scotland were to secede, the international identity of the United Kingdom would not be affected. The United Kingdom Government would continue to exist (although controlling less territory than before) and a new international person would emerge in the form of Scotland. The obligations of the predecessor state, the United Kingdom, would in strict legal theory be unchanged by the diminution of its territory; it would continue to occupy its existing seat in the United Nations and on other international bodies; it would remain a party to all the treaties contracted by it during the period of Union (except those particularly relating to Scotland); and it would be bound by all its existing obligations to external creditors.

There are a number of reasons for supporting this theory of the continuity of the United Kingdom and the novelty of the Scottish state. Initially, nomenclature is of no significance. The removal of one part of a state which identifies itself with a name closely tied to a political relationship with that part of its territory, will have no effect on the question of identity. Loss of territory is equally irrelevant. In international law a state can lose a very substantial portion of its territory and still be the same state in international law. A most persuasive precedent here is the case of the Republic of

Turkey which, after the dissolution of the Ottoman Empire, accepted continuity of identity with the Empire, in spite of massive territorial loss.
Similarly, Paraguay survived the loss of two-thirds of its territory to Brazil
and Argentina after the 1865-70 War. Economic and political predomi-
nance are also factors which may be taken into account, as is shown by the
Partition of India in 1947. In India's case, Pakistan became a new state
while India's identity remained unchanged. India continued as a member
of the United Nations and remained a member of international organisations; Pakistan had to apply for these privileges. The predominant unit,
India, thus survived the loss of territory involved in the creation of Pakistan. Similarly, when East Pakistan separated from West Pakistan to form
the new state of Bangladesh, West Pakistan retained its existing international identity.[26] When, as a result of the Anglo-Irish Treaty of 1921, the
Irish Free State left the United Kingdom, there was no change in the
international identity of the latter. The departure by Scotland from the
United Kingdom likewise should result in no change of the United Kingdom's international identity.

The new state and its obligations
If a sovereign state were to come into existence in Scotland, what would be
its position in relation to treaties currently in force between the existing
United Kingdom and other states? To a considerable extent, any answer to
this questions is complicated by the fact that succession to treaty obligations is currently the subject of a diplomatic conference held under the
auspices of the UN to discuss the state succession proposals of the International Law Commission. Although this conference has not at the time of
writing yet been concluded, it seems likely that international agreement
will be reached on the acceptance of the ILC proposals, thus codifying this
complex area of international law. If Scotland were to attain independence
after the coming into force of the new rules of state succession, then some
of the existing rules would not be applied in its case.

    There are two major approaches to the question of succession to person-
al treaties. In the universal succession view (a view disproved by practice), a
successor state should inherit the treaty obligations of its predecessor; in
the negative view, the successor state inherits no such obligations and
begins its life unencumbered by personal treaties of any sort.[27] In practice,
what has happened in the era of decolonisation has been that although
newly independent states have indicated that they do not consider themselves bound by treaties entered into by the predecessor state, they have
shown themselves to be willing to become party to many of these treaties.[28]
This is particularly the case with certain multi-lateral treaties which are
not primarily political but which are concerned with international co-
operation for humanitarian and related purposes. Since the War, practice
has been confused, with states approaching the problem in a variety of
ways. It has largely been in order to introduce an element of certainty into

practice that the ILC has concerned itself at such length with the question of succession to treaties.

Under existing international law, there are different rules for states coming into existence as a result of secession and those coming into existence as a result of the dissolution of unions. In the case of seceding states, these are not bound by the treaty obligations of their predecessor, a proposition that is supported by a number of precedents.[29] After the secession of Cuba from Spain in 1898, Spanish treaties were not regarded as being binding on the new Republic; with Panama's secession from Colombia in 1903, a similar attitude to Colombian treaties was taken by the United States and Great Britain; and with Finland's secession from Russia in 1919, the attitude of the British Government was that the treaties it had concluded with Russia did not apply to the new Finnish state.

The case of Ireland is particularly interesting from the Scottish point of view. Under the Government of Ireland Act of 1922, the Irish Free State came into existence. In the eyes of the United Kingdom, the Free State was in the position of a dominion and was therefore party in the same way as were the dominions of New Zealand and Australia to British treaties previously binding on them. The attitude of the Irish Free State, however, was that it had seceded from the United Kingdom and was therefore not subject in this way to British treaties. The statement made in 1933 by the Irish Prime Minister, Mr de Valera, provides a frequently quoted classical exposition of the position of the secessionist state in relation to the treaties of the parent state:

'. . . acceptance or otherwise of the treaty relationships of the older state is a matter for the new state to determine by express declaration or by conduct in the case of each individual treaty, as considerations of policy may require. The practice here has been to accept the position created by the commercial and administrative treaties and conventions of the late United Kingdom until such time as the individual treaties or conventions themselves are terminated or amended.'[30] In respect of multi-lateral treaties, the attitude of the Irish Free State was to accede to rather than to succeed to such instruments.

Where a new state comes into existence as a result of the dissolution of a union rather than through secession, there is a presumption in favour of the continuity of treaty obligations based on the principle that the constituent parts of the union had, during the period of their union, legal orders which retain their identity after the dissolution. In the case of the Norway-Sweden Union, which was dissolved in 1905, both Norway and Sweden considered themselves bound by treaties entered into by the Union prior to its dissolution, provided that they were not treaties which were clearly intended to affect only one of the states. International practice in this case was not unanimous (Britain regarded the dissolution as entitling her to re-examine her treaty relations with the Union), but as far as other states were concerned, the Norwegian and Swedish interpretation was accepted. Other cases in which after dissolution of a union the constituent states have regarded themselves as bound by union treaties include the United Arab Republic and the Iceland-Denmark Union of 1918-44.

The ILC proposals

The ILC has proposed certain changes in these rules which could affect an independent Scotland's position in relation to United Kingdom treaties. One of the concepts underlying the Commission's views on succession to treaties is the 'clean slate' principle which allows the new state to begin its existence free from obligations inherited from its predecessor. Although this principle does not further the aim of continuity which many authorities have pursued, it has been widely accepted as a political reality. It is, however, a principle that is to be applied selectively, as the ILC recommends that it be applied only in the case of newly independent states and that in other cases the principle of continuity should be observed.

Between 1972 and 1974 the views of the ILC underwent an important change. In its 1972 draft articles on succession to treaties the ILC distinguished between succession by newly independent states, succession by the constituent parts of dissolved unions and succession by secessionist states. In the case of unions, the parties to the dissolved union were deemed to succeed to union treaties; in the case of secession and of the newly independent state, the 'clean slate' principle was to be applied. In the 1974 draft, the ILC position changed and the distinction between the secessionist state and the former member of the dissolved union was abandoned. The rationale behind this change is made apparent in the commentary accompanying the article. Although the Commission accepts that a theoretical difference may exist between the dissolution of a union and the separation of a part of a state, in that in the latter case the predecessor state continues to exist, it does not accept that the effect of succession should be different in each case. 'In other words,' as the commentary explains, 'it is possible to treat the new states resulting from the dissolution of the old state as parts separating from that state.'[31]

There is an exception to this rule provided by paragraph 3 of Article 33 of the draft. This provides that where part of the territory of a state separates to form a state in 'circumstances which are essentially of the same character as those existing in the case of the formation of a newly independent state . . .' then the seceding state need not be bound by the predecessor's treaties. Certain cases of secession, then, are to be considered as coming within the scope of the rules for newly independent states, though others, whether involving unions or not, will be subjected to a rule of continuity of treaty obligation. The Commission's explanation of this provision is far from satisfactory.[32] Stating that 'at least in some circumstances' the separated territory which becomes a sovereign state may be regarded as a newly independent state (Bangladesh is cited as an example), the Report fails to explain what these circumstances are. In the light of this failure, it might be suggested that the Commission had in mind cases in which parts of the territories of Third World states ('new states' in the strict sense of the term) separate from parent states. It might be possible to argue that such secessions represent the coming into existence of states which have the right to the same treatment as their parent states received, and the peoples concerned (especially where the self-determination argument is used in this area) should not be penalised merely because of delayed parturition.

Yet the obvious question must be raised as to the position of states seceding from the territory of developed states outside the realm of the 'new states'. These states may choose to claim the benefit of the clean slate principle applied to other newly independent territories, and the problem may then arise as to their characterisation in the context of the Article 33(3) exception. If Scotland were to claim that it was emerging to independence in circumstances 'essentially the same' as those of the newly independent states, what would be its position on the inheritance of treaty obligations? The solution adopted by the ILC to this question is that newly independent states will be deemed to have succeeded to treaties if the parties to the treaties agree that this should be the case, or if by reason of their conduct they are to be considered as having agreed. In essence, this recommendation provides a very general justification of previous state practice in respect of succession by newly independent states to bi-lateral treaties. The principal methods by which succession was achieved were (1) through the use of devolution agreements whereby the colonial power reached agreement with the newly independent state as to the inheritance of treaty obligations (this was the case, for instance, in Nigeria, Jamaica and Cyprus); (2) through temporising declarations in which the newly independent state agreed to be bound by treaties for a fixed period (two years or so) but would be assumed not to be prepared to be bound if it did not inform the other party at the end of the period of intention to be bound (this form was adopted by Uganda, Kenya, Malawi and Tanganyika); (3) through the 'Zambian' formula in which an unlimited time for reflection was claimed pending the termination of the predecessor's treaties, but in which succession by virtue of the operation of customary international law was admitted; and, finally, (4) through the use of general or specific declarations. The devolution agreement has in its favour the characteristics of certainty and convenience, yet at the same time it was objected to by the newly independent states on the grounds that they might find themselves burdened with many treaties which they were not particularly eager to accept. The temporising declaration gives the newly independent state the opportunity to consider its position, but has against it the disadvantage of uncertainty on the side of the other party to the treaty.

For many states, the most advantageous position possibly entails the acceptance of the overwhelming majority of its predecessor's treaties. In view of this, there is some force in the argument that the early acceptance of succession to all bilateral treaties should be followed by the weeding out of the few treaties that will be regarded as inappropriate. These can always be terminated according to the normal rules of international law. An independent Scotland might wish to follow this course, or alternatively, may agree to a devolution agreement. Devolution agreements have been extensively used by the United Kingdom in granting independence to colonies, but their effect in international law is questionable. The ILC suggests, in fact, that the treaty obligations and rights of the predecessor state should not become part of the obligations and rights of the successor state merely by virtue of the existence of the devolution agreement.

Multilateral and dispositive treaties
International lawyers disagree on the question of succession to multilateral treaties of a legislative character. In one view, such treaties are automatically succeeded to by the successor state. According to this argument, the consequences for stability and certainty in international relations would be too unpleasant if there were no succession.[33] Another body of opinion takes the opposite view, stressing that the concept of mutual agreement important in the law of treaties would be compromised if multilateral treaties were succeeded to in this way.[34] The ILC's attitude to this question endorses the former view where newly independent states are involved, but favours the latter in relation to other states. From the Scottish point of view, the question of succession to multilateral agreements such as the 1958 Geneva Convention on the Continental Shelf could be of considerable importance; the question of whether or not an independent Scotland would be bound by the provisions of this Convention could affect the techniques whereby ownership of the North Sea oil fields was decided. In this area, it could be to Scotland's benefit to assert 'newly independent' status.[35]

Practice in respect of these treaties varies: in some cases the treaties themselves contain succession provisions outlining the procedure to be adopted by states seeking to take advantage of the provisions of the treaty; in others no such provision is made. The practice of the Office of the Secretary-General of the UN, which acts as depository for a number of multilateral treaties, is to require a formal notification by the new state of succession to multilateral treaties with which the Secretariat is concerned.

Most international organisations require an application for membership on the part of the successor state. The question of membership of the UN may be considered as settled after the elucidation by the Sixth (Legal) Committee of certain principles after the problem of Pakistan's membership had been raised. According to the Sixth Committee, there is a presumption that a state which is a member of the UN does not cease to be a member 'simply because its constitution or frontiers have been subjected to change'. In the event of the creation of a new state 'whatever may be the territory and population which it comprises' and irrespective of whether or not they (the population and territory) formed part of a member state of the

United Nations, such a state must formally apply for membership of the organisation. These rules would certainly require a Scottish application for membership. The rules applied by the IMF are similar, and it is clear that a Scottish state would have to make a fresh application for voting and drawing rights on the IMF. These would be determined according to the economic criteria which are applied by the Fund in granting membership to a new member.[36]

Admission to membership of the EEC is governed by the Treaty of Rome, a multilateral treaty establishing the Community and its juridical order. Although some political controversy has already occurred over the question as to whether an independent Scotland would automatically succeed to membership of the EEC in the event of gaining independence, there can be little doubt that succession would not take place and a new application for membership would have to be made on Scotland's part. This view is based on the argument that the United Kingdom would continue to exist as an international person, with essentially the same obligations and identity as before. In addition, the very nature of the EEC excludes automatic succession to membership; the principle that new states cannot succeed automatically to membership of international organisations (unless specific provision is made for this by the organisations themselves) is one that is recognised in practice and in theory.[37] *A fortiori*, this argument would apply in the case of defence agreements involving alliances and common defence institutions.

Dispositive treaties are another category of treaty which may give rise to succession problems. These treaties are treaties which purport to affect in some way the territory of a state, whether by creating a 'burden' of some sort over the state's territory, or by defining boundaries and hence the extent of the state's territory. Dispositive treaties creating international servitudes are concerned with giving an interest in a state's territory to another state. Examples of such treaties would be an agreement to allow another state fishing rights or the granting of a permanent right to pass through a waterway. Another more controversial form of dispositive treaty might be an agreement granting another state the right to have military bases on one's territory.

Considerable controversy surrounds the whole notion of international servitudes. Some writers deny that such servitudes are competent, on the grounds that they constitute a derogation from the sovereignty of the state. In support of this view there is the fact that international tribunals have frequently declined to endorse the doctrine of international servitudes. Other writers support the notion of the legitimacy of international servitudes, invoking the authority of decisions which seem to give them effect. There is also disagreement on the question of whether dispositive treaties are succeeded to by successor states.[38] Here there is a decision of the Permanent Court of International Justice which holds that such treaties are succeeded to, but international practice reveals little inclination to accept this.[39] Although the International Law Commission concluded that the weight of authority favours succession to dispositive treaties, there are misgivings on the part of the new states to the acceptance of this principle. In the view of these states, to allow a predecessor to burden its successor with limitations on the exercise of its right to use and enjoy its territory poses an unacceptable challenge to the hard-won sovereignty of the former colonial state. In spite of these misgivings, the ILC in its 1974 draft articles included a provision which stated that succession should not affect dispositive treaties.

What would Scotland's position be in relation to dispositive treaties entered into by the United Kingdom conferring 'real rights' on other states in respect of Scottish territory? The sort of treaty which might come into question here would be, for example, one granting fishing rights in Scottish waters to another state or group of states. Such a treaty would be dispositive and would, according to a large body of opinion, be succeeded to by an independent Scotland. If Scotland decided that it was not in her interests to observe these rights vested in the other state or states, it might ally itself with the new states' position and argue against succession to such treaties. With the current division of opinion and with the uncertain state of the decisions on the point, such a course would not be unreasonable. On the other hand, if the ILC proposals win broad approval, such a position would be more difficult to sustain.

Public property

The public property of a state consists of assets directly owned by the state (such as the property of government departments, government installations etc.) and property which is owned by publicly owned bodies. This second category consists of, for example, the property of nationalised industries. The determination of the ownership of such property is clearly not a major issue where a successor state succeeds totally to a predecessor state, but difficulties may arise where, for example, there is a secession. International lawyers have expressed the view that in the latter case, immovable property passes to the successor state if located in its territory, but that this is not necessarily the case with property held outwith the successor state's territory, either in the territory of a third state or in the predecessor state itself. There is also the problem of movable property and here it may be a complicated matter to ascertain what proportion of the movable or incorporeal assets held by the predecessor state can be claimed by the successor state. These movable assets may be situated either within the territory of the successor state or within the territory of the predecessor state. Stated briefly, the traditional rule is that only that movable property which is closely connected with the inherited movable property is succeeded to. Ownership of funds such as state insurance and pension funds remains, in theory, with the predecessor state where there has been a partial succession.[40] There are, however, few clear rules in this area, although a certain amount of guidance can be obtained from a study of practice. In the case of the Partition of India, fixed assets were transferred on a territorial basis and other assets, such as Reserve Bank funds were allocated between the two states on the basis of equitable principles. Military equipment was divided on the basis of one-third to Pakistan and two-thirds to India.[41]

At its 29th Session in 1977, the ILC adopted a set of draft articles on succession to state property which distinguishes between succession by newly independent states, secessionist states and constituent parts of a dissolved union. The basic principle for the passing of state property is laid down in Article 9, which states that state property passes to the successor state if it is situated in its territory. In the case of newly independent states, Article 13 makes two important provisions. Movable state property of the predecessor state, if it is connected with the activity of the predecessor state in respect of the successor's territory, passes to the successor state. More significantly, movable state property of the predecessor state to the creation of which the dependent territory has contributed, passes to the successor state in proportion to its contribution to this property. Agreements may vary this rule, but Article 13 makes it clear that such agreements should not infringe the 'principle of permanent sovereignty of every people over its wealth and natural resources'.

In a case of secession, unless there is agreement to the contrary, the provision is made that movable property other than that connected with the predecessor state's activity in respect of the successor's territory, passes to the successor state in 'equitable proportion' (Article 15 (1) c). Where there is a dissolution of a union leading to the disappearance of the predecessor state, the equitable principle once again applies in relation to the question of movable property of the sort dealt with in Article 15 (1) c.

Applying the existing international law rules and the ILC proposals to the Scottish case, it is clear that Scotland would succeed to immovable property situated in her territory. Movable property designed for specifically Scottish use would pass to Scotland under both the existing and the proposed rules. Thus railway stock, the movable property of various government departments based in Scotland and dealing with Scottish affairs, and the property of Scottish nationalised industries used in connection with the activities of the Scottish branches of these industries, would all pass to Scotland. In the case of railway equipment, a Scottish state would have a strong claim to that equipment which is permanently located in Scotland for use on Scottish track and administered by British Rail in Scotland. While fixed military installations would pass into Scottish ownership, movable military equipment might be said to be not for specifically Scottish use and would not necessarily pass to Scotland under the existing rules. Under the ILC proposals, however, whether Scotland were to be regarded as a newly independent state or as a secessionist state, it would have a claim to a reasonable share of movable military assets located in Scotland. As a newly independent state, this would be in proportion to its contribution to the creation of the property; as a secessionist state, it would be to an 'equitable share'.

The public funds of the United Kingdom as predecessor state would, under the existing rules, remain the property of the United Kingdom. However, practice would suggest the division of these according to 'equitable principles', which is also the approach favoured by the ILC for dissolving unions. In an earlier draft, the ILC recommended that in cases of secession the Treasury of the predecessor state should be apportioned between the predecessor state and the successor state, 'due regard being had to the criteria of viability of each of the States'.[42] Although this provision does not appear in the 1977 draft articles, it is interesting to note that this criterion of viability was dropped in the 1974 draft on the grounds that a seceding territory could not 'realistically expect' to obtain anything more than the assets of the predecessor state which had been specifically allocated for the use of the territory of the seceding state. The principle contained in the earlier draft might well have been used against a state in Scotland's particular position. If a seceding state took with it resources of some importance to the predecessor state, the latter's viability could well be affected and could in this way diminish the seceding state's claim to a share of public funds.

The question of succession to the assets of the British National Oil Corporation could prove controversial. These assets are the property of the United Kingdom, but it would be argued that they are connected with the activity of the predecessor state in the successor's territory. In these terms, they may fall under Article 15(1)b of the ILC proposals and would therefore pass to Scotland. Alternatively, if they were not regarded in this way, they would be the subject of 'equitable' division.

It is obvious that the provision that property should be divided on 'equitable grounds' is a formula that hardly provides much clear guidance. It would be difficult, however, to be more specific without providing an arbitrary and unworkable rule of thumb. The 'equitable' formula and, in the case of the newly independent state, the 'contribution' formula provide no more than a starting point for what must inevitably be a complex process of negotiation. They do, however, give the successor state a clearly expressed right to participate fairly in the assets of the predecessor state and as such provide a bargaining weapon.

Public debt

The public debt of a state consists of funds owed by the central government to internal creditors, funds borrowed abroad by the central government, and other borrowings by bodies within the public sector. If Scotland were to secede from the United Kingdom, the question would arise as to what would be the obligations in respect of these debts of the new Scottish and the remaining United Kingdom Governments. As far as internal debts are concerned, the Scottish State may assume responsibility for the repayment of bond-holders within its territory. This responsibility need not involve any assignation of the debt, as the existing debtor could retain responsibility to make payment on contributions being made from the Scottish Government. External debts would pose greater problems of allocation. In the United Kingdom, outstanding external debts contracted by the central government stood at the beginning of April 1977 at a total only slightly higher than external debts contracted in other parts of the public sector.[43] The former were made up of borrowing from the International Monetary Fund, from other governments, market borrowing and the issue of foreign currency bonds to sterling holders. Within the category of borrowing from other governments is included long-term United States and Canadian credit together with more recent inter-governmental borrowing.

There are at present few rules in international law on the question of succession to the public debts of a predecessor state, although practice affords some guidance. In theory, when a part of a state secedes, the predecessor state from which it secedes is not relieved of liability for the payment of public debts. The predecessor remains the debtor in the creditor-debtor relationship it has established. There are, nonetheless, certain debts for which the successor will be liable, these being the local debts contracted in the name of the seceding territory. Debts which are contracted by the predecessor state for the sole benefit of the seceding territory also fall within the category of local debts.

Continental writers have made a distinction between *dettes hypothequées* and *dettes hypothequaires*.[44] The former (debts secured over physical assets) are said to survive the change in sovereignty over the territory concerned, but the latter (debts connected with a particular source of revenue) are said not to survive the change. The implication of this is that should a state contract on the understanding that repayment should be made from funds derived from a particular source of income (for example, concession revenues), the fact that the territory producing the revenue in question comes under the sovereignty of the seceding state will not suffice to transfer responsibility for the repayment of the loan to the seceding state. In Scotland's case, the implications of this are that a Scottish state would be able to argue that any loan contracted by a United Kingdom Government prior to Scottish independence and contracted on an understanding to repay out of oil revenues subsequently coming within the control of Scotland would not, *prima facie* at least, be the liability of the Scottish state.

As far as the general public debt is concerned, although international law does not at present require it, practice recognises the partition of the debt between the predecessor state and a seceding part of its territory. There is sound justification for this principle: a state losing part of its territory may find it difficult to repay international loans, and this inability could severely damage the interests of creditors and the interests of the predecessor state. The principle of unjust enrichment is also significant here in that the successor state will possibly have benefited economically from the loans procured by the predecessor and it is inequitable that it should enjoy the benefit without accepting part of the responsibility for payment.

The principle of repartitioning accepted, there remains the problem of deciding on what grounds this repartition will be made. Various criteria have been suggested, each of which may be helpful in reaching a decision but none of which need, in itself, be regarded as being the exclusive basis of repartition. These criteria have included relative populations (*Scotland 1980* assumes that this will be the basis of partitioning of the United Kingdom debt — an assumption not supported in international law); contribution to national revenues; and ability to pay. The last two factors are the criteria which have been employed in practice. After the First World War, the successor states to Germany assumed responsibility for portions of the German Empire's debt, the basis of partition being the ratio between the average revenues between 1911 and 1913 of the territories concerned and the total German imperial revenue.[45] With the partition of India, India remained the debtor state, but Pakistan assumed part of the Indian debt by becoming a debtor to India for the relevant portion. In the negotiations preceding partition, Pakistan urged that her share of the debt should be determined on the basis of the contributions by Pakistan's territory to the central government. India argued that population should be taken into account alongside the criterion of financial contribution. In the end result, under the terms of an agreement of 1st December, 1947, Pakistan's contribution was declared to be 'equal to the accountable value of all the property to which Pakistan had succeeded, plus 17·5% of the surplus of the obligations of India over its assets'.[46]

Applying the existing rules to the Scottish case, in so far as international law and practice provide a guideline, Scotland could be expected to assume responsibility for a portion of the United Kingdom's external debt. Debts to the IMF, regarded by many as being closely linked with North Sea oil, would not be regarded as being the particular obligation of Scotland as they are not secured or hypothecated on the oil reserves. At the same time, the utilisation of an ability to pay argument could require Scotland to assume a fairly substantial responsibility for external debts in general. Other public sector borrowing would be the responsibility of the Scottish state if it involved debts incurred for Scottish purposes by specifically Scottish institutions. Loans incurred by the British National Oil Corporation, for example, such as the $825m loans of June, 1977, would be the responsibility of Scotland to the extent to which Scotland succeeded to the assets of the Corporation.

The inadequacy of the existing rules on this question will be partly remedied if the ILC proposals on the matter are generally accepted. Under Article of the 1977 draft, the passing of state debt where there is a secession is to be determined by agreement between the predecessor and successor states. In the absence of agreement, this article provides that 'an equitable proportion of the State debt of the predecessor State shall pass to the successor State, taking into account, *inter alia*, the property, rights and interests which pass to the successor State in relation to that State debt'. For newly independent states, the ILC suggests that debts should pass to the successor state only by agreement. Such agreement would be reached, Article 22 states, in respect of 'the link between the State debt of the predecessor State connected with its activity in the territory to which the succession of states relates and the property, rights and interests which pass to the newly independent State'. Finally, the agreement must not infringe the permanent sovereignty over natural resources doctrine, nor should its implementation 'endanger the fundamental economic equilibria of the newly independent State'. (Article 22(1)2.)

If Scotland were to be considered a seceding state without any claim to 'newly independent' status, in the unlikely event of agreement proving elusive, the ILC proposals would envisage its assuming its fair share of the United Kingdom debts. If Scotland were to succeed to the larger part of the oil reserves, no doubt it could be argued by the United Kingdom that a proportion of the United Kingdom debt is oil-related, in that it was incurred to facilitate oil exploitation. This would mean that Scotland might have to assume a larger part of the United Kingdom debt than might otherwise have been the case. If Scotland were to be regarded as a 'newly independent state', the only way in which any part of the debt would pass would be by agreement, and even then, Scotland could claim under Article 22 that the assumption of a major share of the debt would compromise its ability to exercise sovereignty over oil resources or would prevent the implementation of a plan for economic progress through industrial renewal.

Concessions

A new Scottish state may for social and economic reasons wish to make changes in agreement reached between the predecessor state and commercial companies. In a later chapter, Tony Carty discusses how this might arise in relation to the licences under which foreign oil companies currently extract oil from the United Kingdom sector of the North Sea. His contention is that oil companies would argue that the current United Kingdom regime of oil licences grants what amounts to a right of property in the oil to the companies. To interfere with this would involve questions of acquired rights and compensation. Here we look merely at the contractual question in general, leaving aside the property element which is fully explored below.

A Scottish Government could interfere with the concession contracts granted by a predecessor United Kingdom state without invoking any issues of state succession. It would not be necessary for such a government to argue that the contracts had lapsed on the change of sovereignty if it wished to invoke a general regulatory power to achieve changes in a matter such as depletion rate in oil fields. This regulatory power flows from the fact that such contracts involve important considerations of public policy and hence should be considered in a different light to that in which ordinary contracts between private individuals are viewed. The 'national interest' element in these contracts makes it possible to distinguish between two forms of provision within the contracts: those that are principally contractual and those that are regulatory. The 'contractual' provisions are ones in which a government is more strictly bound than the regulatory conditions, which may, in certain circumstances, be extensively changed by the unilateral action of the government party.

There is a growing view that concession contracts are not properly viewed within the sphere of private law at all but should be considered as consisting of both private law and public law elements. This view was expressed by the Permanent Court of International Justice in the *Lighthouses* case,[47] and is reflected in the writings of international lawyers. Friedmann, for example, finds the most appropriate analogy for the concession contract in the administrative contracts of French law, as developed also in the Belgian and Italian courts.[48] The most important element in the administrative contract is the recognition of the existence of certain unilateral powers that can be exercised by the state party in the national interest. Although there is no direct counterpart of the *contrat administratif*, Mitchell has argued that there is a discretion to act unilaterally in government contracts under English law.[49]

Even if a government may have extensive powers to change the regulatory provisions of a contract, it may still wish to repudiate the contract in its entirety. To what extent is a successor state, faced with contracts which it dislikes, entitled to repudiate its predecessor's contractual obligations? International law lays down no clear rule on the matter and authorities have expressed different views. One contemporary international lawyer, Robert Delson, has suggested that there are four possible courses that can be followed by a new state.[50] Firstly, a new state may be subrogated to its predecessor's contracts and be bound to a greater extent than the predecessor state; secondly, the new state may be bound to the same degree as its predecessor (in the event of non-subrogation, indemnity being required to the same extent as would have been required of the predecessor); thirdly, that there is no subrogation *ipso iure*, but an option exists to subrogate (involving less compensation than would be due from a predecessor); and fourthly, there may be a presumption against subrogation, although the option to subrogate exists.

This range of possibilities reveals the lack of agreement on the question of whether concession contracts survive a change of sovereignty. Authorities on the matter are divided. In one view, the successor state need not consider itself a party to the contract, unless it wishes to do so, and the agreement can thus be repudiated. In the opposite view, the contract survives and the successor state takes the place of its predecessor. An analysis of writings on this question shows that it is the former view which is dominant and that successor states need not consider themselves bound. O'Connell states this position in one of his earlier writings:

'Upon change of sovereignty the successor State does not automatically inherit the rights and duties comprised in the contract of concession. These come to an end with the extinction of the personality of one of the parties to the contract, or the obliteration of its sovereignty in the territory which is subject to the operations of the concessions. To admit the contrary would be to admit the doctrine of universal succession with all its implications.'[51] Other authorities support this view,[52] though it is consistently stressed that in a case where the successor state does not observe the contract, the 'equities must be satisfied' and compensation paid.

The decisions of international tribunals reveal no agreed view on the question of survival. In the *Mavrommatis* case[53] the Permanent Court of International Justice held that concessions granted by the Ottoman Empire to a Greek citizen resident in Palestine were succeeded to by Great Britain as mandatory power in Palestine. The court held, moreover, that in such cases the principle of subrogation applied in international law. The *Lighthouses* case in 1956[54] did not state so bald a principle, although the tribunal of arbitration clearly favoured respect for existing concession rights. In other cases, there has been either judicial hostility to the survival of concessions,[55] or unwillingness to support the notion that concession rights cannot be extensively altered by the successor state.[56]

O'Connell's more recent writing on the matter seems to show a significant change of view. Abandoning the position that concession contracts should not survive, he argues that international law should now favour succession to such contracts. The arguments which are used to underpin this view are based on the degree of autonomy in contracts which former colonial territories possessed, and on the fact that the new state will be in a position to use the instruments of nationalisation to achieve precisely the effect that could be achieved if it were to regard the contract as having lapsed on the change of sovereignty.[57] The principle of non-survival, O'Connell argues, was based on the assumption that the new state would otherwise have no means of ridding itself of unwelcome contractual obligations. Once this is recognised as no longer being the case, the main rationale for the principle disappears, though of course the problem of compensation remains. Certainly an assessment of practice amongst the new states of the former colonial world shows that the vast majority have continued to honour the contracts entered into by their predecessors and that there has been no widespread assertion of the automatic lapsing of the contractual rights of aliens as a result of a change in sovereignty.[58] Because of the greater regulatory powers given to governments under such contracts and because of the extensive acknowledgement of the right of the new state to renegotiate obligations which are incompatible with its social and economic policy, it may indeed be more convenient for a new state to accept the survival of concession contracts.

This last right, the right to make alterations in the contract, receives wide recognition. One writer classifies it with the right to repudiate completely odious concessions or concessions violating public policy.[59] Others are more cautious, and define it as a right to renegotiate objectionable features of an inherited contract. Certainly the power of the successor state to legislate in respect of the vested rights inherited from a predecessor state is not disputed. The mere fact that a right is inherited from a predecessor does not mean that it has a special status of immunity conferred upon it. Rights of ownership of property (rights *in rem*) conferred by a predecessor state enjoy no status greater than that enjoyed by similar rights conferred under the juridical order of the successor; all that they receive is the normal protection afforded by international law to alien property.[60]

The options open to a Scottish government in respect of concession contracts would seem then to be:

1. To argue that the contracts survive but to approach the problem of depletion control, taxation etc. from the point of view of the exercise of the regulatory power which the contracts imply. This 'police power' might allow for fairly substantial control of oil interests in the national interest, and conservation of a scarce resource would be a powerful justification for its exercise. The difficulty with this approach is that if the intervention is sufficiently serious, it may constitute an interference with 'property rights', as discussed in the treatment of oil below.

2. To accept that the contracts survive but to argue that international law allows a successor state to renegotiate them in order to bring them into line with its own policies. There is authority for this which, as stated above, enjoys wide acceptance amongst international lawyers. Further authority can perhaps be added by introducing into the argument the question of permanent sovereignty over natural resources.

3. To argue that the contracts lapse by virtue of the change of sovereignty. In such cases, the 'equities' must be settled and compensation paid for any interference with the property rights of the companies.

There is reasonably strong authority in international law for this view, but whether or not a Scottish Government would wish to pursue it would depend on their assessment of the practicalities of their position and their relations with the international oil industry. Being the most radical position, however, it is possible that it is the option which would provide the greatest room for manoeuvre.

3
Land

Tony Carty and John Ferguson

Monday 20 June 1977   *Written*

House of Commons

50   Mrs Margaret Bain: *to ask the Secretary of State for Scotland, what record is being maintained of private land transactions in Scotland in which ownership of land is transferred furth of Scotland.*

51   Mrs Margaret Bain: *To ask the Secretary of State for Scotland, what estimate has been made of land in Scotland currently owned by: (a) Germans, (b) Americans, and (c) Belgians; and if he envisages a limit being placed on foreign ownership of Scottish land.*

52   Mrs Margaret Bain: *To ask the Secretary of State for Scotland, what steps he is taking to prevent the speculative sale of Scottish land to owners and developers furth of Scotland.*

Mr Harry Ewing:
My Rt. Hon. Friend is not satisfied that there is a need for action in these directions.

Scottish Office

INTRODUCTION

Control of the ownership and use of natural resources is frequently a major political issue. For the small state, the question can be particularly important. Lacking the domestic capital and technology for the development of resources, it must rely on foreign funds and expertise. Often these are seen as rapacious and strong internal political pressure builds up for the policing of foreign interests or for their nationalisation. Where the resources consist of mineral wealth or oil, there are major difficulties in limiting foreign control, largely because the market outlets are abroad. Where the resources are agricultural, although external control may still be a problem, the small state will be in a slightly stronger position because of a lesser degree of dependence on external markets.

In many cases, the external ownership of land is seen as a very much greater threat than the external exploitation of other natural resources. For reasons of social psychology, the land is an asset which is vested with particular, almost symbolic significance. The external ownership of land may be perceived of as being little short of external control of territory, and there is consequently a particular sensitivity to the issue, irrespective of whether there is any real difference in the use to which land is put under external or under domestic ownership.

In the small state, the external ownership of land may be a particularly acute problem, particularly when it is underpopulated and has considerable tracts of 'vacant land'. This will tend to be cheap. When such a state borders on a larger and wealthier neighbour in which pressure on land resources is acute, the pattern of land ownership and purchase will reveal heavy external buying. The result of this will inevitably be the disruption of domestic agriculture, the weakening and eventual dispersal of rural communities, and, in extreme cases, emigration. That will be the pattern unless, of course, the state takes action to control land purchase and land usage. Most states retain the power to do this, limiting, with varying degrees of efficiency, the extent to which external ownership will be allowed and the uses to which land will be put.

In most Western European countries, controls are placed on the purchase of land for speculative or other purposes which are not conducive to the survival of agriculture and the agrarian community. This has a direct effect on the purchase of land by aliens. The striking exception to this is the United Kingdom, where no such restraint is exercised. Anyone can purchase land in the United Kingdom, irrespective of their motive. Planning permission is necessary for certain changes of use, so it may be difficult to develop agricultural land for recreational or tourist purposes, but there is otherwise no restriction on allowing land to lie fallow, phasing out agriculture in favour of sport, or for speculating in rural land and consequently hastening inflation in land prices. Land use control through planning restrictions is, moreover, an unsatisfactory means of controlling land abuse for another reason. Frequently the only interest that a local authority will have will be the encouragement of revenue producing activities on the land. For this reason, Switzerland has recognised that this control should not be exercised by local authorities but by central government.

In Scotland, the problem of external ownership has traditionally been particularly serious. For historical reasons, land in the Scottish Highlands has long been available for latifundia purposes, as it passed out of the control of the Highland clans and as the Highland population was systematically cleared by large farming or sporting interests. Political sensitivity to the matter is widespread, although this has yet to be translated into effective political action.[1] Most Scots know that vast tracts of Scotland, particularly in the Highlands, are owned by absentee landlords, and the issue occurs with great regularity in most discussions of Scottish political and social questions. This discussion can frequently be extremely emotive, relying more on unsubstantiated generalities than on facts. This may be because very few people know what is going on in land purchase today. Who owns the land and who is buying it? Politicians, even local politicians speaking of their own areas, will often be unable to give an answer. Because of the system of land conveyancing in Scotland, nobody knows who owns Scotland, in spite of the publication of useful studies such as John McEwen's *Who Owns Scotland?*.

Scotland's land register, the Register of Sasines, is well known to be defective in a number of respects regarding information on land purchase. There is no legal requirement that a deed be registered with the Register, and consequently many purchases do not appear on the search sheets. Even where an estate is registered as having changed hands, the search sheets need not indicate the acreage involved and the price paid, and they are even less likely to do so in the case of sub-sales. (These are sales where there is an intermediate purchase between the seller and the ultimate buyer, usually occurring within a few days.) Beneficial ownership is usually unascertainable where land is held by trusts or by foreign-registered companies, the latter being especially significant in this study. These defects are hardly surprising, since the Register of Sasines is merely a conveyancer's convenience and does not purport in any way to monitor the details of estates or the intentions of purchasers, as does the legislation of other countries such as Norway, Sweden, Denmark, West Germany, France, Switzerland and the Republic of Ireland. Hence information about the character and intentions of purchasers, which may be readily available in those countries, has had to be inferred either from the Register itself (where it provides any information), or gleaned from local sources.

This study aims to establish two things. Initially it deals with the pattern of land purchase. Who is buying Scottish land, and for what purposes? On the basis of empirical researches (research which is continuing: we merely state here our results to January 1978), it is shown that Scottish land is being purchased at a significant rate by external purchasers, some known, others sheltering behind trusts or companies.[2] Nobody can ascertain precisely who owns the land, but one can identify a distinct and indeed overwhelming pattern of foreign acquisition. This fact is recognised by the Scottish Landowners' Federation in their submission to the Northfield Committee, where they point out that 'nearly all estates sold in the Highlands in the last three years have gone to foreigners. This is a significant trend which must give rise to local concern and would be quite unacceptable in the long term if continued . . .'. The Committee received similar representations from the Scottish branches of the National Farmers' Union, but the Committee's brief is limited to an examination of monitoring procedures and, in view of British membership of the EEC, it will be

unable to do anything about the problem unless it recommends standards
of control applicable to UK nationals as well as to aliens. Yet until action is
taken, the predictions of one leading British land economist of the widespread acquisition by aliens of land in the United Kingdom will continue
to be proved correct.[3]

The second objective is to show how the state, and even the small state,
can control the process of external acquisition and can decide how land is
to be used. This is not a radical programme, but is something undertaken as
a social duty by most Western European governments and also by certain
Canadian provinces and American states. Here, at least, vulnerability can
be accepted without defeat and decisive steps can be taken by a small state
to dictate the way in which it wants its most significant natural resource to
be used. It is possible that accusations of discrimination and xenophobia
may be raised against a state undertaking such a programme, but it must be
emphasised that all that such a state would be doing would be following the
standards of behaviour accepted by Western European states.

PART 1

A STUDY IN LAND PURCHASE

Patterns of purchase
The North of Scotland and particularly the Highlands are almost unique
in Western Europe in a number of ways. Perhaps the most significant is the
peculiar legal framework prevailing. The complete absence of legal control of rural land inevitably attracts foreign purchasers who are constrained
by their own national laws. It is quite unusual to be able to dispose of land
suitable for, or at least traditionally employed in, agriculture, forestry or
other primary land uses, without any guarantees at all as to the future uses
to which the land might be put. However, equally remarkable is the
unique character of the Scottish Highlands, the only region in Europe in
which no measure of land reform has ever been attempted, save for legislation affecting crofting tenure. The sheer size of many estates makes individual purchases significant in themselves because of the vast acreages
which change hands. The political, social and economic consequences of
such purchases have major implications both at local and national level
and yet they depend upon the personal choice of a very small number of
individuals who are very often ill-informed even as to their own best
economic interest let alone that of local communities.

The land use potential of much of Scotland's upland areas is, of course,
a matter of hot dispute. Whether improved farming techniques, sophisticated systems of reclamation and grazing control and scientific land management could significantly increase the productive capacity of the land is
open to question in a number of Highland areas. Nonetheless, informed

opinion suggests that there is room for considerable improvement and the evidence of the Hill Farming Research Organisation demonstrates that productive capacity could be doubled for certain agricultural activities.[4] However, recent foreign purchases add a dimension which will hinder any political choices made by any future Scottish Government. They appear to be falling into two broad categories; some are designed to develop a tourist market which is mainly foreign and exclusive in character. This can only make more difficult any development or even regeneration of rural Scottish communities, particularly since it is well known that sporting and other recreational activities conflict with primary uses of land. Perhaps even more serious are the very common speculative purchases of land which serve not merely to disrupt continuity in its use and management, but also artificially inflate the price of rural land generally. This makes it all the more difficult for local persons to engage in or expand farming activities, but it also places obstacles in the way of public authorities who may wish to acquire land compulsorily where owners, foreign or national, are proven guilty of misuse or underuse of their land. How in this situation can a satisfactory measure of compensation be found when land prices themselves are highly questionable?

Whatever controversy may exist in Scotland about land potential, it must surely cause serious misgivings that at present most of its European neighbours are agreed that recreational, tourist and investment activities in rural land, especially by companies, are very much to be discouraged.

Tourism and Recreation
There appear to be two strands in estate ownership within this category at the present time and although both require a high degree of exclusivity for sporting purposes, the basic reason for purchases are different. A purchase may be made for a profit motive arising out of the sporting potential of the estate, stalking, grouse shooting and salmon fishing. The Highlands represent one of the few remaining wilderness areas left in Western Europe and have undoubted sporting attractions because of this. It is not therefore difficult to develop the area as an exclusive hunting, shooting and fishing preserve for those who have the financial means, and, indeed, the requisite social credentials. The sums involved both for the purchase of the estate and subsequent development often appear disproportionate even to the possible yields of this exclusive tourist market.

In other cases, purchases are for private personal use although equally exclusive as the first. It may well be that in a number of cases the costs of the estate are supported by some private letting or renting of shoots or salmon fishing. Perhaps the main motive behind such purchases is that of the non-capitalist latifundist who sees his land as an object of social prestige and status, an extension of the personality of the owner, which may be so even in the case of company purchase. In our analysis these purchases are distinguishable from straight land speculation (although not perhaps as secure long-term investment) by the fact that the land is not resold within a short space of time.

The evidence which allows this broad distinction to be made can be extracted from local sources and inferred from the character of the land and the identity of the purchaser. For instance Durness Estate (Sutherland Appendix) appears to fall mainly within the first category. The estate consists of high grade salmon fishing and deer stalking. Local sources have recently stated that Katz, a Dutchman, is in the process of completely renovating Smoo Lodge, the main estate house, at considerable cost. The owner has publicly stated that the estate will afford him a personal amenity.[5] However, the fact that he has also purchased Ben Damph Estate at Loch Torridon (Ross and Cromarty Appendix) where he has applied for planning permission for more than thirty executive type chalets easily allows the inference that he has a definite commercial interest in these areas. Indeed, he has sold off a part of Durness Estate to Taekele Soepboer, a fellow Dutchman who owns a holiday complex on Brin Estate in Inverness-shire (Inverness-shire Appendix).

An apparently clear case of individual purchase is the Foich section of Braemore Estate (Ross and Cromarty Appendix) which is collectively owned by a Dutch family and local information suggests that it is used for family leisure purposes. This analysis appears to us to lead to a similar differentiation in Tables 1 and 2.

Of particular interest in the purchase of sporting estates is the Enessey Company Limited who are one of the biggest investors in Scottish real estate. Their purchases range from Moray to the island of Harris and include the massive Mar Lodge Estate in Aberdeenshire. Their investment in sporting land first appears in 1963 when the name of Gerald Panchaud appears in the Register of Sasines in association with the Ashdale Land and Property Company Limited, who together sold Mar Lodge to Harlow and Jones (Investments) Limited, of whom G. Panchaud is a director.

Their activities in Scotland are principally directed towards the establishment of a major tourist leisure and recreation organisation specifically catering for the upper end of the foreign market. Their acquisitions include 61,200 acres at Mar Lodge, 15,000 acre Tulchan Estate in Moray, their most recent purchase being the 62,500 acre North Harris Estate which they acquired in January 1977. The cost of purchase and development of these estates has been high; Harlow and Jones spent £150,000 in the early sixties in an attempt to develop skiing at Mar Lodge; Slater Walker (Moray Appendix) are reputed by Panchaud to have invested over £700,000 in modernising Tulchan Estate, with a further £100,000 being spent by Enessey in their first year of ownership. Enessey are currently engaged in a similar exercise at their North Harris castle, and hope to complete their development programme in time for the start of the 1978 season. Panchaud, in a letter to James McKillop of the *Glasgow Herald*,[6] says 'Enessey's two properties, as well as Mar Lodge Estate, is an invest-

TABLE 1

Commercial purchases

Estate	County
Ben Damph	Ross & Cromarty
Kindeace	,, ,,
Brin	Inverness-shire
Kilmartin	,, ,,
North Harris	,, ,,
Tulchan	Moray
Durness	Sutherland
Mar Lodge	Aberdeenshire

(Mar Lodge price not included)
Total acreage   180,328
Total purchase costs   £2,376,000

TABLE 2

Individual purchases

Estate	County
Braemore (Foich section)	Ross & Cromarty
Rhiddoroch East	,, ,,
Dervner	,, ,,
Knockie & Dalachapple	Inverness-shire
Ardochy	,, ,,
Craskie & Invercannich	,, ,,
Black Corries	,, , part in Argyllshire
Kerloch, Tilquhillie & Invery	Kincardineshire
Ledmore	Sutherland
Lower Dess	Aberdeenshire
Lesmurdie	Banffshire
Dunbeath	Caithness

(Kerloch price not included)   Total acreage   88,466
(Lesmurdie acreage not included) Total purchase costs   £1,071,178
(Foich acreage includes Strone section)

ment in tourism aimed at the top end of the market for which the highest standard is demanded. We aim for overseas visitors and their families. Individuals requiring sport only are not profitable.' This is why Mar Lodge, Tulchan Lodge and Amhuinnsuidhe Castle, by next year, will be able to accommodate 80 people, all in bedrooms each with private bathrooms, and with 'furnishings, public rooms, service and food equal to the best anywhere'. This high quality accommodation and service in conjuction with access to some of the finest sporting ground in Scotland suggests that Enessey are guaranteed a thriving market, already confirmed by full bookings for Tulchan and Mar Lodges during the 1977 season. They are basically looking towards future returns on investment and have stated that so far, even taking into account their 1977 marketing successes, their returns have not matched investment. However, with the cost of accommodation rising fairly rapidly and the actual returns on the varied sporting activities offered by Enessey, their investments seem to be assured a fairly rosy future. Fairly typical costs of field sports of the type being marketed by Enessey are likely to fall within the following range, although it should be noted that particularly good salmon beats or deer forests can generate much higher profits for the owner. A two-day grouse shoot of seven to ten guns would cost about £2000 on an average moor, but as Her Majesty the Queen's recent purchase of Delnadamph Estate indicates, even for Royalty the cost of this exclusive sport is becoming not inconsiderable. Included in the £2000 is an allowance of a brace of grouse per gun, the supply of beaters and transport to and from the butts. Out of the day's sport the owner retains the rest of the bag; on an average shoot about 160 brace over two days, these retail for £3-4 per brace. On estates in the top bracket, where 2000 brace is not uncommon, the cost for one party can rise to as much as £7000 per day.[7] Stalking also attracts a well-heeled clientele. For the privilege of shooting a stag, the hunter can expect to pay between £70 and £120.[8] Hind shooting, which takes place later in the year, costs less, the range being from £24 to £30 for each beast. The venison itself does not belong to the hunter, it remains the property of the estate owner and is normally sold on the European market, ultimately retailing for as much as £5 per lb. Surprisingly, Panchaud seems to be pessimistic about potential returns from this side of the business unless his clients also avail themselves of his complete package.

The North Harris Estate is particularly well suited for the development of salmon, sea trout and sea fishing, all of which are central to this Enessey project. The cost of killing this game fish (salmon) varies but the average current costs including boat rental and the hiring of a ghillie would work out about £60 for each fish taken. Some stretches of river are rented out for £500 to £700 per week, with particularly good beats rising as high as £250 for one rod per week. Enessey are setting their tariff in the region of £500 for a double room for one week, thus the profits to be made out of their accommodation and sporting provision are by any measure fairly healthy. Nor is this limited to the stalking and salmon fishing seasons.

Investment — Genuine and Speculative
Genuine purchases are distinguishable from speculative ones simply by the pattern of resales taking place within a short period of time, eighteen

months or less, or by the accumulation of numerous purchases by the same individual or company, in the same or adjacent counties. Resale and subdivision of holdings is a fairly common feature of recent purchases. It appears that farmland, forests and other non-sporting land are often purchased at a fairly realistic price and yet resold very quickly for double or treble the price with no apparent change in the land use itself. One case is that of Greengate Limited (Ross and Cromarty Appendix) who purchased the Tarbat farmlands and foreshore in November 1971 for £80,000. This estate changed hands twice to related companies and culminated in July 1976 with the estate being purchased for £600,000. The inflation of the initial purchase price took place within the umbrella of one parent company.

Greengate Limited were also involved in the purchase of the West Highland estate of Drumchork (Ross and Cromarty Appendix), buying the largest section of the estate in 1972 and the remainder in 1974. Both of these sections were resold in exactly the same way as the Tarbat Estate, the new owners being associates of the same group involved in the Tarbat purchase, the final price being double that which Greengate originally paid for the estate.

Similar inflation has also occurred where an individual has purchased an estate. One Dutchman, Hellinga, bought the farm of Easter Brockloch (Moray Appendix) in March 1977 for £55,000. Within the same month he sold off two sections of the farm, 25 acres fetching £15,000 while 84 acres required the purchaser to raise a standard security of £52,700.

Perhaps a more significant case of this type of speculation concerns the Camster Burn Estate in Caithness (Caithness Appendix). On 12th April, 1972 the Camster Estate was sold by John Darmady, a local sheep farmer, to a company known as Ideal Citrus Sales (Europe) Limited. Their purchase consisted of 1600 acres of rough grazing lying on a deep bed of basin peat, costing £1500. Ideal Citrus commenced business by selling off small plots of land as building sites, the sums involved at this stage being fairly small (Caithness Appendix). In June and July 1972, they disposed of 10 acres to another property development company and a further 225 acres for £11,250 to one Leslie Roberts, described in the Register of Sasines as a director, although of what there is no indication. At this point another property investment company, Sunningdale Securities, appeared on the scene. They purchased three blocks of land between October 1972 and January 1973 (Caithness Appendix) amounting to 1600 acres for a total price of £4000. Sunningdale began at once to sell off small plots for building purposes. From a total of 302 small sales they have grossed £68,261. Over and above this, they have also sold off four larger units of land to a number of property developers (Caithness Appendix), these dealers being Mitchells (Cuthbert & Gartland), Leslie Roberts and Cutland Properties Limited, the total sum involved being £187,274. Although Sunningdale Securities have disposed of a considerable proportion of their original purchase, they still have an interest in the estate, their most recent sales taking place in the summer of 1977. Of the secondary purchasers, the most significant groups appear to be Mitchells (Cuthbert and Gartland), Leslie Roberts and Cutland Properties.

In January 1973 Roberts sold off 73 acres to Bernard Mackeonis for £22,000. In March 1975 he sold a further 60 acres to the same purchaser for £78,000. A further 91 acres were disposed of in February 1977 to Ghazi Orfali of Abu Dhabi for £40,500. We have no information whatsoever on the United Arab Emirate's connection, how it was established or how the estate was portrayed in terms of investment, thus Arab motives remain a mystery in this context. Perhaps Orfali did not know the history of the Camster Burn site or the physical nature of the terrain. However, Orfali himself began selling in April 1977 when he parted with five acres to a fellow countryman for £6500; also in April 1977 he sold another unit of similar size for the same price. His most recent sale was on 29th April, 1977 when he disposed of 10 acres to another Arab buyer for £13,000. Bernard Mackeonis has also been active in the Arab market, selling off a section of his 60 acres to an Ismail Fatah for £3900 and in December 1976 a further area to Sheik Khazal of Abu Dhabi for £17,500. Mackeonis's largest sale was to Mitchells Estate Agents, when 88 acres changed hands in September 1974 for £45,200. Both Mitchells and Cutland Properties follow a similar pattern of small sales directed at would-be home builders (Caithness Appendix). As recently as January 1978, we made enquiries to the local planning department in Wick who advised that no building had taken place on the site; outline planning permission had been granted for the site as a whole, but no detailed permission had been granted for the individual plots. Their opinion was that the site was unlikely to be built upon because of the deep blanket of peat bog and mentioned difficulties relating to road building as well as supplying domestic water, the nearest suitable supply being four miles away from the Camster morass.

Other forms of estate purchase and resale in small units have been evident in Scotland recently. One which has attracted considerable publicity has been the activities of Wood and Leisure Land Division of the Australian Land Sales organisation. Wood and Leisure Land got under way in 1973 after Frank Chapman, owner of Australian Land Sales, had his activities restricted in the Antipodes when British investment was curtailed with Australia no longer being in the Scheduled Territories. Through Wood and Leisure Land, Australian Land Sales launched a sophisticated campaign which laid out the attractions of investments in small sections of Scottish timberland, both in terms of the amenity value of the investment and the future profits these would realise.[9] In 1973, Australian Land Sales purchased woodland in Aberdeenshire and Banffshire (Aberdeenshire and Banffshire Appendices) amounting to 592 acres for £232,000. They began selling plots of timber, four to six acres in extent, at an average price of £2933, their total income so far being £158,083 from 57 units in Aberdeenshire and £273,190 from 90 units in Banffshire. These blocks are managed by the company on the purchaser's behalf. The purchaser has no rights on the land other than the timber itself. Potential investors were advised that at 1973 prices the total financial yield on investment could range from £750 to £1780 per acre over a twenty-year time scale. There is no indication that Australian land intend to do anything more on this land. It is already wooded, and by local accounts managed competently. The invitation to purchase is on the basis that there will be a sky-rocketing of prices at a later date, as has already happened with farmland.[10]

TABLE 3

Investment and speculation

Resale of part or total estates

Estate	County
Drumchork	Ross & Cromarty
Tarbat	,, ,,
Kindeace	,, ,,
Easter Brockloch	Moray
New Banchory	Kincardineshire
Overscaig	Sutherland
Blackhill and Longhaven	Aberdeenshire
Cobairdy Group	,,
Glennie Group	Banffshire
Camster	Caithness
Glendessary	Inverness-shire

(Kindeace also appears in Table 1. Durness Estate is not included in the total.)
(Longhaven acreage not included)
Total acreage   48,216
Total purchase costs   £2,313,490

Larger profits are probably to be made in selling land to local authorities or commercial enterprises for building purposes. In Kincardineshire, S. A. Germont (whose beneficial interest is located in Geneva, although the company is incorporated in Panama) bought 52 acres of farmland in 1969 for £4500 (Kincardineshire Appendix). A number of sales took place between 1970 and 1975, mainly to Kincardine County Council and private developers; these resulted in a return of £136,297 to Germont on their investment, as well as interest on standard securities to one particular company. This land, originally farming, has been divided up in a way which can only be inflationary both in terms of local primary land use and property development.

Land more suitable for sporting purposes has not in the main included this type of speculation, possibly because considerable profit can be made out of the recreation industry itself. Nonetheless, a few cases do occur which indicate substantial short-term profits through sectional reselling. The Dutchman, Katz, purchased Durness Estate in December 1976 for £50,000 and then resold 4800 acres to a fellow Dutchman for £36,000 (Sutherland Appendix). Overscaig Estate, also in Sutherland, appears to embody similar factors. Originally purchased by a Dutch company in 1965 for £7500, it was considered worth at least £50,000 on a Bond of Credit in 1968, but fell in value in a sale in 1973 to £27,000. Finally, less than half of the estate was sold for £105,650 in 1975 and on the same day a mere one-tenth of the estate was sold for the same sum as the original purchase price for the whole estate (Sutherland Appendix).

Accumulation of Holdings and Sitting Investments
One series of purchases may be characterised as land accumulation. Here a company may intervene frequently on the market, gathering up a large number of holdings, perhaps without any clear intention of running them as a single unit. The scale of such operations makes it difficult for smaller farmers to bid successfully for plots adjoining their own land or acquiring single holdings as a farming unit. There may be a number of reasons for the cumulative purchase of land; one possibility is to 'sit on' the land thereby securing a long-term profit from rising values in farmland, another is to use it as a shield against inflation and possible instability in the national currency. A third explanation may lie in the potential of the land for purposes other than farming, which could relate to a variety of forms of development. This form of speculation is best illustrated by reference to Bocardo Société Anonyme of Lichtenstein (Ross and Cromarty and Sutherland Appendices) who, during a four-year-period have acquired extensive farmlands in the North East of Scotland. While their purchases do not appear to be critically significant in terms of total acreage, nor is the land especially fertile compared to other regions in Scotland, the location of their acquisitions does suggest a deliberate underlying pattern. Bocardo have bought more than 3463 acres of farmland at a cost of £1,417,316. Much of this investment is tied up in land which Government advisers have defined as prime sites for oil and gas pipeline landfalls. It is suggested locally that Bocardo's most recent purchase, Balnagall Farm, is one of the sites currently being considered as a landfall for the Mesa Oilfield. Whether this is accurate or not is difficult to ascertain at this stage; what is certainly true is that Bocardo now have in their possession much of the land which could be brought into play in any future development of consequence in this area.

Bocardo is only one of a number of interlinked companies, in Britain or abroad, nominally under the control of Mohammed Al Fayed, a petrodollar millionaire of Egyptian origin, whose business tentacles spread out from

Dubai, his adopted home in the United Arab Emirates. The *Glasgow Herald*, in a report on Al Fayed on 1st December, 1975, gives an interesting account of the activities of this Arab group in Scotland, but the important details remain hidden in a web of associated companies and undisclosed beneficiaries protected by the laws of Switzerland and Lichtenstein.

TABLE 4

Accumulation of holdings

Bocardo purchases	*County*	
Newton Farm	Ross & Cromarty	
North Balkeith	,,	,,
Mid and South Pithogarty	,,	,,
Fendom Hill	,,	,,
Kingscauseway and Heathmount	,,	,,
Summerton Farm	,,	,,
Balnagall	,,	,,
Balblair	Sutherland	

Hellinga purchases		
Kindeace	Ross & Cromarty	
Blervie	Moray	
Easter Brockloch	,,	
Greenburn Farm	,,	

See also Katz, Ben Damph and Durness
Soepboer, Brin and Durness

TABLE 5

Sitting investments

Estate	*County*	
Braemore (Strone section)	Ross & Cromarty	
Fannich	,,	,,
Eishken	,,	,,
Pitmain	Inverness-shire	
Struy	,,	
Forglen	Banffshire	
Mey	Caithness	

Total acreage	142,057
Total purchase costs	£1,707,122

Methods of Purchase

Many estates simply appear on the open market, either in trade magazines or through the publicity of estate agents. The attraction of land in Scotland is tied to sheer availability (especially in the absence of legal regulation), and the price itself which is often anything from 40% to 50% lower than on the Continent; this applies to both agricultural and sporting land. The effect of the attractive market position in this country has meant an upsurge in purchasing in the last five years. Although many of the purchases are public, a significant number are highly secretive. The only explanation can be that many individuals and companies deem it expedient to remain anonymous. What is shown here is the deliberatively secretive character of some purchases which have taken place recently.

Secrecy is maintained through bearer shares in companies registered abroad. The Enessey company of Lausanne illustrates both how this system operates and its implications. They, at the latest count, own Tulchan, Mar Lodge and North Harris estates. The negotiations which were undertaken prior to the purchase of these estates were secretive, particularly in the case of the latter, and although the knowledge that these estates were to be sold or 'change hands' was available locally or in the public press, the background information on the new purchaser was lacking. In the North Harris deal, neither the local populace, nor the *Glasgow Herald* who were conducting an insight investigation into foreign ownership in Scotland,[11] were able to establish who the new owners were or what future purposes were intended. So although a background picture has been built up, it is only with the name of the directors. The names of the beneficial owners remain hidden behind the bearer shares. Panchaud of Enessey (Executive Director) has stated in a letter to James McKillop of the *Glasgow Herald*, that he personally has no shares in the company, nor is he a nominee for anyone. He will not divulge who, in fact, the beneficial owners are, except that they are Swiss. He claims that this anonymity is not unusual in so far as it is the invariable custom in Switzerland in both private and public companies to guarantee anonymity. This being so, he maintains that there is no case for disclosure in Scotland. Although Enessey appear in the Register of Sasines as being registered in Switzerland, the address being 1, Galeries Benjamin Constant, 1002 Lausanne, further investigation has revealed that Enessey are, in fact, a company incorporated in Panama. Enessey Panama was set up in March 1975, its stated business 'to engage in any commercial or industrial enterprise', with directors in Montreal and London, including Gerald and Paul Panchaud in Lausanne.

Somewhat similar secrecy surrounds the Tarbat Estate in Easter Ross (Ross and Cromarty Appendix), which was sold by the Trustees of Lord Elphinstone in November 1971. This estate comprises 500 acres of farm, woodland and foreshore. The purchaser, Greegate Limited, registered in Jersey, paid £80,000. In November 1971, Greengate also bought the adjacent area, Croy Wood (Ross and Cromarty Appendix), for £15,000. Most of their acquisition was sold in May 1975 to a company known as Quartet Holdings, registered at Suites 2/3, Gibraltar Heights, Gibraltar, the selling price at this stage being £50,000. In July 1976, Quartet Holdings disposed of their property to Garrulus Glandarius Limited, a company registered in the Channel Islands. The transaction covered the 500 acres including the mudflats foreshore area. The price was now £600,000. Greengate have also been active elsewhere in Scotland, having made significant purchases in the Gairloch area of Wester Ross (Ross and Cromarty Appendix). In October 1972 they bought most of Drumchork Estate for £17,500, following this up in May 1974 with a further section of Drumchork costing £8000, the total amounting to just over 20,000 acres. In February 1975 they disposed of the larger part of the estate to Longfields Investments for £50,000, and in March the residue passed to Ballina Investments for £8000, both of whom are reputed by local sources to be associate companies of Greengate. Greengate are recorded in the Register of Foreign Companies in Edinburgh as being located at Regency House, Saint Helier, Jersey, as are Ballina Investments and Longfields Investments. In the Tarbat Estate transaction, a feature of considerable significance is that Greengate Limited, Quartet Holdings and Garrulus Glandarius all share the same parent company, Turquand, Barton, Mayhew and Company, a firm of chartered accountants based in London, all being nominees of this organisation.[12]

Consequently, it appears reasonable to assume that local sources are correct in suggesting that Ballina Investments and Longfields Investments Limited, by their association with Greengate Limited, are also subsidiaries or nominees of Turquand, Barton, Mayhew and Company. Laurence Monument, a senior partner in Turquand's Jersey office, who also appears as a shareholding beneficiary in Garrulus Glandarius, has stated that he has no idea what Turquand's development plans for these estates are, and further insists that Garrulus Glandarius are not beneficial shareholders in the purchase of Tarbat Estate. They are merely acting as nominees for the parent company. It also appears that Turquand's Jersey office are reluctant to divulge who has beneficial interest in these companies and who subsequently profited from the vast price increases resulting from the internal transactions which have taken place between them.

In none of these purchases does Turquand's name appear; all deeds in the Register of Sasines are recorded under the names of their nominees. One possible explanation for this seeming confusion is that a British parent company may avoid its disclosure duty when having 5% or more shares by having its beneficial interest located in nominee companies registered in Jersey and Gibraltar where there are no disclosure duties. Not merely is the cumulative purchase of land concealed but also at least two other possible disadvantages arise. Firstly, these transactions are bound to inflate the prices of neighbouring land, and secondly, although up until now they are merely accounting transactions, one must suppose that at some stage the land itself will be put onto the open market; how otherwise can one explain the fact that the land is being put to no use at all? Although these transactions are recorded in the Register of Sasines, Tarbat and Drumchork Estates were never advertised in the normal way, perhaps an inevitable aspect of internal selling.

Secrecy is obviously a matter of degree. The absence of public monitoring allows an individual to sell land abroad to his own nationals who may or may not be able to assess what the local 'real' price for land should be. It allows the accumulation of holdings without attendant unfavourable publicity and the selling off of land at apparently improbable prices. The purchases and sales of the Dutchman, Hellinga, illustrate this point. In these instances, effective ownership does change hands but resale seems to be restricted to fellow countrymen of the seller, at least in the case of Kindeace Estate (Ross and Cromarty Appendix). In December 1976 this farming estate was bought by a Dutch cattle breeder, Johannes Hellinga, for £460,000. It would appear that Hellinga initially intended establishing a cattle breeding and collection station in which he would purchase cattle in the Highland markets and would keep them at Kindeace until sufficient numbers had been gathered for transportation to European markets. These plans seem to have altered and Hellinga has been selling off sections of Kindeace to fellow Dutchmen in a system of closed selling. The sense in which it is closed is not known, since no information is available as to whether Hellinga knows the subsequent purchasers personally, or whether the land is being advertised for sale outwith Scotland. These sales have brought in no more than £418,343. It is not known what proportion of the whole estate this represents, although it has been established that they were sold between March and October 1977.

The most recent occurrence of significance at Kindeace has been Hellinga's application to the local council for planning permission to develop what appears to be a large-scale tourist enterprise. Local sources state that he first sought permission to build 400 chalet type houses on the Burrock's section of the estate. This was modified a few weeks later, and planning consent was sought for 10 housing units which were scheduled for residential purposes, these being phase 1 of a reduced building programme which grew out of the initial planning application. Hellinga is reputed to be acting as an agent for two unnamed Dutchmen and a series of companies have been set up with their registered offices in Inverness.

Hellinga also bought Blervie Estate in February 1977 for £75,000 and in March he bought Easter Brochloch Farm for £25,000. In the same month he once again sold off part of the latter, 25 acres for £15,000, the buyer being a Scot, and in April of the same year a further 84 acres were released to one James Munro who raised a standard bank security in that property of £52,700. Hellinga continued to be active in the field of farm purchase, buying Greenburn Farm in Aberdeenshire in June 1977 for £67,000, and is stated by local sources to have purchased the farm of Edderton Mains in

Easter Ross, although this has not yet been confirmed in the Register of Sasines.

PART II

STANDARDS IN WESTERN EUROPE

Monitoring
How could there be any objection to knowing who are the beneficial or effective owners of Scottish rural land? It is true that neither a Register of Deeds (Sasines, as in Scotland) nor a Register of Title need fulfil this function. Their function is merely to ensure a private purchaser that his newly acquired title is secure. As such, neither need be public at all. However, once it appears open to question that land mobility is always working to the benefit of the community, the very least one can ask is simply who are the purchasers of land and perhaps even what are their intentions. This does not in itself imply control or restriction, but merely that the information should exist. It constitutes the very basis of a considered judgement about what the public interest may require.

In Scotland at present the primary obstacle in the way of obtaining this information is that many companies buying land are not subject to the Companies Act 1976 which requires that shareholdings of more than 5% have to declare their beneficial ownership. The Act does not apply to the Channel Islands and Gibraltar. Nor is it applicable to alien companies particularly bearer-shareholding companies. The effect is not quite that one does not know the future intentions of the companies. The same is true in the case of individuals. This uncertainty is merely an aspect of the absence of any public control of rural land sales. Rather, the danger is that secrecy may be concealing the fact that in a given number of land transactions the same persons may be operating through different companies. Even if no objection is taken to accumulation or subdivision of landholdings the possible inflation of prices resulting from 'unreal' sales may be thought to serve no useful purpose.

This is a problem which most Western European countries and even a few of the states of the United States and provinces of Canada do not have to face, simply because they do not consider it sensible that rural and especially agricultural land should be sold to companies at all except in very limited circumstances. There are laws in Switzerland and Canada especially designed to prevent foreign controlled companies from purchasing land. They contain elaborate attempts to define how much influence aliens must have before they can be said to control a company.[13] However, these definitions assume that alien ownership is itself undesirable. Perhaps the most suitable monitoring legislation is the Irish Land Act 1965.[14] Section 54 as a whole is designed to ensure that purchases, particularly of farmland by aliens, occur only when the Irish Land Commission considers them to be in the public interest. To forestall the possibility that the alien avoids all monitoring by setting up an Irish company, the Act effectively places the onus of all companies to indicate who are their beneficial owners. In this way the Land Commission can learn of the hazards likely to arise from the character of the effective ownership of the company.

In Ireland, whenever a body corporate wishes to buy land, it must come to the Irish Land Commission and indicate to it the persons who control the company. Control means the power of a person to secure by voting shares in that company or a voting power in relation to that *or any other body corporate*, or by the Articles of Association or other document regulating that *or any other body corporate* that the affairs of the first mentioned body are conducted in accordance with the wishes of that person. The simplicity of the procedure is that should it appear at a later stage that the Land Commission was for any reason misled, *e.g.* as to the true nature of the effective ownership of the company, or dissatisfied with the use to which the land is put, it has very wide powers of compulsory acquisition.[15]

Monitoring could be made more complete by requiring that any person, trust or institution which could possibly be acting on behalf of an alien, should declare for whom he or it is acting. If one wishes to preserve confidentiality, the sale need not proceed. This minimum level of publicity has been regarded as essential in Switzerland in order to supervise adequately the spread of foreign tourism within the country. Swiss Law presumes that notaries, legal advisers and companies, particularly those engaged in property dealings, are acting for aliens until they prove otherwise. In Sweden, a special Nominee Company Act 1925 provides that where any person or company acts as a decoy for someone ineligible to purchase property, a court may divest the property. This is over and above the rule that companies dealing in real property must declare who benefit from its bearer shares in order to give the State a clear picture of the extent of alien ownership.

The monitoring process is facilitated on the continent by the Cadastre. This is a public register of the quantity and value as well as ownership of immovable property compiled to serve as a basis for taxation. Its public function inevitably makes it much more informative than the conveyancer's register of deeds or titles. The latter may give some general description of land use but will not provide a fertility classification. Nor will it provide a list of the properties belonging to each owner.[16]

Obviously the whole issue of monitoring is a matter of balancing the value of confidentiality with that of publicity in the interests of possible public supervision for whatever reason. The Inland Revenue authorities have the power to pierce the veil of foreign registered bearer-shareholding companies for the purpose of capital transfer tax when the companies are acting for the benefit of persons in the UK. This information is not, however, available to the public.[17]

Purchase Control

The patterns of purchases of rural land described in this study are very widely regarded in other countries as warranting close control, if not complete prohibition. In Scotland, estates are being bought by individuals and companies with a view to resale by lots within a short space of time. Estates are accumulated for no obvious economic or social purpose. Land which is possibly of agricultural or other primary land use is being developed commercially as a tourist enterprise without any effective public judgement as to the economic or social value of this activity. It is well-established international practice that states may control or exclude any alien individual or company engaged in such activities without fear of accusations of xenophobia, commercial protectionism or any other form of isolationism. This is because most states regard such practices as clearly contrary to their own public policy regardless of whether they are perpetrated by aliens or by their own nationals. Indeed, provinces and other states within federations usually have the power to control the character of rural land ownership regardless of the incidental effect which this may have on aliens.

Rural land is very widely seen as outside the normal course of commerce, national or international. The farming community needs at least some protection from the business community and the recreational or other demands or urban society. The political and social processes which have facilitated this development are perhaps not as important to Scotland as an understanding of the exact nature of what has now become common practice. Scotland's room for manoeuvre in terms of the reactions which it might provoke is very wide provided any proposed restrictions are not directed against aliens and alien companies as such.

a. Investment and companies

Hostility to companies investing in land has its roots in the basic political judgement that only those actually intending to work land should be allowed to purchase it. Concern at a rural community of owner-occupiers being transformed into tenants of managers of absentee landlords looms very much larger than any attempt to assess exactly the benefits of stimulating private investment in agriculture, forestry or even recreational activities. The most common world-wide public control of land use is the prohibition on the holding of land by other than physical persons. As J. Masrevery, a leading lawyer in the UN Food and Agriculture Organisation, put it '. . . by creating the obligation to farm one's land directly and personally the legislator has sought to make the tenure of land a matter of individuals and to create and strengthen the physical links between man and the land'.[18]

An illustration of the introduction and history of such legislation may be found in developments in forestry in Sweden at the turn of the century. Major sawmill companies acquired so much forestland from yeomen that by 1906 the companies had accumulated 5 million hectares of land or 36%

of all privately owned land in Northern Sweden. As is usual in questions of
land politics, a violent reaction occurred. 'People were afraid that too much
felling would occur and also that the agricultural holdings in the northern
province of Norrland would disappear. But above all, they pointed to the
social perils of replacing the landowning farmers by a poor and dependent
class of tenant farmers.'[19] In 1906, a Company Act was passed banning the
acquisition of real estate by companies and associations. A Surveillance
Act of 1909 was designed to provide a guarantee that farming on land
owned by timber companies would not be discontinued. By the 1960's,
rapid progress in mechanisation of forestry appeared to give new advantages to large-scale enterprise. So the Land Acquisition Act 1965 granted
county agricultural boards a discretion to admit persons, physical or judicial, engaged in an industrial or commercial activity for processing of
agricultural or forestry products or for distribution of agricultural products,
where the main intention is to permanently utilise the products from the
property acquired in the business activity. Farmland was in fact being
abandoned and it was felt that only the introduction of processing companies could ensure rational land use. However, the boards have a wide
power to favour private farmers wishing to purchase land, especially where
this would lead to more rational holdings for them. In fact industry has not
been interested in purchasing rural land for the purposes envisaged by the
Act because the profits, particularly the international markets in forestry
products up to 1969, have not been adequate.[20]

Legislative policy is much more unambiguous where a company purchase is supposed to have the character of passive investment, though here
the prohibition applies equally to individuals. Of course a distinction between active and passive investment is very difficult to draw. A company
will purchase land with a view to eventual sale presumably taking advantage of an increase in land prices (*i.e.* not directly connected with a primary
land use enterprise *e.g.* a 'hedging' against inflation). Assets superior to
those of an individual farmer will allow a company to bid so much more
than an individual farmer. This serves to accentuate further the basic
objection to passive investment in land, that the difference between capital
tied up in land and the return which a productive use will yield is unnecessarily enlarged.[21] The view taken of the effects of company investment as
such will inevitably be tied to a political judgement about the importance
of maintaining farmers as owner-occupiers or of furthering the goal of
family farms. In Denmark, Norway, France and, perhaps to a lesser extent,
West Germany, there is very little possibility of an individual, not to mention a company, making a purchase which has the character of a passive
investment.

Definition need not be difficult if it is assumed that a non-farmer's
intentions in purchasing land will in some sense amount to a passive
investment. The Danish Agriculture Act 1973 prohibits companies, co-
operatives or other institutions from acquiring land without special per-

mission, and permission is only granted for special purposes such as agricultural research and experiments etc. A purchaser must *inter alia* have farming as a main occupation and take up residence within six months from the time of purchase. This legislation has recieved support from farmers primarily because it serves to reduce the inflation of land prices though the public policy is more generally to ensure that land is kept in good agricultural use.[22]

Investment may be attacked more directly in terms of the intention of an owner to resell the land or part of it within a short space of time, or simply to buy or sell land at a price judged, in some way or another, to be out of proportion to the return which a productive use of the land might yield. In Norway, the licensing authority must be satisfied that the purchase is not an investment, for instance that it is intended to resell the land shortly or that the purchase is itself one of a series, leading to an accumulation of holdings. Furthermore, the County Agriculture Committees have a duty to intervene where a property is being offered for sale at a disproportionately high price.[23] The French *Societes d'Amenagement Foncier d'Entablisse-ment Rural*, better known by its initials SAFER occupies a position very similar to the County Agriculture Committees. They may intervene when a price is too high and exercise a prior right of purchase at an adjudicated price. Their resale prices are comparatively low and, being taken as reference prices for the region, have a definite stabilising effect on the agricultural market.[24]

A purchase may be thought to have an unsound effect on the distribution of agricultural units. There is undoubtedly a political judgement involved in supposing that an accumulation of holdings could lead to a reversion of the 'credo' of the French Revolution. This explains the strict rules on amassing of holdings in many Western European countries.[25] However, the restrictions are themselves only part of a more general public power to prevent rural land transactions which are considered to be economically unsound. For instance the Danish and West German legislation both ask in almost identical terms whether the sale leads to an unsound division of land and in particular whether, in the case of subdivisions, the remaining units are viable. These controls are an integral part of the system which allows objection that the price paid is excessive and which invites agricultural authorities to exercise the right of pre-emption to ensure more rational economic use of rural land. Undoubtedly the context in which this public control is usually exercised is a land policy of consolidation of small holdings. Resales might only undo this policy. Yet the general legal regime clearly assumes that patterns of sales of rural land can be disruptive of rural land use and as such they need to be monitored.[26]

b. *Tourism, recreation and primary land use*

Tourism and recreation needs are normally understood as simply two possible uneconomic uses of land. As such they are prevented by not allowing a person without farming or forestry competence to acquire land. Because of the relatively small size of the land holdings in Western Europe, the problem does not take on the same dimensions as in Scotland. In Sweden, West Germany, France and Ireland, it is the part-time or 'hobby' farmer and the 'week-end' or 'second residence' which are resisted as clearly uneconomic uses of rural land. However, Ireland and Switzerland afford more particular policies towards the 'recreational industry'.

Swiss policy is that land sales ought to be confined to Swiss citizens and to those aliens who work on the land or in some other way are permanently bound to it.

In 1972 the Federal Council reported to the Federal Assembly that a national solution to the problem continued to be necessary. Local planning authority was inadequate. It was essential to make clear that resistance to the powerful purchasing power of aliens was much more important than the short-term profits to be obtained from speculation in land prices. Mountain areas are not benefited if large areas are occupied by people who are only there on vacation, clinging together in groups disrupting the local community, whose infrastructure they do nothing to maintain. The powerful foreign purchasing powers has been leading to a factual monopoly of land. Indeed, the absence of a ceiling on the price they are willing to pay for land serves only to cause a general inflation in the economy given the central importance of land prices.[27]

Residences may be purchased by aliens who show that they will have a genuine connection with their chosen district. For instance they may intend to exercise a profession there on a permanent basis or contribute to cultural and educational institutions, have relations or a business which warrants actually living on the spot. The would-be purchaser may justify his connection in any other way which does not amount to an admission that it is no more than a holiday or other temporary interest. However, the connection must be very close and the Federal/Kantonal authorities must be consulted before permission is granted. These are responsible for safeguarding the public interest. Of course, the alien who settles permanently in Switzerland is not subject to these restrictions. However, he may buy only one residence, may not resell it for 10 years, and may not lease it. In areas already dependent upon tourism, the Swiss have found it useful to qualify certain places as especially vulnerable. Where there has been a considerable increase in alien influx, *e.g.* more than 10% already, or more than 100 cases within 10 years, no more permissions are allowed. In some towns, such as Lucerne and Montreux, purchase is completely prohibited.[28]

In Ireland the policy of the Land Act 1965 is primarily to discourage the view that there is farmland easily available. An Irish policy of land consolidation makes it desirable that land which comes on the market should be used to enlarge existing uneconomic holdings. However, the land Commission will exercise its discretion under the Land Act 1965 sect. 45 to allow aliens to purchase land where no primary land use is in issue. Though the matter is entirely within the judgement of the Commission, a number of examples are given.

These do appear to afford a possible characteristation of remote, very marginal land as distinct from farmland, even if they do not take adequately into account social consequences of tourism and the recreation industry. Perhaps they are worth listing:

(a) Parcels of land not of any significant size having regard to the quality of the land and local conditions generally.
(b) Large mansions and grounds which have become insupportable for the local purchaser.
(c) Remote estates of low agricultural value, unsuitable for afforestation.
(d) Existing *bona fide* stud farms (with reservations as to acreage) being sold as going concerns.
(e) Transactions in which the applicant can show that he is going in for some special line — preferably one with export possibilities — and that he has the necessary expertise and capital to back it up.[29]

Some modifications of Irish policy are having to be made as a result of EEC membership.

The Problem of Discrimination
Are there not considerable hazards in a small state with an open economy choosing to close most if not all of its rural land to aliens, whose purchase money could possibly be described as foreign investment, at least in the literal sense that foreign money is coming into Scotland? The Western community is drawn together in a series of bilateral and multilateral conventions, the most important of which, for Scotland, is the Treaty of Rome.

These guarantee freedom of commerce and a right of establishment. In fact, this objection is very easily met except perhaps in the case of individuals purchasing holiday homes (see below). Scotland needs only ensure that the controls it introduces are not discriminatory against any particular category of persons *per se.*

The question of discrimination has arisen recently at constitutional level in Canada and Ireland. In Canada, the British North America Act gives the Dominion competence with respect to the admission of aliens, including foreign companies (Article (91)25 BNA), while the provinces are competent to define property rights (Article (92)13). Prince Edward Island has passed legislation excluding any non-resident of PEI holding title to property beyond 10 acres or shoreland beyond 5 chains. The objects of the legislation are to combat declining agriculture, holiday homes and land price inflation. Its constitutionality has been upheld by the Canadian Supreme Court.[30] The Province of Ontario has resorted to taxation to control non-resident ownership. But this roundabout approach now seems superceded by the Supreme Court decision.

In Ireland, an Inter-departmental Committee on Land Structure Reform has also been concerned by the problem of discrimination. In Ireland it is accepted that about half the agricultural land transactions on the open market represent purchases by persons not farming full time. This factor, along with speculative and sitting investment purchases, contributes to inflated land prices and diminishes the capacity of smaller landholders to compete for land. The Committee has been advised that to declare categorically that purchases by certain designated classes would be disallowed is probably contrary to Articles 40 and 43 of the Constitution. However, it recommends that a new land agency should regulate sales (the Land Commission has merely a power of compulsory purchase) to improve the competitive position of the smaller farmer and to ensure that land passes into the control of those most likely to use it effectively. The grounds of possible prohibition are familiar, amassing of land, possible absenteeism or part-time farming and incompetence.[31]

The Treaty of Rome Article 52 guarantees a right of establishment to citizens of member states, *i.e.* to participate in non-salaried activities, the running of businesses and companies, but only within the conditions established by the law of the host state for its own nationals. The EEC Commission has already approved the Danish Agriculture Act 1973 despite its exclusion of investments, land accumulations and purchases by non-farmers.[32] The legislation was intended to exclude not merely large numbers of Dutch and Germans purchasing land on the West Coast of Denmark, but also urban Danes, especially of course from Copenhagen.

The Norwegians and Swedes have legislation expressly discriminating against aliens. The Norwegians passed legislation very soon after independence with a view to excluding Swedes from purchasing land. However, they find now that the controls of the Koncession Act are quite adequate. The Swedish Law was concerned with foreign companies which had begun to buy forest and mining land. This is now, in any case, very difficult. Exceptions for aliens bring the law very close to other rural public law in its effect. If the alien wishes to farm and is domiciled in Sweden, or if he needs the estate for another trade activity in Sweden, he may be allowed to buy the land. The authorities administer this legislation closely in co-ordination with the Land Acquisition Act.[33]

Although the legality of the Danish legislation has not been adjudicated by the Court of Justice of the European Communities, one may assume that it would take into account international practice with respect to the scope of a right of establishment. Given the importance of the US in world agriculture it merits particular attention. In an exhaustive study of US practice it has been shown that even with a broadening of the right of establishment after 1945, the United States expressly reserves the right of the US to limit or exclude alien activity in the exploitation of land and natural resources. If exercised, this reservation could prohibit aliens from agricultural and mineral resource development. The effect is that treaties do not limit state statutes on agricultural or other rural land. For the most part the states do not exclude aliens but the policy has been at various stages in US history, especially the 1870's/80's, to exclude aliens, *e.g.* English nobility, acquiring large holdings. At present the family-farms acts of eight states in the upper Mid-West and the Great Plains discourage investment in agricultural land by corporations not engaged primarily in agricultural activities or closely held family-farm corporations.[34]

The Scandinavian legislation should be perfectly adequate to exclude most of the purchases described in this study. It would be entirely open to a Scottish Goverment to restrict rural land purchases by aliens to a certain size, to require that they themselves come to Scotland, reside on the land and exploit it as their main occupation, provided only that it does not subject aliens to any special treatment.

However, somewhat different questions are posed by restrictions on individual recreation *per se*. In an independent Scotland these are much more likely to be directed specifically against aliens. Complete prohibition of purchases of holiday homes etc. by aliens is certainly within the competence of a sovereign state but it would be an unusual development in Western Europe.[35] It might be more diplomatic for Scotland to accept the moderate restraints imposed by the Treaty of Rome, which does allow restrictions on all the common market freedoms (of goods, labour, capital, Articles 38, 483, 56(1)) wherever public policy requires it. A recent court decision has said that the treaty requires: '. . . in addition to the perturbation of the social order which any infringement of the law involves . . . a genuine and sufficiently serious threat to the requirements of public policy affecting one of the fundamental interests of society . . .'.[36]

Discussion in Sweden in 1975 concerning the tightening of the law on alien purchase of holiday homes indicates how even a state not a party to the Treaty of Rome feels constrained by a notion of international public policy. More than 50% of alien purchasers were German and they tended to concentrate in the most densely populated parts of Sweden. Swedes felt that such a pattern of purchases could lead to the formation of ghettos where not only other aliens but even Swedes would be unwelcome. The law did not react crudely. It distinguished aliens who had a special connection with Sweden (*e.g.* regular holidaying for many years), from other aliens. The former could purchase homes where they pleased while the latter were confined to less densely populated areas.[37]

Compensation

Suppose that a Scottish Government decided to 'roll-back' the pattern of alien purchases which has already occurred, what kind of reaction could it expect from abroad? Would it have to pay full market value of the land or the price which a seller would be prepared to sell at? Could it achieve acceptable use of the land through taxation or primary land use regulations without having an accusation of 'creeping nationalisation' levied against it? In all probability Scotland's room for manoeuvre would be extremely wide. Compulsory purchase legislation need merely form part of a much wider legislative programme which introduces standards of control of rural land regarded as unproblematic elsewhere. Cries of acquired rights and the sanctity of property enjoy very much less international support in this area than in others such as a taking of businesses or urban property.

Legal standards concerning primary land use, *i.e.* quite simply obligations to plant crops, graze animals, etc., are very uncommon in Western Europe largely because the land tenure system renders them unnecessary. However, where special regulations on land use do exist, they are not considered to justify compensation being paid for inconvenience. For instance, when a West German state recently passed a statute compelling landowners to maintain a minimum level of cultivation of marginal land for environmental purposes no compensation was paid. The duty of the landowner arose out of a social obligation of property.[39] In Switzerland regulations which require that land remain in agricultural use are not regarded as necessitating any recompense except perhaps where it is clear that particular owners were on the point of converting the land to another more profitable and, of course, publicly accepted form of use. Indeed, it is proposed to compulsorily lease marginal land which is being neglected, without paying compensation. The reason is simply that in no way can it be said that such a law '. . . prevents an existing use or a very probable use in the near future, or renders very difficult a use for which the property is suitable.'[40]

In developing countries outright expropriation of rural land owned by aliens has been much more common than what might be called 'creeping nationalisation'. However, this has largely been due to factors which need not affect Scotland. The emotive or symbolic effect of treating the alien as especially harmful could not so easily be achieved by the imposition of regulations for which there is not an adequate administration to enforce. It is nonetheless accepted that a state may impose maximum/minimum levels of production in a crop considered socially desirable, *e.g.* in conformity with national food policy it may introduce price controls, marketing restrictions and even progressive *ad valorem* taxes on land with higher rates on high acreage-units, which can nonetheless be avoided by selling off the land.[41]

The enforcement of standards respecting land use is notoriously difficult. There is not much room for disagreement about the best possible use to which land might be put. It is not only developing countries which despair of deciding — *i.e.* conclusively for the sake of a once and for all court litigation — how much different communities or persons could make so many types of land yield. The Swedes and the Irish have both experienced great difficulty in attempts at effective control.[42] So it might be more realistic for a Scottish Government to accept that it cannot hope to persuade many of the individuals or companies to conform to its social and economic policies by anything short of a compulsory taking. What will then be the measure of compensation?

In Western Europe perhaps the standard imposed by Norwegian law could be taken as most appropriate for Scotland. It arises within a context common to Denmark, France and, to a lesser extent, West Germany. In Norway, as has been seen already, when the County Agricultural Committee exercises a right of pre-emption it may object that the purchase price of the property exceeds its operative agricultural value and require that the amount due shall be determined by valuation. The background to this is the Norwegian Expropriation Compensation Act (26/1–73 No. 4 esp. sect. 4) which applies to all compulsory acquisition of land. Valuation is based on the current use of the land, and changes in land use may be taken into account if they are within the framework of existing operations. Thus profits obtainable from better agricultural methods would be owing but not from a different use which is regarded as contrary to public policy, such as an exclusive and large-scale tourist or recreation enterprise. In any event market price is not a determining criterion for the simple reason that, with respect to rural land sales, prices are controlled.

In developing countries the problem of compensation to aliens does not present itself in quite the same way. Land reform legislation is usually punitive in the case of completely or partially neglected land. The reasoning is that even the theory of acquired property rights supposes that land will be put to some use, that the owner will not simply 'sit on' the land, but work it to provide a return. If he does not, there is no occasion to compensate him. This underlies the 1967 Land Reform of the Christian Democrats in Chile.[43] However, aliens are usually active in quite intensive cash-crop plantation agriculture. These enterprises will, in all probability, have been in existence for many decades. They may well pose questions about foreign control over natural resources which cannot be resolved by improved standards of primary land use and labour conditions. Tea and rubber plantations resemble oil fields much more than rural land speculation or a recently developed tourism which may disrupt local communities and future land development plans. They date back to colonial and neo-colonial times and raise much wider questions about unjust enrichment of Western companies in the past and unfavourable terms of trade between the West and the Third World at present. Needless to say, compensation which is paid is never the full market price, but it is difficult to draw conclusions from such practice which are relevant to the Scottish situation.

Appendix to 3: Examples of land sales in eight counties of Scotland

Seller	Purchaser	Estate	Type	Acreage	Date	Price £	R

Caithness

Seller	Purchaser	Estate	Type	Acreage	Date	Price £	R
Trustees of Betram Currie	Harry E. Blyth (American)	Dunbeath	Sporting	32,000	11.4.68	83,000	
Harry E. Blyth	Dunbeath Estate Ltd	,,	,,	,,			
William Sinclair	Marinus Kloet (Dutch)	Mey	Farmland	2,972	2.3.77	120,000	
John Darmady	Ideal Citrus Sales Europe Ltd	Camster	Rough grazing and peat moor	1,600	12.4.72	7,500	
Ideal Citrus	Lewferran Property Co Ltd	,,	,,	10	23.6.72	600	
,,	Anthony Leslie Roberts	,,	,,	225	19.7.72	11,250	
,,	Sunningdale Securities Ltd	,,	,,	696	11.10.72	2,000	
,,	,,	,,	,,	600	8.11.72	1,500	
,,	,,	,,	,,	225	18.1.73	500	
Sunningdale Securities Ltd	Cuthbert & Gartland (Estate Agents)	,,	,,	41	24.1.73	4,750	
,,	Anthony Leslie Roberts	,,	,,	29	30.3.73	6,264	
,,	Cuthbert & Gartland	,,	,,	28	14.3.74	11,260	
,,	Cutland Properties Ltd	,,	,,	450	14.11.74	165,000	
Cutland Properties Ltd Standard Security to	Property and Financial Syndications Ltd	,,	,,	450	18.9.75	162,000	
Anthony Leslie Roberts	Bernard Paul Mackeonis	Camster	Rough grazing and peat moor	73	16.1.73	22,000	
,,	,,	,,	,,	60	5.3.75	18,000	
,,	Ghazi Orfali (Abu Dhabi)	,,	,,	91	24.2.77	40,500	
Ghazi Orfali Standard Security to	Anthony Leslie Roberts	,,	,,	91	24.2.77	34,500	
Bernard Paul Mackeonis	Cuthbert & Gartland	,,	,,	88	20.9.74	45,200	
Cuthbert & Gartland Standard Security to	Bernard Paul Mackeonis	,,	,,	88	,,	26,000	
Bernard Paul Mackeonis	Ismail Abdul Fatah (Abu Dhabi)	,,	,,		25.10.76	3,900	
,,	Majid Sheakh Khazal (Abu Dhabi)	,,	,,		6.12.76	17,550	
Ghazi Orfali	Mohammad Taisseer	,,	,,	5	6.4.77	6,500	

eller	*Purchaser*	*Estate*	*Type*	*Acreage*	*Date*	*Price* £	*Resale*
(Abu Dhabi)	Sheheda (Abu Dhabi)						
,,	Lufti Hassan Abu Hishmeh (Abu Dhabi)	,,	,,	5	6.4.77	6,500	
,,	Tamima Tawfik Al-Dabbas	,,	,,	10	29.4.77	13,000	

Sample of Typical Small Purchases

Cuthbert & Cartland	Eric Leslie Smith	Camster	Rough grazing and peat bog		18.8.73	1,000	
,,	Peter Charles Norman	,,	,,		17.8.73	120	
,,	David Michael Page	,,	,,		17.8.73	240	
,,	James Lang Reid	,,	,,		17.8.73	340	
,,	Graham George Langford	,,	,,		3.6.75	550	
,,	Ian Batchelor	,,	,,		6.8.75	220	

No indication is given in these sales of acreage, merely a plot number.

Total number of small sales   70
Total purchase costs   £29,202

Sample of Typical Small Purchases

Sunningdale Securities Ltd	Susan May Benns	Camster	Rough grazing and peat bog	2	29.4.76	165	
,,	Francis Ian Dochert	,,	,,	6	28.5.76	850	
,,	Kenneth Walter Simpson	,,	,,	$\frac{1}{3}$	8.6.76	240	
,,	Shakuntla Devi Nandi	,,	,,	5	9.6.76	2,780	
,,	Peggy Joan Tewkesbury	,,	,,	$\frac{1}{6}$	11.6.76	90	
,,	Shifau Abimbola Kazeem	,,	,,	$\frac{1}{2}$	14.6.76	270	
,,	Bertha Mary Stearn	,,	,,	$\frac{1}{3}$	17.6.76	180	
,,	Barry John Edmonds	,,	,,	$1\frac{1}{3}$	25.4.77	231	
,,	Michael Seager Harvey	,,	,,	1	27.5.77	165	
,,	Gerald Brooks	,,	,,	$\frac{1}{2}$	19.7.77	280	
,,	Charles Ejimofo Osakwe	,,	,,	$\frac{1}{2}$	18.8.77	270	

Total number of small sales   302
Total purchase costs   £68,261

Banffshire

David George Sharp	Dr Viet Christian Aldinger (German)	Lesmurdie	Sporting		20.3.74	10,000	
Trustees of Sir George Wm Abercromby	Cement Industries now Forglen Estate (Hong Kong) Ltd (Hong Kong & Kuala Lumpur)	Forglen	Sporting and farming	285	2.12.74	300,122	

Seller	Purchaser	Estate	Type	Acreage	Date	Price Re£
Johanna Mary Riddoch	Australian Land Sales Ltd	Glennie	Woodland	275	12.2.74	232,000
Executors of Joseph Riddoch	,,	Towie	,,	65	7.3.74	
		Saterslack	,,	26	,,	In
		Rennies	,,	8	,,	Cummulo
		South Catstone	,,	22	,,	Aberdeen
		Ardmeallie	,,	4	,,	

See also Aberdeenshire

Total number of small sales	90
Total purchase costs	£273,190

Aberdeenshire

Seller	Purchaser	Estate	Type	Acreage	Date	Price
Major Henry Charlton Park	Barnard Robert van der Ham and Alida Moerman van der Ham (Dutch)	Lower Dess	Farmland and sporting	404	27.8.76	256,400
Gordon Rhind	Johannes Hellinga	Greenburn Farm	Farmland	163	30.6.77	67,000

See also Ross and Cromarty and Moray

Seller	Purchaser	Estate	Type	Acreage	Date	Price
Trustees of Princess Arthur of Connaught	Enessey Company through Gerald Panchaud	Mar Lodge	Sporting	61,200	1.9.63	

See also Ross and Cromarty and Moray

Seller	Purchaser	Estate	Type	Acreage	Date	Price
Ronald Mervyn Titcombe (Australian)	Mayfair Commercial Services, Ltd 9 Rue D'Anjou Paris 75008	Blackhill Cruden Bay	Quarry	112	19.8.77	3,000
,,	,,	Longhaven	Farmland		21.10.77	10,000
Johanna Mary Riddoch	Australian Land Sales Ltd	Cobairdy	Woodland	297	12.2.74	232,000
,,	,,	Huntly Lodge	,,	24	,,	
Executors of Joseph Riddoch	,,	Slobach	,,	17	7.3.74	In Cummulo Banff
,,	,,	Ardmiddle	,,	35	,,	
,,	,,	Raemurrack	,,	14	,,	

See also Banff

Sample of Typical Small Purchases

Seller	Purchaser	Estate	Type	Acreage	Date	Price
Australian Land Sales Ltd	Malcolm Rutland Shaw	Cobairdy	Woodland	4¼	21.3.74	2,800
,,	Mary Gay Platt	,,	,,	7½	21.3.74	4,850
,,	Roy Brealey	,,	,,	3¾	21.3.74	1,901
,,	George Richardson	,,	,,	5½	21.3.74	2,325
,,	Michael Barker	,,	,,	5	7.1.75	2,650
,,	Annelore Haseler	,,	,,	6	10.3.75	3,325
,,	Raymond Cappi	,,	,,	3¾	12.3.77	1,900
,,	Samuel Davidson	,,	,,	5	30.6.77	2,632
,,	Christopher Berkley	,,	,,	5	12.8.77	2,100

Total number of small sales	57
Total purchase costs	£158,083

eller	Purchaser	Estate	Type	Acreage	Date	Price £	Resale

Sutherland

eller	Purchaser	Estate	Type	Acreage	Date	Price £	Resale
Trustees of Ian McGregor Campbell	Balnagown Castle Properties Ltd	Balblair	Farming and hill ground	1,856	20.8.76	235,100	
Balnagown Castle Properties Ltd	Bocardo S.A. (Lichtenstein)	,,	,,	,,	21.7.77	466,908	
Thomas Ian Robinson	Sijtze Katz (Dutch)	Durness	Sporting	20,000	20.12.76	49,200	
Sijtze Katz	Taekele Soepboer	,,	,,	4,858	19.1.77	36,000	
Blue Star Line	Ursula Schwab (German)	Ledmore (Part of)	Sporting	9,000	1.7.77	69,000	
Ursula Schwab Standard Security Co	Nicolaus Stark Bank (German)	,,	,,	,,	,,	,,	
Rural Reconstruction Ltd	N.V. Landbouw Exploitatie Maatschappij (Dutch)	Overscaig	Sporting	5,800	9.6.65	7,500	
N.V. Landbouw Bond of Credit Co	Hollandsche Bank-Unie N.V. (Dutch)	,,	,,	,,	4.4.68	50,000	
					Discharged	14.2.73	
N.V. Landbouw	W. Duits B.V. (Dutch)	,,	,,	5,800	14.2.73	27,000	
W. Duits B.V.	Exploitatie Maatschappij (Dutch)	,,	,,	2,135 Hctrs	5.6.75	105,650	
W. Duits B.V.	Doeke Bakhuizen (Dutch)	,,	,,	165 Hctrs	5.6.75	7,728	

Kincardineshire

eller	Purchaser	Estate	Type	Acreage	Date	Price £	Resale
Johnstone & McCombie Ltd	Germont S.A. (Switzerland and Panama)	New Banchory	Farmland	52	24.2.69	4,500	
Germond S.A.	Kincardine County Council	,,	,,	2	9.2.70	2,500	
,,	Cumming & Dempster Motor Engineers	,,	,,	3	10.1.73	1,000	
,,	George Wimpey & Co	,,	,,	5	23.7.73	10,725	
,,	Ingasetter Ltd	,,	,,	4	5.12.74	1,000	
,,	Kincardine County Council	,,	,,	4	20.1.75	32,025	
,,	George Wimpey & Co	,,	,,	18	31.3.75	32,297	
,,	Muirtack Estates Ltd	,,	,,	5	5.12.75	37,750	
,,	Albert McIntosh Bldr	,,	,,	7	9.12.75	19,000	
Muirtack Estates Ltd	Albert McIntosh Bldr	,,	,,	2	6.2.76	1,000	
Muirtack Estates Ltd Standard Security Co	Germont S.A.	,,	,,	3	25.3.76	37,750	
Muirtack Estates Ltd	Pitlochry Knit Wear Company	,,	,,	·224 Hect	16.8.76	30,000	

Seller	Purchaser	Estate	Type	Acreage	Date	Price £	Resal
Sir William Gladstone	Per Hegard (Norwegian)	Kerloch, Tilquhillie and Invery	Sporting and farmland	10,000	1.6.77		

Moray

Seller	Purchaser	Estate	Type	Acreage	Date	Price £	Resal
Trustees of Countess and Earl of Seafield	Tulchan Estate Company Ltd	Tulchan	Sporting	15,000	26.4.73	1,425,000	
Tulchan Estate Company Ltd Standard Security to Trustees of Countess and Earl of Seafield	Slater Walker Ltd Tulchan Estate Company Ltd	,, Straan	,, Woodland	134	6.11.73 27.3.75	8,716	

Slater Walker Discharge Standard Security 9.3.76

Seller	Purchaser	Estate	Type	Acreage	Date	Price £	Resal
To	Bestward Estate Company Ltd Formerly Tulchan Estate Company Ltd) Sermon Lane Investments Ltd						
Bestward Estates Company Ltd	Enessey Company S.A. (Switzerland and Panama)	Tulchan and Straan Wood	Sporting and woodland		9.3.76	1,225,300	

See also Aberdeenshire
Inverness-shire

Seller	Purchaser	Estate	Type	Acreage	Date	Price £	Resal
Enessey Company S.A. Standard Security to	Bestward Estate Company Ltd	Tulchan and Straan Wood	Sporting and woodland		9.3.76	493,300	
Enessey Company S.A.	James McDonald	Tulchan Dalvey Farm	Farmland	(part of) 2·25	2.12.76	6,000	
,,	Bestward Estate Company Ltd	Tulchan Discharge Standard Security	Sporting		15.3.77		
,,	Frederick Roy Rutter	Tulchan Shennach Farm	Farmland	(part of) ·50	28.3.77	6,000	
,,	Major John Keith Hayes	Tulchan	,,	(part of) ·50	18.7.77	2,500	
Col. Michael Hardinge Houssemayne du Boulay	Johannes Hellinga (Dutch)	Blervie	Farm and woodland		23.2.77	75,000	
,,	,,	Easter Brockloch	Farmlands	117	7.3.77	25,000	
Johannes Hellinga	Alexander Mackenzie	,,	,,	(part of) 25	24.3.77	15,000	
,,	James Munro	,,	,,	(part of) 84	11.4.77	52,700 Standard Security	

See also Ross and Cromarty
Aberdeenshire

Seller	Purchaser	Estate	Type	Acreage	Date	Price £	Resale

nverness-shire

Seller	Purchaser	Estate	Type	Acreage	Date	Price £	Resale
ohn Trotter	*Taekele Soepboer* (Dutch)	Brin	Sporting and farmland	360	14.1.77	57,000	
		See also Sutherland					
David Wathen	Scotrex B.V. (Dutch)	Kilmartin	Holiday Centre	15	1.8.77	55,000	
"	"	Kilmartin Farm	Farmland	1,930	23.9.77	135,000	
Ashdale Land and Property Co	Samuel Clifford Hardy (American)	Knockie and Dalachapple	Sporting	2,597	27.8.70	60,000	
ilversands Holiday Parks Lossiemouth Ltd	Luc Marie Joseph Delamaire (French)	Ardochy	"	310	18.1.77	39,900	
Frederick Wm. Dalgety	Guenther Ernst Roedel (German)	Craskie and Invercannich	"	155	6.5.77	50,000	
Sir Hereward Wake	Enessey Company (Switzerland and Panama)	North Harris	"		10.1.77	235,000	
Trustees of Henry Rice Nichol	Rodolphe Roger Baudouin de Spoelberch (Belgian)	Black Corries (Part in Argyllshire)	"	10,000	1.10.75	87,900	
Teocarlo Ltd	Jacob Cremer (Dutch)	Pitmain	"	9,900	. .68	41,000	
acob Cremer	Cremer Oil Co Texas, U.S.A.	"	"	"	. .72	182,000	
Donald Cameron of Locheil	No. 26 Trustee Company Incorporated	Glendessary	"	13,200	29.11.73	905,165	
No. 26 Trustee Company Standard Security	Slater Walker Securities	"	" D'charged	13,200	14.3.77	106,237	
No. 26 Trustee Company and Mathews Wrightson and Ltd	Viscount Pollington	Glendessary North	Sporting	860 (part of)	20.1.75	84,991	˄
"	Post Office Staff Superannuation Scheme	Glendessary North West	"	702 (part of)	20.12.76	36,500	
Viscount Pollington	"	Glendessary North	"	860	20.12.76	48,890	
No. 26 Trustee Company	Perfidia Investments Ltd (Channel Isles)	Glendessary	"	10,600	14.3.77	106,000	
Perfidia Investments Ltd Standard Security	Brothock Trustees Ltd	"	"	10,600	14.3.77	30,000	
ngus Spencer Nairn	Over Rankeilour Farms Ltd (Channel Isles)	Struy	"	20,000	5.8.73	200,000	
ishken Estate Co Ltd	Ralph Austin Dubery (French)	Eishken and Parc Deer Forest	"	41,000	12.9.77	50,000	
"	Constructions Architectures Urbanisme S.A. (French)	"	"	40,000 (part of)	12.9.77	190,000	

Seller	Purchaser	Estate	Type	Acreage	Date	Price £	Resale

Ross and Cromarty

Seller	Purchaser	Estate	Type	Acreage	Date	Price £	Resale
Volstead Properties Ltd	Bocardo S.A. (Lichtenstein) Business address: Rue du Rhone, 92 Geneva	Newton Farm	Farmland	63	6.9.73	15,000	
Sir Hugh Rose	Bocardo	North Balkeith Farm	,,		30.10.74	267,000	
,,	,,	Mid and South Pithogarty Farms	,,	247	,,	In Cummulo	
,,	,,	Fendom Hill	,,	85	,,		
Trustees of Wm. Alexander Mackay	,,	Kingscauseway Heathmount	,,	567+	26.5.75	105,000	
Balnagown Castle Properties Eire	,,	Balnagown Castle	Castle Policies		16.9.75	466,908	
Executors John Ormiston Gordon	,,	Summerton Farm	Farmland		16.10.75	27,500	
Ross Estates Company Inc Eire	,,	Balnagown Castle (part of)	Grounds		26.10.76	1,000	
Executors John Ormiston Gordon	,,	Balnagall Farm	Farmland	340+	5.9.77	66,000	

Bocardo *see also* Sutherland

Seller	Purchaser	Estate	Type	Acreage	Date	Price £	Resale
Jermeh Hugh Dewhurst	Hendrik Jan Engelbert van Beuningen and relatives (Dutch)	Braemore (Foich section)	Sporting	14,000 (part of)	21.10.76	55,000	
Jeremy Hugh Dewhurst	N.V.Beheersmat Schappij Festeyn (Dutch) Now Belegginsmatt Schappij Festeyn (Dutch)	Braemore (Strone Section)	,,	14,000 (part of)	21.10.76	100,000	
Timothy Walter Sandeman	Malie-Geod B.V. (Dutch)	Fannich	,,	10,000	19.5.76	140,000	
Major Cecil Geofrey Braithwaite	Anne Arnoldus Nicolai (Dutch)	Ben Damph	,,	14,023	10.9.76	Price not known	Sub Sale
Anne Arnoldus Nicolai	Saitjze Katz (Dutch)	,,	,,	,,	10.9.76	160,000	
Peter Esme Brassey	Gerardus van (Dutch)	Rhiddoroch East	,,	10,000	19.6.61	225,000	
Dorothy Anne Balean	Greengate Ltd (Channel Isles)	Drumchork	,,	20,048	13.10.72	17,500	
W. McLean and Bank of Scotland	,,	,,	,,	(part of)	17.5.74	8,000	
Greengate Ltd	Longfield Investments Ltd (Channel Isles)	,,	,,	20,048	10.2.75	50,000	
,,	Ballina Investments Ltd (Channel Isles)	,,	,,	(part of)	5.3.75	8,000	
Trustees of Lord Elphinstone	Greengate Ltd	Tarbat	Farmland and foreshore	500	24.11.71	80,000	
,,	,,	Croy	Woodland	178	24.11.71	15,000	

Seller	Purchaser	Estate	Type	Acreage	Date	Price £	Resale
Greengate Ltd	Quartet Holdings Ltd (Gibraltar)	Tarbat	Farmland and foreshore	500	13.5.75	50,000	
Quartet Holdings Ltd	Garrulus Glendarius Ltd (Channel Isles)	,,	,,	500	22.7.76	600,000	
Major Robert George Pollock-McCall	Johannes Hellinga (Dutch)	Kindeace	Farmland		21.12.76	460,000	
Johannes Hellinga	Johannes and Hermanus Huis in Het Veld (Dutch)	Kindeace Easter Coillymore Farm	Farmland	(part of) 147	2.3.77	25,238	
,,	,,	Kindeace Bardentyre House and Farm	,,	(part of) 190	10.6.77	47,058	
,,	Tjeert Zijlstra (Dutch)	Kindeace Inchfuir Farm	,,	(part of) 255	25.8.77	148,900	
,,	Marius van Ooijen (Dutch)	Kindeace	,,	(part of) 429	9.9.77	169,767	
,,	Den Heuvel (Dutch)	,,	,,	(part of)	4.10.77	27,380	
		Hellinga *see also* Aberdeen					
Derrick Thomas Allan	Claude Marie Balteau (Belgian)	Dervner			25.7.75	20,000	

4
Oil

Tony Carty

If a new Scottish state came into existence with the political slogan 'It's Scotland's Oil' still fresh in the electorate's mind, what could be done to translate such a slogan into action? The popular idea of this slogan is that it means that Scotland would be entitled to a major share in the North Sea oil fields, and indeed much of the discussion on this topic has been limited to talking about who would inherit what on the dissolution of the United Kingdom.[1] Such discussion is valuable, but there is another very much more difficult issue to be faced. Assuming that the delimitation lines were drawn up and a new Scottish state found itself with control over a portion of the North Sea fields, what could it do with them? If Scottish politicians argue (as many of them do) that an independent Scotland could virtually have its own way in relation to depletion control, participation and taxation, they are ignoring a number of very important questions. Any attempt by an independent Scotland to change the conditions under which multinational oil companies currently operate in the North Sea would bring the new state up against the opposition of an international industry of very considerable power. The oil fields which will be commercial if Scotland were to come to independence within the next few years are mainly in the hands of the oil majors and the US oil 'independents'. A newly created small state would therefore be facing the combined power of companies the size of Shell, Exxon, Texaco and BP. These companies now enjoy powers which appear to impose even further limitations on the slogan 'It's Scotland's Oil'.

The problem that a Scottish state would have to consider is one of deciding just how far it could hope to push the oil majors. For this reason, it is essential that a Scottish Government should understand how ownership and control of oil are exercised in the centres of the oil industry, which would constitute its immediate framework of action. In the Scottish debate, the United Kingdom oil regime has been contrasted with the experience of OPEC and Norway. An 'empirical' assessment of Scotland's position might involve asking to what extent do the optimal interests of a small state such as Scotland correspond to Norwegian and OPEC practice. This would involve an assessment of the urgency of a change in depletion policy[2] and a weighing of this against the possibility that the oil companies might threaten to withdraw their operations, it being more economical for them to exploit their offshore US licences.[3] However, the very first question to be answered is whether a Scottish Government would have the right to revise the United Kingdom oil regime — it is, after all, argued that UK licences prior to 1974 grant ownership of the oil to the companies. Any speculation as to company manoeuvres would be premature before this fundamental issue were faced.

There is a major ideological cleavage between the oil companies and the majority of oil producing states. A leading petroleum economist[4] has said that legal claims in the oil industry consist of blanket ideology in which economic self-determination (the position of the oil-producing states) is pitted against the property-centred arguments of the oil companies. In common with states of the Third World, the oil producing countries argue that each state has a right of sovereignty over its natural resources, and that this right cannot admit of any exercise to its long-term detriment. The oil companies assert that an interest acquired in a natural resource is an 'acquired right' and cannot be taken away without prompt and effective compensation. While it is true that between the OPEC states and the oil companies there was a commercial compromise which reflected the economic balance of power, it would be rash to conclude that the doctrine of 'acquired rights', the property of companies operating in foreign jurisdictions, does not enjoy wide force within the West itself. It is against this complex background of conflicting interests and ideologies that a new Scottish state would have to act. Here we consider what arguments the oil companies would present against any attempted Scottish interference, assessing them in the light of the uncompleted so-called OPEC Revolution, which has left international standards and the location of power within the oil industry so very uncertain.

PART I

THE INHERITANCE

The UK legal regime is so confused in conception that a new Scottish Government could be certain only on one score, that there will be no agreement among *interested* parties about the rights which have been conferred on the oil companies. The view which is developed here is that the companies, foreign and UK, will insist that their rights are proprietary and not contractual, *i.e.* the UK Government has transferred ownership of an asset, the oil, to the companies. This transfer is complete and hence it cannot be taken away by such 'creeping nationalisation' as a taxation or depletion regime which substantially deprives the companies of the profits which they obtain from disposal of 'their' oil. Despite the extreme ambiguity of the UK legislation itself it is nonetheless clear from the attempts of the Labour Government to renegotiate the licences after 1974 that it has accepted this company position. The licences are therefore not contracts in the sense that they constitute a continuing relationship between two sub-

jects dependent upon their particular character and hence bound to lapse
where one subject disappears. An example of such a contractual relationship would be where a US company agreed to supply the UK Government
with continuously updated naval defence equipment.

The basis for the proprietary claim of the oil companies will be the
terms of the production licences themselves. The terms are, however, not
very clear. The central element of a licence is that the state transfers its
property in the natural resource to a private company upon certain conditions. The Petroleum (Production) Regulations 1976 Sched. 5, cl. 2 (made
under the Petroleum and Submarine Pipelines Act 1975) provide:

> 'In consideration of the payments and royalties hereinafter provided and
> in performance and observance by the Licensee of all the terms and
> conditions hereof, the Minister, in the exercise of the powers conferred
> upon him by the Act of 1934 [Petroleum Production Act] and the Act of
> 1964 [The Continental Shelf Act] hereby grant to the Licensee during
> the continuance of this licence and subject to the provisions hereof, *to
> search and bore for and get, petroleum in the seabed and subsoil under the
> seaward area* . . . etc.'.

There is bound to be fierce disagreement about the meaning of this form of
words. It does not grant the companies as unequivocal a property right as
did the Middle East concessions. For instance, Article 1 of the 1933 Concession Agreement between Aramco Oil Company and Saudi Arabia
grants to the former '. . . the exclusive right for a period of 60 years . . . to
explore, extract, treat, manufacture, transport . . . carry away and export
petroleum . . . etc.'. These same terms were used for Kuwait, Iran, Libya
and other Middle East states.[5] Certainly the quite explicit character of
Article 1 contributed to Saudi Arabia losing an arbitration case against the
Aramco Company, a holding company for major US oil companies. It tried
to break into the disposal stage by granting Aristotle Onassis a priority to
transport the oil. Nonetheless the Tribunal decided at a more general level
that disposal of the oil was the very essence of the concession, extraction
being a preliminary stage, in itself of little significance. In particular it
said:

> '. . . the concession has the nature of a constitution which has the effect
> of conferring acquired rights on the Contracting parties. By reason of its
> very sovereignty within its territorial domain, the State possesses the
> legal power to grant rights which it forbids itself to withdraw before the
> end of the concession . . .'.[6]

Oil company lawyers have already made clear how they understand the
terms of the production licence. For instance, R. Bentham of British
Petroleum accepts that the licence terms do not on the face of it convey a
right of property, but this is only because it is doubtful whether the UK
itself has title under international law to the resources as they exist in the

strata on the UK continental shelf. This is why UK legislation distinguishes between onshore and offshore oil. The 1934 Act, sect. 1(1), refers to
'the property in the petroleum existing in its natural condition in strata'
vesting in the Crown, whereas the 1964 Act, sect. 1, vests in the Crown 'any
rights exercisable by the UK outside territorial waters with respect to the
seabed and subsoil and their natural resources . . .' without defining these
rights. So, argues Bentham, oil in its natural state belongs to no-one until it
is captured. It is the granting of the exclusive right of capture which is
decisive, though '. . . the earliest stage at which it can be said with certainty
that the Licensee is the owner of the petroleum is when the petroleum
actually reaches the well-head . . .'.[7] Bentham refers to a legal decision,
the *Singapore Oil Stocks* case,[8] which treated an exclusive right to explore
and exploit as amounting to a right of ownership. Where companies are
extracting oil in accordance with ordinary commercial practice '. . . they
had actual possession of the oil in the reservoirs, and this, combined with
the sole right to dispose of it, gave the appellants as complete a title to the
oil as it was possible for anyone to have during the period of the concession . . .'.

There seems to be no doubt that the UK has given the oil companies, up
until the most recent round of licences, all the property which it considers
it has. This is especially significant since the reservations about transfer of
property can only be presumed to have come from the UK side. In none of
the depletion and participation renegotiations did the UK dispute that
the companies had as complete a title as possible in the oil. Indeed, the
object of 'renegotiation' was to recapture the property. However, one has to
admit that it may be difficult to see the UK taxation system in such terms.
The system seems to be based on the assumption that the licence confers
on the licensee a mere temporary property right for the purpose of exploration and production. Taxation is based upon a supposed fair return upon
capital invested and it is at least possible to argue that it is not understood as
some kind of 'property tax'.[9] If this is true it may possibly transform the
entire supposed 'property right' of the companies into a purely contractual
relationship, *i.e.* finance and expertise in return for an agreed level of profit.
Should so much be established the way would be wide open to argue that
the UK has merely entered into a contract with the companies to extract oil
at very great speed in return for a very high level of profit in order to satisfy
the UK's balance of payments difficulties. Whether this is the case can only
be seen in the context of a complete analysis of the UK oil company
'package', itself a part of international oil industry practice.

Depletion
Depletion control is probably the main issue with respect to which a Scottish Government would differ from existing UK policy. It might try to
argue that, at the very least, such a control does not affect title to the oil as
directly as a claim to participation in existing licences. Indeed it might not

inconceivably claim that by imposing a depletion control a Scottish Government prevents the oil companies from ever 'capturing' property in the oil. However, the UK Labour Government did not take this view in its 'renegotiations' with the oil companies. Instead both sides accepted that depletion policy was crucial to profitability and that a reduced rate of extraction could render the licence completely worthless. The Government did place on the statute book a power to control depletion 'in the national interest'. There is ultimately no limitation to the use of this power as a matter of domestic UK law. However, the oil companies insisted that the rate of extraction was central to the whole production enterprise and this position was not disputed by the UK Government. It claimed merely that any and every government must have a power of last resort concerning depletion of a natural resource. There was no change in government policy which was to encourage investment and continue to issue licences on the basis that the rate of extraction of oil would not be restricted. To put it quite simply the UK has not exercised depletion control.

The UK Government accepted on several occasions that the rights of the oil companies affected its power to impose depletion controls. The well-known Varley Statement (6th December, 1974) assured the companies that:

'. . . depletion policy and its implementation will not undermine the basis on which they have made plans and entered into commitments'.

In the House of Commons Debates, when it was argued that licences are property rights in the petroleum won, Benn, the successor to Varley as Energy Minister, spoke of control in the sense of a legal framework, *e.g.* taxation, health and environmental regulations, changes in currency valuation, as cases of '. . . wise legislative protection without in any way impacting upon the basic property rights which, rightly or wrongly, were embedded in the contracts to which the previous Government assented'.[10]

The issue of the exact limits of company rights never came to a head for the simple reason that the interests of company and government never clashed. The view of the oil industry was that the amount of and profits from sales of oil are basic to the decision to undertake operations. Their reaction to the 1974 White Paper[11] was that being forced to operate below capacity would discourage exploration effort, *i.e.* they threatened to discontinue projected investment. The Chairman of Esso Petroleum Co, A. W. Pierce, insisted that '. . . the economic consequences of production at well below the levels for which the installations were planned are very serious unless there are compensatory correctives . . .'.[12] Jesse Wyllie, the President of Gulf Oil, Eastern Hemisphere, was even more hostile to the disruptive effects of what he saw as arbitrarily defined reductions.[13] For its part the Government was anxious to increase rather than decrease the rate of oil extraction and did not wish to do anything to discourage this. Its view was merely that a power of depletion control — in the Petroleum and Submarine Pipeline Bill — was no more than the back-up powers which any state must have.[14] From the start, the White Paper itself did not speak of exercising the power for some years to come.[15] So the Government proposals to act 'in the national interest' included acceptance that the problem remained '. . . how investment security and cash-raising would be affected if the Government prevented companies developing their fields or altered production plans once fields were already in action . . .'.[16] The Labour Government did not reverse the decision made by previous governments, that the balance of advantage for the UK lay in the fastest exploitation possible.[17] On the contrary, the large allowances on corporation tax and the deferment of petroleum revenue tax reflect the continued desire of the Companies, banks and the Government to extract the oil as quickly as possible.[18]

The depletion control powers under the Petroleum and Submarine Pipelines Act 1975 (Sched. 2 Part II cols. 15, 16) may best be seen as no more than an assertion by the UK that it is not to be outdone by other countries which claim sovereignty over their oil, especially with the ever present possibility of an energy crisis. The legislation does not reveal the object to be achieved by control 'in the national interest', a matter firmly within the discretion of the Minister of Energy. This appears to allow the Government maximum flexibility in dealing with the companies. However, the Minister is expected to approve programmes which specify, *inter alia*, the maximum and minimum quantities of petroleum for each calendar year or other period specified, which he will approve. If he chooses to modify this he must give notice after due representation heard. In practice the Government has given the companies a free hand in determining so-called production profiles, with automatic approval for the whole lifetime of the field. Even for controls envisaged for future oilfield projects, any system of time-staged consents will involve a minimum flow to ensure an economic return on investment.[19]

Participation
Nothing more clearly demonstrates the right of the oil companies to the oil they 'capture' than the failure of the UK to renegotiate existing licences. The sole purpose of the Labour Government was to obtain part ownership of the oil through an equity share in the licences. For the most part it had to settle for a very limited right to purchase the oil from the companies at 'market' price. There, even more than in the case of depletion control, the UK seems to have been attracted by developments in OPEC states and Norway, yet unwilling to risk questioning the proprietary rights of the companies.

The rationale of participation was not to nationalise the oil companies outright but to follow a trend in oil producing countries, which ensured an active role for the state in partnership with the companies. However, participation in this sense had a short life in the Middle East and it later became clearer that the UK understood participation as a means to give the nation direct title to oil produced, control over its disposal and, eventually, through BNOC, to acquire its own knowledge of oil production.[20] The White Paper of August 1974 did not spell out what it meant beyond referring to the Norwegian 'carried interest' system whereby the state has an option to acquire ownership with a specified proportion of costs, *i.e.* usually after a field has been discovered but before it has gone into production.

However, when the question of compensation received closer scrutiny it was realised that expenditure on a vast scale was involved and this led the Government to launch its 'no-gains no-loss' principle. The companies would not lose financially from participation and the Government could avoid any immediate large-scale expenditure. Not to have paid any compensation and yet to have taken an equity-interest was seen simply as contrary to international law and likely to provoke a confrontation with the US.[21] Indeed, a government working paper of May 1975 accepted the full proprietary interest of the oil companies in proposing compensation not merely for a share of future development costs but also for the post-tax revenue lost by the companies as a result of participation.[22] However, the idea of the Government handing over capital to the companies ignored the economic reality that it was the UK Government which needed oil company capital to finance its policy of speedy, large-scale oil production. In late 1975 drastic escalation of development costs intensified the UK need for capital at a time when the whole development programme towards self-sufficiency seemed likely to be 'postponed' for six to 10 years.[23] The companies were 'responding'. The rate of ordering of new production equipment and even the rate of drilling activity fell off. The Cabinet was anxious for 'industry co-operation' and hence the no-gains no-loss principle was issued.[24]

As for the results of the participation renegotiations the British Government '. . . obtained an oil purchase agreement that they chose to call a participation agreement' (Dam). Although some success was achieved with Gulf and Conoco none of the other major oil companies (BP, Shell, Mobil, Exxon, Texaco) allowed any significant part of production and even refining and marketing to be disturbed. They appealed to the no-gains no-loss principle with almost complete success.[25] In particular, Shell and Esso operate jointly in four of the declared commercial fields. By 1982 they should be producing about one-third of current UK oil consumption, particularly from the Brent field. Six months hard bargaining produced a refusal to compromise on their ambition to retain control over all the oil they expect to produce from UK oil fields. The 1976 Shell UK Review and Accounts described the majority-state participation in their existing licences over commercial fields as allowing the Government to be a joint licence holder '. . . but the companies will retain full beneficial ownership of all petroleum and related assets. The entire Shell share of foreseeable North Sea crude oil production, all of which will be required to support

Shell's UK refining and marketing activities, will be secured for the company's own use. Furthermore, there will be no change in the Shell position as operator responsible for the total management of all activities with the ability to exercise decision-making control. . . .' The UK option to buy is tied to a duty to sell back to the companies, to satisfy their UK refinery needs. At most it may serve to give the UK priority over EEC countries in an energy crisis and to contribute to the policy of ensuring that two-thirds of refining takes place in the UK. Nothing better was obtained with Mobil and Texaco. Gulf and Conoco did not object to options to purchase 51% of their oil partly because of their limited UK refining capacity. Even BP may buy back in the period 1979 to 1981 a major part of the 'government oil' subject to BP providing equivalent amounts of oil from production sources elsewhere. After 1981 further arrangements will be a commercial matter between BP and the Government.[26]

Taxation

Nothing may seem more obvious than the power of Parliament to tax as it pleases commercial activities within its jurisdiction. Indeed an American commentator (Dam) maintains that the UK Government avoided confrontation on the 'licence issue' because it found that it could obtain the same ends through regulation and taxation. Any claim that the licence itself could be used to restrict such powers would imply that a different tax/regulation regime would be required for each licence.[27] The last point is open to the simple objection that licences are largely model clauses in statutory regulations. More generally, as a matter of international practice it has not been accepted that taxation, any more than a regulatory power such as depletion control, could be used to take away the economic substance of a licence. This practice has had a marked influence on the Norwegian experience. The companies usually took the precaution of including clauses in the agreements precluding substantial revision. These specified that the concession was exempt from taxes or any other measures which would render it more onerous. However, these clauses, known as Law Stabilisation Clauses, have not been regarded as necessary. The contract itself is enough.[28] The distinction between contract/licence and regulation/law was irrelevant in the traditional system. The terms of exploration were agreed mutually whether this was a personal contract with a sovereign ruler, such as in Qatar and Abu Dhabi, or a contract confirmed by legislative act as in Saudi Arabia, or whether the company merely accepted a petroleum law, as in Iran or Libya.[29]

It may well be that the UK Government considers itself free to alter the taxation rate as it pleases, that the 'no-gains no-loss' financial guarantee which it applied to the participation negotiations does not apply to taxation matters. The companies may have no explicit assurance against severer taxation. However, close analysis of the changes in taxation after 1974 suggest rather that investments have been made on a certain scale on the basis that the taxation laws would continue to guarantee a particular return notwithstanding a number of possible vicissitudes. The changes as against the pre-1974 period were designed to remove only glaring anomalies. Nonetheless, whether the UK itself could use its taxation power to remove the advantage of owning and disposing of the oil is not at all conclusive of the question whether Scotland could treat the UK-oil company relationship as contractual, and therefore confined to them, rather than proprietary. In the sphere of taxation this distinction between contract and property may seem to be nominal. Is the UK taking a proportion of the net value of the oil as it is sold by the companies or is it granting a fair return on capital invested? Surely the basis on which the oil company/UK proportions are assessed is what matters? This assessment has clearly been profoundly influenced by the special economic circumstances of the UK. Still this may be too narrow a definition of 'proprietary' interest. Capital has already been invested and ownership of the oil transferred. So it might be said that more severe taxation of the substance of the right to sell the oil is not permitted.

The taxation policy of the post-1974 UK Government was to close tax loop-holes in oil company activities, especially their capacity to reduce taxes on North Sea activities by setting against them capital invested or loss incurred elsewhere and their opportunity to reap the windfall of world oil price rises of 1973. Legally this policy was unproblematic. The initial terms of the licences only stipulated that UK taxes would apply but they did not specify that the rate of tax should be the same as that applied to other commercial operations, nor the rate at which North Sea oil profits would be taxed.[30] The ring-fence tax system whereby each field is taxed separately is not so much a centre of possible future controversy[31] as the Petroleum Revenue Tax and the exemptions from its application. Undoubtedly this tax is designed to encourage a very rapid expansion of oil production in the North Sea, *i.e.* a taxation rate more favourable to capital than that prevailing in Norway and the Middle East. The return on capital is supposed to be at least equal to what could be earned in the best alternative use. Hence quite inevitably the initial 'tax-offer' has a certain binding character. As MacKay puts it '. . . the producer should obtain terms which guarantee him a payment equivalent to his transfer earnings, *i.e.* a payment just sufficient to induce the producer to continue to employ his productive resources in their current use rather than transferring them elsewhere'.[32]

The Petroleum Revenue Tax (PRT) is designed to ensure that a definite measure of profit accrues to the companies even though the full extent of profit to be obtained from the sale of the oil cannot be known in advance, *e.g.* because of fluctuations in levels of production or in world oil prices. That is, the tax is designed to guarantee a certain return on capital invested. To the extent that in any given year PRT would reduce the return on a field before corporation tax to less than 30% of capital expenditure measured on the basis of historic cost, PRT will not be imposed. Above this 30% a tapering provision ensures that PRT will not be greater than 80% of the amount by which the profit exceeds 30% of the capital expenditure to date. The 30% safeguard will have the effect, taking into account the deductibility of PRT for corporation tax purposes, that PRT will not cause the rate of return on capital invested to fall below about 15%.[33]

However, the effect of certain PRT exemptions is to postpone its operation for a number of years. Each oil field is given an allowance (OTA sect. 8) of half a million long tons. Also an uplift of 75% is allowed ostensibly (sect. 3/5) because interest on loans taken out by the companies to finance development is not deductible.[34] Uplift can be carried forward to a second 'chargeable' period if it is not used in a first, postponing the onset of tax and thereby significantly cushioning the disincentive effect of PRT.

It would certainly be open to both the UK and a future Scottish Government to improve upon the administrative efficacy of this tax regime. There may be difficulty in establishing satisfactorily whether certain company 'costs' are true capital expenditures. A tax may be based on a premise which turns out to be clearly mistaken, *e.g.* where taxation is deferred because it is supposed that revenue will come much later than an initial capital expenditure and this turns out not to be the case. It might be more effective to have a field variable tax, reference price for each barrel of oil, allowing an 'equivalent reasonable return', *i.e.* allowing for what the Government considers normal development expenditure for a field. The onus could then be on the companies to prove, for instance, that the special geographical conditions required further expenditure etc.[35] However, it could hardly be open to the UK, at least, to argue that the oil companies would have invested in the UK North Sea sector in the same fashion even if they had received only more 'normal' rates of return on capital invested.

PART II

THE OPEC REVOLUTION

The essential result of the OPEC revolution is that the oil, as a natural resource, belongs to the state. Oil companies may be hired on a contractual basis to assist in the extraction of the oil. They may be needed for their capital, or, much more likely, for their technical expertise. For each of these they receive an agreed return. The state determines, as a matter of its own public policy, the level at which the oil is to be extracted, the price to be charged, to whom it shall be sent. The relationship with the companies can only be contractual and not proprietary. Their purely financial reward is not significant when compared with the total revenues obtained from the sale of the oil.

The juridical basis upon which OPEC states repudiated the traditional concession system was simply that it purported to transfer ownership of the oil to the oil companies and that this was beyond the normal powers of a sovereign state. Natural resources belong *as a matter of inherent right* to the state in whose jurisdiction they lie. The power of the oil companies at the production stage of the oil industry lay in their ownership of the oil. They could decide how much of it they wished to extract and dispose of, and at what price. They had to pay first royalties and then a proportion of the profits, about 50%, but their ownership of the oil meant that the state had no possibility of ensuring that the oil resource could be developed in accordance with its own view of its national interest. It had the mere possibility of disposing of the revenue.

If a radical Scottish Government decides that oil within its jurisdiction is to be extracted at a rate which it considers to be in the national interest, if it insists that it has a sovereign right to determine what is an appropriate rate of return for the services which the companies render or to whom the oil is to be sold, it is asserting quite simply that the oil belongs to the state, to Scotland.

It is not a question of respecting the private property rights of the oil companies in licences granted by the UK but subjecting them to different public law restrictions such as depletion control and taxation of profits. To regard as decisive the capacity of a Scottish state to formulate its own public laws is to ignore the key significance of company ownership of the oil.

Nor is it possible to argue that the licences are mere contracts which lapse with the secession of Scotland from the UK. The UK has purported to transfer ownership of the oil to the companies through its equivalent of the traditional institution of the concession, *i.e.* the production licences. If Scotland wishes to modify its inheritance it can only do so on the basis that no aspect of the supposed company ownership of the oil can stand in the way of the Scottish national interest. Scotland's newly acquired independence does not in itself diminish the radical nature of its claims against the oil companies. Traditionally 'private property rights', *i.e.* 'acquired rights', were not affected by state succession. Their more precarious position at present is due entirely to the general hostility of newly independent states to alien private property rights especially those over natural resources, no matter when they were acquired.

OPEC states could have argued, and in some cases they did, that the concessions which they had given to foreign oil companies were invalid because they were never made freely. Iran and Iraq were hardly independent states when oil concessions were extracted from them. Political intrigue and even coercion reached such a high peak in the Middle East after 1918 that they were not acting as free agents.[36] Even where overt political pressure was not exerted the states concerned existed at a level of political and economic infancy. A chief legal adviser to OPEC 1967-1970, Zabariya, insists that they knew nothing at all about the nature of the petroleum industry, its international character and especially the full financial implications of discoveries. The oil companies had taken advantage of them.

This argument applied especially to the Arab Kingdoms and Sheikdoms of the Persian Gulf.[37] The position of OPEC states was then, at least in their own view, not basically different from that of a radical independent Scotland which claims that it is not bound by licence agreements which the UK has granted.

However, rather than ask if renegotiations of the concessions could produce balanced or fair terms, OPEC decided to revoke them completely and take over direct ownership of the oil. They came to realise that individual concessions did not reflect the true nature of the international oil industry. For the major oil companies they were only the starting point giving the companies exclusive control of production. Since oil was in excess supply the companies guaranteed their own profits by agreeing among themselves from which country to 'lift' oil, *i.e.* levels of production, and where to refine and retail it. Hence they could assure for themselves a margin of profit — the difference between the cost of production, including taxes paid for the oil and the retail price which they fix — which was quite independent of the taxing power of the state.[38] At first in 1971 OPEC seems not to have realised this. The so-called Teheran Agreement was designed to increase the financial take of the OPEC states involved (Libya concluded a separate agreement) by increasing tax by 5 cents per annum per barrel with a 2·5% allowance for inflation. The oil companies insisted that the agreement amounted to a settlement of the limits of the Government take. Yet their control of the oil meant that the price could be passed on to consumers. The Shah of Iran warned at the time that more effective means would have to be found to prevent companies doing this.[39] The OPEC revolution consists precisely in the realisation that control of the oil itself was the key to effective seizure of oil revenues, their central objective.

This policy brought OPEC into radical conflict with the oil companies. These latter never accepted the legality of its actions. They merely adapted to an economic reality which they could not avoid. For Scotland perhaps most relevant are the 'participation' negotiations between the 'moderate' Persian Gulf OPEC states and the oil majors. Of course, the latter saw participation as upsetting the financial balance of the Teheran Agreement. No matter what the proportion of equity-sharing between host states and oil companies, any loss of ownership of oil was bound to affect profits. The companies were willing to accept it, if at all, only on a no-gains/no-loss basis.[40] So OPEC would have to compensate the oil companies for the difference between the tax-paid cost of the oil, *i.e.* what the oil companies themselves had to pay to extract and export their own oil at present, and the 'market price', namely the price at which they sold it. The companies insisted that in normal commercial practice they should receive the loss of earnings at at least their capitalised value, reckoned on a discounted cash-flow basis, at least until the expiry of production rights. In other words, the oil companies fell back on their rights under individual concessions, precisely as they were to do with the UK Labour Government after 1974. The legal position, in their view, was that the concessions gave the right, for risks undertaken, to produce and sell crude oil for a given number of years.[41] In view of the magnitude of the risks and costs incurred it had always been recognised that a reasonably long concession period must be allowed. If a proportion of contractual rights is surrendered beforehand the loss of earning potential must be made up.[42] So the companies insisted on the right to buy back the 'equity crude', which they would lose through participation, automatically and at a price no more than 5 cents a barrel above present tax-paid costs, *i.e.* on a no-gains/no-loss basis.[43] OPEC was unanimous in rejecting this view.

After some hesitation even Saudi Arabia decided that compensation would be on the basis that the oil belonged to the host state. The General Agreement on Participation of 1st October, 1972[44] provided only for up-dated net-book value of company assets, *i.e.* written down book value adjusted for inflation. Oil was to be sold to the companies at approximately market price. This was only 6% of the compensation which the companies had requested. In other words, as the Libyan Oil Minister put it, book value meant no compensation for future profits gained on the sale of the oil owned in any case. The fund of capital invested would alone be returned. Suppose an oil company spent 100 million Libyan dinars and then recovered 60 million dinars in production: 40 million would remain to be paid.[45]

When participation was fully implemented it could only leave the oil companies with management and long-term supply (crude oil) contracts. When Kuwait decided upon 100% participation it merely invited BP and Gulf to negotiate the details of implementation of its decision. The principle of transfer of full ownership of the oil to the state was assumed and the questions remaining were merely the details of net book value of assets, administration of the industry and marketing of the oil abroad. Production and pricing were not part of the contractual relationship. The Government must remain free to adapt the exploitation of its natural resources to the 'objective conditions of the international oil industry'.

It is vital for a radical Scottish Government to realise that the oil companies did not accept this 'revolution' until they were subjected to superior economic force. They had learned since the confrontation with Libya over price increases in 1970 that oil producing states could survive much longer without the revenue of the oil than they could dispense with their sources of supply. Seven months of confrontation meant that Libya gained quite small price increases by making a credible threat of outright take-over of all company assets.[46] Henceforth, OPEC took the view that negotiations were merely a tactic used by the companies to delay interminably and circumvent issues. The October 1972 General Agreement, the first stage in the participation 'process' merely provided for 25–51% participation staged over several years, yet Yamani disclosed afterwards that this had only been obtained through a collective threat of effective unilateral action.[47] In 1973 oil price rises convinced OPEC that nothing less than complete ownership of the oil was enough. The companies never accepted this in negotiations. So OPEC taxed away the difference, first by increasing the tax reference price in October and December 1973 and then by raising taxes and royalties on 'equity crude' to remove the distinction between it and oil which the companies bought back from the governments. Only after this did the 'breakthrough' in participation negotiations come.[48] The use of taxing power was explicitly directed to put an end to the concession system and it was not merely an integral part of a continuing concession system. The companies had to accept it because the cartel formed by OPEC cut them off from alternative sources of oil and they could expect no diplomatic support from Western states which were not interested in the structure of the oil industry so long as the supply of oil continued.[49]

The exact extent of the OPEC revolution has to be understood. The oil companies were never threatened with extinction. OPEC merely asserted control over the production/upstream stage of activities, which were safely within their national jurisdiction and where unilateral action was possible. Indeed, the whole purpose of the participation process, at least in Yamani's view, was to keep the co-operation of the oil companies in downstream (refining and marketing) activities, essential to maintaining the cartel price for the oil. The companies continue to fulfil the 'management' role of so regulating oil production that supply does not exceed demand[50] and, with assured long-term supplies, the oil companies were encouraged by OPEC to transfer their profits into 'downstream' activities. In other words the OPEC revolution still meant no gains/no losses for the companies because they merely transferred their profits from upstream activities.[51] Their agreements with OPEC, which they see purely as a matter of commercial advantage and not of legal principle, are nonetheless quite tolerable to them.

Scotland, OPEC and the question of succession

If Scotland achieves independence, the foreign, and especially US, oil companies will argue that changes in the Constitution of the UK are irrelevant to their private rights. They will have the support of the same 'classical' international law which accepted the inviolability of the traditional oil concessions '. . . Traditional state succession involved only the substitution of one sovereign, who was often a monarch, for another and left the legal relationship between individuals intact'. The law was reinforced in the nineteenth century by the *laissez faire* doctrine of property.[52] It was reaffirmed by the case-law of the World Court in the 1920's.[53]

The traditional law of state succession is now highly controversial precisely because the distinction between private rights and public institutions is widely regarded as unsound. Particularly, economic concessions involve a political judgement by a state that property otherwise normally public should be transferred to private bodies. If one considers that '. . . the political regime of a given community is linked to the private property

regime in the territory which it controls . . . (it) is therefore not surprising
that failure to respect acquired rights in cases either of succession or of
non-succession constitutes a fairly marked trend in modern times . . .'.[54]
However, conversely, where states or individuals see no reason for questioning the value of private property they need not be expected to move
away from the traditional law of state succession. In the case of Scotland
the law will not be somehow controversial in the abstract. The same parties
will be in dispute over the legal nature of the licences themselves. The oil
companies will point out that there are virtually no cases in the modern
practice of states where successor states have claimed the right forthwith
upon change of sovereignty to repudiate contracts. The repudiations come
later and have all the characteristics of an ordinary expropriation.[55] Examples from state practice where the successor state has claimed to be free
to disregard acquired rights have characteristics perhaps similar to those of
OPEC states but irrelevant to the UK situation. For instance, Ghana abro-
gated concessions granted to UK, Dutch and South Africans on the ground
that those granting them, being illiterate, had not understood the full significance of the instruments. The consideration was illusory and the
profits excessive. Similarly the Mobutu Government in Zaire revoked Belgian concessions because Belgians had acquired rights without payment to
the detriment of the indigenous population.[56]

The UK licences were in no sense similar to contracts won from illiterate Ghanaian chieftains, or to Royal Belgian handouts at the height of the
imperial era, any more than they were a product of political intrigue in the
semi-anarchic, chaotic conditions following the fall of the Ottoman Empire. The oil companies would presumably argue that, within the context
of normal Western commercial practice, they accepted in good faith the
decision of a democratically elected government in one of the oldest of
European states, that its offshore natural resources could best be exploited
through private enterprise. On that basis they invested very large amounts
of capital and expertise in return for the right to property in the oil.

The difference between UK and Scottish 'interests' may be seen in
terms of how to organise the oil industry. In substance this comes to
nothing more than a reversal of public policy, a second attempt, after the
failure of the post-1974 UK Government, to bring offshore oil extraction
under public control. As such, it is undoubtedly permissible for a Scottish
state to have a different view of what the public interest requires concerning public control of private enterprise. However, differences between
Scottish and English authorities need not be expected to concern the oil
companies. In view both of the remoteness of Scottish independence and
of the wide room for disagreement within Scotland itself about suitable
policy, the companies might argue that in no sense have they entered into
commitments in bad faith.[57] The situation does not even remotely resemble an agreement between the UK and the oil companies, months
before an independence referendum, to supply the UK economy with oil

on especially favourable conditions. The oil installations remain intact, the revenues continue to flow. Scotland can step into the position of the UK without frustrating the terms or operation of the licences. The companies may argue that any 'taking' of their assets without full compensation is an interference with private rights.

Should a radical Scottish Government choose to assert full control over its offshore oil industry in the manner of OPEC, it will not be able to pay full compensation. The two courses are mutually incompatible. Compensation would be paid for the oil and yet the basis for its action is that the oil does not belong to the companies. A no-gains/no-loss approach will leave the companies in command as it did in the UK negotiations. Hence it has to be accepted that a radical Scottish Government would in effect be opposing the private property rights of the companies. Nor can this be avoided by reference to any supposed equities of the situation. Such formulae usually refer to situations in which some compromise may keep an enterprise going to everyone's satisfaction, *e.g.* the Austro-Hungarian railway network after 1918.[58] The organisation of the oil industry is politically highly controversial and the two better-known alternatives oppose themselves in the Scottish situation just as they did in the Middle East in the early 1970's.

PART III

NORWAY

Norway presents itself as a very attractive model to a radical Scottish Government. A State Oil Corporation (Statoil) has primary responsibility for the development of offshore oil, itself owning the major share of the production licences. The oil companies receive a rate of return of no more than 20% on the capital invested. The oil has been, and continues to be, extracted at a rate which is determined by Norwegian authorities. Norway is a small nation, whose economy has such limited energy requirements that a major part of its oil may be exported. It must face economic issues not unlike Scotland's, major ones being whether it is economically more sound to take oil revenues now or to keep oil in the ground, and whether too large an oil surplus, bringing with it a rise in the exchange rate, might damage its trading competitiveness.

However, Norway's relations with the oil companies have developed entirely differently from the UK's. For this reason alone its experience cannot be seen as modelled on, or even significantly affected by, the OPEC experience. There has been no confrontation with the oil companies. Indeed, there has been no need. Since the end of the 1960's the latter have not been given a decisive place in the Norwegian oil industry, *i.e.* the ownership of oil. Before the OPEC revolution had even begun Norway's Labour Government had decided that since Norwegian private capital would be unable to intervene significantly in the offshore operations, state capital should take the initiative. This decision was taken as soon as oil was discovered in significant quantities in the North Sea. Its policy has always been directed to the future, and never retrospective. Peter Nore, a Norwegian political scientist, emphasises that Norway:

'. . . has scrupulously refused to change existing concessions but has just imposed tougher and tougher terms for each additional round of licences. The only exception was excess profits, a point not excluded even under existing licences . . .'.[59]

Norway began in 1965 with a concession system like the UK's but it was tightened up as soon as oil was discovered. Participation began to be discussed as early as 1968 but was rejected in so far as it would involve risk capital, *i.e.* engagement in a field where oil might never become commercial.[60] The carried-interest system, the right to take a percentage ownership share in a proven field upon payment of a share in exploration costs already incurred, was introduced in 1969, after oil had been discovered, but only up to 17·5%. The licensing went forward very slowly until 1974. The increases in state participation in 1971–1972 were due to 'farm-in' agreements.[61] Discussion about a state oil company began in a committee of the Norwegian Parliament in 1970 and a state-owned holding company was proposed to ensure a more active government role in all stages of the oil industry. This was approved in June 1972. All existing government participation rights would be consigned to 'Statoil'. In a resolution of 16th May, 1973 the Storting (Parliament) agreed that all future oil agreements would be made on Norway's behalf by Statoil. Only in 1974 was there another licensing round in which nine licences were granted to Statoil on a 100% basis and nine on a 50–80% basis.[62]

The reason for the delay in awarding further production licences until 1974 seems to have been primarily that Norway wished to define its policy towards foreign oil companies quite clearly before committing itself. Norway was in no need to hurry the volume of extraction and indeed chose at this stage not to grant licences as a means of 'macro-volume' control (the fewer oil fields the less oil extracted). It felt that a slower build-up of production would suit better its capacity to absorb revenues and its trading competitiveness.[63] However, in view of the technical limits which may stand in the way of depletion controls it is perhaps more important for a radical Scottish Government to understand the nature of Norwegian commitment to state participation. Total Norwegian investment in the North Sea by 1974 came to $1·5 billion as compared to $2·9 billion for total private investment in the economy. The decision to commit such sums was in large part due to a tradition both of state socialism and economic nationalism. Once it became apparent that private Norwegian capital would be unable to participate effectively the State took an initiative which was facilitated by an almost unique political tradition which had brought about the highest taxation rate in the West, at 47%.[64]. In other words, a society in which there is a broad consensus on a role for state capitalism committed itself to substantial capital expenditures.

Norwegian depletion control and taxation demonstrate both an acceptance of the doctrine of acquired rights and the possibilities of extensive control over oil operations in the North Sea. The terms of the production licence do not seem to indicate any concern about the nature of the rights which Norway has over resources under its continental shelf. The Royal Decree of 31st May, 1963 provides that the seabed and subsoil are subject to Norwegian sovereignty in respect of exploration and exploitation of natural deposits. An Act of 21st June, 1963 No. 12 sect. 2 declares that the right to submarine natural resources in the ocean areas referred to shall vest in the state. The production licences themselves seem to provide clearly for a transfer of ownership:

'A (production) licence gives the licensee exclusive rights to exploration for and exploitation of petroleum deposits in the area to which the licence is applicable.'[65]

The Norwegian Government has never disputed that once a licence is granted the power to regulate it is limited. With minor exceptions operation of tax laws with respect to licences has not been altered. The excess-profit tax is seen as a special case.

Depletion control
There are two ways in which depletion control may be understood. Attempts are made to relate the general level of extraction of oil to national economic goals. Or one endeavours to ensure the best use of a particular oil field in the national interest. Norway has sought to achieve the first type of control mainly by limiting the number of licences issued to oil companies. This method is clearly very haphazard as one cannot know in advance how much commercially exploitable oil will be discovered as a consequence of the licences granted. Notwithstanding anxiety in 1974 about an excessive rate of production, it now seems that a much slower rate of production (37 million tons (m.t.) for 1978, 65–70 m.t. in the 1980's, instead of 60 m.t. in 1978 and 90 m.t. in the 1980's) is encouraging a consensus for a faster rate of production. The Finance Ministry sees oil not as disruptive of a full-employment economy as much as a counterbalance to 'hit' traditional industries such as shipbuilding, metals, textiles etc. Oil revenues are needed for the balance of payments deficit of 14%.[66]

At least as much difficulty exists in controlling the operation of particular fields if the licence holder is a foreign company, because it is pure chance if the global company interest in volume is the same as Norway's.[67] It is accepted that once production licences have been awarded control possibilities are limited. A wide power to impose controls in the interests of conservation exists. This power is understood to cover bad production methods and also the production rate which is optimal by financial and community standards.[68] However, there does not seem to be any question of limiting oil fields for which permission to extract has been granted. The right to produce and carry away oil, once granted, limits a power of depletion control.[69] Yet, were the authorities to reserve the right to make drastic changes, this would make it impossible to plan operations and enter into long-term supply contracts. The Norwegians try to draw a balance between economical operations and the right of authorities to regulate unsatisfactory development. They cannot decide once and for all, expecially because of the need for data on the productivity of the reservoir. Until 1978 Statoil's technical expertise only goes as far as the exploratory phase and does not include development technology, *inter alia,* competence in reservoir techniques, evaluation of reserves and recovery rates.[70] Nonetheless, offshore installations are accepted as being subject to stresses of an altogether different dimension from onshore ones. It is calculated they will have a life of 20 to 25 years. In the last years of a well, forms of secondary recovery, *e.g.* gas injection, may be necessary to maintain production. Hence a production plan will grant the operator some security about future supplies but allow the Government to modify it in the light of future production figures.[71]

Taxation by means of participation

A central part of the Norwegian reappraisal of its oil industry was that private companies, Norwegian and otherwise, may be engaged in the exploration and production stages and will receive suitable compensation. But in the future they will have the right to exploit these natural resources in exceptional cases only. However, this does not mean that Norway asserts a right to tax all licensees as it pleases. The decision was taken as a point of departure that there was to be no separate tax system for the oil companies though small tax alterations were made between 1965 and 1972.[72] This position has not altered and the considerable increase in income is due to state participation. Thus the farm-in agreements after 1972 produced the first sharp increase in revenue going to the state, with one case of 50% participation increasing the government 'take' to 70–75%. The 1974 licence round '. . . gave the state a sliding participation-scale of 50-80%, a policy which will give a maximum government take of 85%'.[73] Under production licences 038/042 Statoil is not charged for any costs related to any deposits before it is declared commercial. Statoil must cover its proportional share of future costs. Increases in government take have been on the basis that very large funds have been invested and part of the income has to be regarded as yield on invested capital and compensation for business participation risks. Where there has been 100% state participation all the economic rent goes to the state.

There is a Norwegian equivalent to the UK PRT. The Ministry of Finance considered that no question of company rights was involved because the latter had little reason to expect a very major impact on their profits as a result of the price explosion of 1973. The additional revenue should go to the state because it relates to exploitation of a natural resource which is the property of the state. Previous tax rules had been based on the internal situation in the 1960's and early 1970's. The special tax adds 25% to the ordinary company tax. A reasonable return on capital invested must allow for the highly technical development risks. Still the companies say that when they evaluate future projects they reckon on a 20–25% return. The tax rules, in the view of the Ministry of Finance, will reduce the rate of return relatively little when the present rate is about 20%.[74]

PART IV

LEGAL RIGHT AND ECONOMIC POWER

If the oil companies and a radical Scottish Government both insist upon the most obvious view of their respective rights the outcome can only be confrontation. Indeed, there may simply be a legal/ethical dilemma due to the UK assurances upon which the oil companies appear entitled to rely and which, nonetheless, bequeath an inheritance very restrictive for a new Scottish state. In such circumstances it might be thought that a compromise could be reached. Yet predictions about the form of a compromise are so difficult precisely because there is an issue of principle involved in any accommodation which the two sides may be willing to make. For instance suppose the oil companies accept an effective reduction of their return on capital to 10–15%. Does this mean a Scottish state has a sovereign right to impose the taxes it judges appropriate? If it does, the companies have not achieved real security for their interests. Hence they are better advised to refuse to make concessions from the very start and insist upon their acquired rights. This is precisely how they behaved in Libya in 1970 when an oil producing state first attempted to negotiate a moderate (44 cents a barrel) increase in 'government take'. The oil companies considered that a question of principle was involved in accepting that their property interest in the oil concessions could be modified whenever an oil producing state considered its 'take' inadequate. Even when Libyan coercion was clearly prevailing the oil majors purported to increase the posted price of oil unilaterally.[75] The same taxation agreement could be taken to mean that Scotland, for its part, accepts a duty to consult with and obtain the approval of the oil companies for every change in its policy. The argument for compromise supposes that there is a simple formula which defines the difference between Scottish and UK interests and which therefore facilitates a once and for all accommodation with the oil companies, following independence. It is at least as likely that a Scottish Government would be uncertain about how its oil policy might develop and, at the same time, determined only to enter into provisional accommodations with the oil companies.

So it would be wise for a Scottish state to wonder what might happen if the oil companies were to refuse to renegotiate the UK 'inheritance'. Suppose Scotland then acted unilaterally, imposed depletion controls, took majority shares in a number of licences upon payment of book-value compensation and increased taxation on the remaining licences. The oil companies respond by withdrawing from their North Sea operations. What are the dimensions of the conflict which Scotland has on its hands?

The oil companies should be able to launch a major diplomatic campaign simply on the basis that security of property is essential to their commercial activities. They will presumably be most able to impress this fact upon their economic partners, which include a very significant part of the Western banking and insurance community, particularly in the United States. The very dimensions of their own operations are bound to impress the governments of Western states which are at present dependent on the companies not merely for the supply of crude oil but also for refining and marketing. However, the oil companies will have to be very careful about this aspect of their campaign if only because of their own dependence upon the long-term supply contracts with OPEC states. They will not be willing to provoke Western governments into revising the nature of their relationship with OPEC, *i.e.* their acceptance of the oil companies as intermediaries. An essentially related part of their diplomacy will be to persuade OPEC that it is not to its advantage to disturb their co-operate relationship with oil companies, banks and Westerm industry for the sake of relatively small alternations in the legal regime of a Western state.

For its part Scotland may suppose that it needs a credible alternative diplomatic strategy. This is because of the central place of the major oil companies and US independents in present North Sea operations and the considerable technical if not financial difficulty of opposing them without the assistance of OPEC. There may be very little possibility of refining and marketing existing oil and developing new fields without impressing upon the companies the possibility that, for the sake of their Scottish assets, they may be putting their place in the international oil industry in question. It is quite undisturbed at the moment and likely to remain so unless a new conflict of interest arises between oil companies and governments.

Oil and money

The major oil companies dominate existing North Sea operations. For oil and gas reserves of about 15,760 million barrels at least 9300 are in the hands of the 'seven sisters' and 3300 belong to US independents. Oil production estimated for 1980 follows the same pattern. Of a total of 2670m b/d (thousand barrels per day), 1800m b/d will come from the 'seven sisters' and 640m b/d from independents.[76]

The finance for the first major phase of fourteen oilfields has been £10 billion. There are at least twelve fields waiting to be exploited and so a continuing £2 bil. p.a. seems to be likely into the 1980's. A new figure of £8 bil. in the next three years alone will make the sums involved from 1972 to 1985 about £23 bil.[77]

There are two principal ways the majors and independents are financing their operations, self- and project-financing.[78] Both mean that the North Sea operations are closely tied to a very wide range of banking interests. The majors, such as Exxon, Shell, Mobil, Chevron, have found as much as two-thirds of the finance through normal corporate borrowing. However, these companies are themselves very closely linked to major banks.

The US Senate Committee on Government Operations showed that the top fifty US bank trust departments controlled 28·87% of Gulf common stock holdings, 12·7% of Mobil, 12·328% of Texaco and 13·248% of Philips. An example of a full 'breakdown' is Mobil where the seven largest New York banks have 17% and other banks 9·7% of the total shares, including virtually all of the largest accounts.[79] Another key element is the role of managing underwriters. These are financial institutions which assemble and represent a group of partners in bidding for a company financing. Of the $9·3 bil. raised between 1945 and 1972 Morgen Stanley alone raised 40%, and more or less equally for Mobil, Shell, Exxon and Texaco ($400–650 mil.). Interlocking directorates between the majors and US banks such as Chemical, First National City, Bank of America, mean that directors have intimate knowledge of one another's operations and inevitably tend to harmonise them. It should not be left unmentioned that the nineteen largest US insurance companies have $5·6 bil. in oil common stocks, usually about 10% of their assets.[80] The combined assets of financial institutions linked to the oil companies in 1972 were, very roughly, $140 bil. for banks and $60 bil. for insurance companies.[81]

Project-financing links the banking community directly to the oil fields themselves. The Forties Field (BP), the Piper Field (*inter alia*, Occidental, Thomson Group) and the Ninian Field, have been financed by a vast number of banks including Lazards, Morgan Guaranty, National Westminster, an international consortium, the International Energy Bank (IEB) and a London Consortium of Lasmo/Scott.[82] UK Government regulations ensure that the licensees may not sell, in any form short of the petroleum resources themselves, the economic rent involved in the licences. The Ministry of Energy can and does approve assignments. A forward-purchase system was used in the BP/Forties case and the Government has agreed that 'in the event of a default or some action on the part of BP that would normally lead to revocation, the banks could in effect take over the licence on exactly the same terms and conditions as other licencees'.[83] In the BP case the lending banks have established a financing company which agreed to buy the oil from BP as it was produced. The banks give the money to the finance company which gives it to BP. The oil is sold to the finance company which requires BP to repurchase it, hence generating the revenue within the financing company which it pays to the banks to service and repay the loans. The Lasmo/Scott London Consortium has introduced oil production stock units entitling holders to 8·75% of Lasmo's income from Ninian. Instead of a fixed interest payment there is an entitlement in the holder to receive half-yearly payments related to the value of the production from the field in the relevant half year. In the Piper Field, in its loan to the Thomson Group the IEB undertook a share of the risk themselves in exchange for a royalty on the estimated reserves of 640 mil. barrels of oil, unless the loss was caused by British Government measures.

The world-wide operations of the oil majors
The support which oil companies might receive from banks should arise quite simply out of an economic partnership. The significance of the vast oil-company network of transport, refining and marketing in Western Europe and North America is much more difficult to assess.

Scotland would have to refine and market its oil, assuming that it had the expertise to continue production. UK policy has been to ensure that at least two-thirds of its North Sea oil will be refined and marketed here, an essential part of its entire oil policy. Of UK refining capacity, the oil majors control, in thousands of tons, 125,860 as against 15,000 for others. Given that British courts did not recognise the legal effect of the Iranian nationalisation of oil without compensation, the oil companies could find justification for refusing to refine nationalised Scottish oil within the UK.[84] Of course a political limit to this policy lies in how the UK itself reacts to such a drastic eventuality. The problem the oil companies face with the UK, as with the most likely alternative markets for Scotland, the EEC and the US, would be how to persuade them to accept oil from sources other than the North Sea.

At present, overwhelming quantities of oil are coming to Western Europe from the Middle East under long-term supply contracts between OPEC and the oil majors. It is then for the most part refined by the same majors. In 1974 Western Europe imported 9480m b/d, 69% of its needs, which compares with a maximum Scottish figure of 2670m b/d in 1980[85] (that is, assuming virtually all UK oil goes to Scotland). The OPEC revolution has left the oil majors in control of supplies. Aramco (an oil major consortium) manages about 92% of Saudi Arabian oil, while in Iran about 80% is managed by the former consortium, (Iranian Petroleum Consortium). Kuwait 'changed its majors' as Gulf and BP now have 50% but the rest goes to Shell and Exxon.[86] BP alone supplies the EEC with one-tenth of its total oil demand, refining 40 million tons in France, Holland and West Germany alone in 1976. It markets most of its own oil. Shell alone processed 1699m b/d in Europe in 1976. Texaco's refining within the EEC is over 532,000 b/d in the same year. Exxon refined within Europe

1737m b/d in 1976 and sold in Europe 1943m b/d. Mobil refines almost one million b/d within the EEC and sells about 703m b/d.[87]

The position of the oil majors in the United States is even more unambiguous. The US percentage of world oil reserves is declining rapidly *vis-à-vis* the Middle East. From 1953 to 1973 those of the latter went from 51·5% to 60·9% while US reserves dropped from 30% to 8·6%. The major discoveries of Alaska seem to be only sufficient to replace existing reserves as they run out. In 1976 imports were 40% of domestic requirements compared to 33% in 1973, while in 1974 29% came from the Middle East. As of 1970 the twenty largest oil companies control 94% of US domestic reserves, 86% of refining capacity and 79% of domestic gasoline sales.[88]

OPEC today

The potentially unstable aspect of the oil industry's vast organisation is, of course, the long-term supply contracts with OPEC. These contracts rest on little more than mutual convenience, the volumes to be 'lifted' by the oil companies are flexible and prices contain three-month re-opener clauses. Their duration is limited to five-yearly intervals. They have been described as 'contracts' of long intention rather than long-term contracts.[89] Indeed, at the height of the crisis in the 'negotiations' for 'participation', OPEC states, such as Iran, Saudi Arabia and Kuwait, threatened to sell their oil to other companies. For instance, the Shah of Iran had *carte blanche* assurances from national oil companies in West Germany and Japan in readiness to put up any amount of capital for export production of oil in return for preferential long-term supplies. In the case of Kuwait a long drawn out confrontation with BP and Gulf was resolved only by their outbidding the Japanese. Saudi Arabia 'shelved' at the last moment a massive offer of crude oil for direct sale following its 'breakthrough' on 'participation' negotiations.[90]

OPEC's capacity to disturb the Western economy is further enhanced by its place in Western and especially the Eurodollar market. Arguably the least of a radical Scotland's difficulties would be to find the finances for future oil developments. Morgan Guaranty estimates that the foreign investments of OPEC should total $205 bil. by the end of 1977, though most of the yearly balance of payments surplus comes from Saudi Arabia, Kuwait, the UAE and Qatar. Arab finance managers have preferred highly liquid investments. In 1977, of $125·5 bil. in identifiable instruments $72·4 bil. were in bank deposits. The Bank of International Settlements estimates that in 1976 OPEC were net suppliers to the Eurodollar market of $33 bil., the main net suppliers by a very long margin. At the same time, the Arabs are dependent upon the Western financial markets. More especially the US financial institutions, so closely connected with the oil companies, such as Morgan Guaranty, Chase Manhattan and the Bank of America provide the necessary professional management to ensure a profitable home for Arab capital. The training of Middle East banking staff could take ten to fifteen years. Nonetheless the Arabs are very anxious to develop their financial institutions. The Saudi International Bank in London is facing up to a major problem in diverting oceans of liquid deposits into investment projects. Arab banks, especially Kuwaiti, are very active on the Eurodollar market, where they are estimated to have about a quarter of the business transacted.[91]

CONCLUSION

Statistics of economic activity provide no indication of political strength. This discussion has highlighted a number of uncertainties. How hard would the oil companies try to persuade Western governments not to accept Scottish oil? Indeed, would they stand a chance at all, given the conduct of European national oil corporations in 1973–1974? Would they consider that enough was at stake to risk the loss of so much of their North Sea holdings? Perhaps they might treat Scotland as a precedent and see defeat as having consequences for their largely successful resistance to Carter's energy policy. For its part, supposing a Scottish Government adopted policies as clear-cut as OPEC's, could it hope to persuade OPEC to anticipate any pressure which the oil companies might put on Western governments? Could it convince OPEC that questions of principle were involved which it could not be seen to neglect? Could it act as a catalyst in provoking Western, or at least European states to try to revise their relationships with the oil majors? Given the terms of the oil debate in Scotland until now, Scottish independence could initiate a serious rethinking of the role of the oil majors in the Western European economy.

But if there is one thing that is clear in the murky world of oil politics, it is that any Scottish Government which wishes to reform the present UK framework will have to be radical. To argue that one can regulate the depletion rate, without at the same time claiming ownership of the oil, is too timid an approach to be an effective weapon at the negotiating table with the oil majors. The essence of the matter is the ownership of the oil, and if a Scottish Government wants to break up the present UK legal regime, it will have to face that fact. Assuming that it does grasp the nettle, it is a nice question whether it will have the political skill to push the oil companies far enough to effect reform, without pushing them so far as to make them put into effect any threats they may make to call a halt to their North Sea activities.

5
Trade

Dermot McAleese

INTRODUCTION

Political independence implies a great deal more than regional devolution. It confers on the independent government the power to implement whatever economic measures are deemed appropriate for the national good, to choose its own system of taxation at whatever rate and in whatever form it chooses, to control the level and allocation of government expenditure, to monitor the national debt and to formulate economic plans. The first, if not the sole, responsibility of an autonomous government is to the people it governs, without the necessity of referral to a higher authority or reference to 'metropolitan' interest groups.

Such, at any rate, are the fruits of independence considered in the abstract. The reality is usually a good deal different. Severe constraints are imposed on the type of economic policy that can be implemented. Some of these constraints are externally imposed, or dictated by the 'dependent' relationship between ex-colony and the metropolis; the most important constraints, however, spring from internal factors, from attitudes of mind and habits of thought deeply ingrained in the people whose independence has been achieved.

The aim of this chapter is to examine the economic consequences of political independence in the context of small open economies. Economists sometimes define a *small* economy as one which has to take the ruling international prices of traded goods as given, *i.e.* the price of its exports is determined irrespective of how much it supplies and the price of its imports is independent of the volume of domestic demand. The definition can be extended to include the stipulation that capital outflows and inflows into a small economy will not affect the prevailing world level of interest rates, etc. Clearly, Saudi Arabia would not qualify as a small country by this definition, despite the comparatively small size of its population, since the volume of Saudi oil production plays a key role in determining the world oil prices. But countries like Scotland, the Republic of Ireland, Denmark and Norway would satisfy the criterion of smallness. An *open* economy is characterised by a large volume of external trade in relation to domestic trade. The degree of openness is conventionally measured by easily accessible ratios such as the ratio of exports and/or imports to GDP. Most small countries are also relatively open economies, although this association is not logically necessary. The Scottish economy conforms to the normal pattern in this regard. Data in the 1973 input-output table suggests extremely high trade ratios of 60% for exports and 64% for imports (inclusive of trade with the rest of the UK).[1] By international standards, therefore, Scotland satisfies fully the criteria of smallness and openness.

The small, open (trade-dependent) nature of the Scottish economy has a number of implications for economic policy in an independent Scotland. First, the heavy leakage out of the economy through imports restricts the effectiveness of fiscal policy. A second consequence of high trade dependence is the limitation it sets on a small economy's ability to control domestic prices and insulate them from world trends. With fixed exchange rates, increases in world prices tend to frustrate domestic price stabilisation policies by raising the price of imports and also by exerting strong upward pressures on export prices. In this way, world inflation is 'imported' into the economy from abroad. Thirdly, changes in the terms of trade (*i.e.* the ratio of export to import prices) exercise a very important influence on real income in a small open economy compared with larger economies. Fourth, cyclical swings in the economies of its major trading partners will be transmitted very rapidly to the Scottish economy. The ability of the Scottish authorities to insulate the economy against these trends is limited. Normally, the main constraint is seen as originating in the balance of payments. Thus, a fall in exports following a downturn in the world economy cannot be counteracted by an expansionary fiscal policy without incurring a balance of payments deficit. In Scotland's case, North Sea oil will presumably remove this balance of payments constraint, but formidable administrative and institutional constraints on the effectiveness of stabilisation policies will remain.

There are other aspects of small size which deserve mention. Kuznets[2] identifies two potential advantages: (a) small countries can fit more easily into the interstices of the international trade network than larger countries and (b) small size is conducive to greater community feeling, resulting from more even income distribution and closer ties among its people, than large countries. The first point carries much weight — a small country, for example, can expand its manufactured exports to larger countries more or less at will, with much less risk of inciting a protectionist reaction in its export markets, or turning the price of its exports against itself, than a larger country would incur. Similarly, small size enables a small country to get away with minor departures from orthodoxy in the field of trade and industrial policy which would arouse hostile comment, if not even retaliation, in the world community were a larger nation to adopt the same practices. Although minor from a world perspective, these slight deviations from the rules can bring major and quite disproportionate benefits to the small country concerned.

It is (as Kuznets[3] himself accepted) rather more difficult to pass judgement on whether small size necessarily brings with it greater social cohesion and, even if it did, whether this would necessarily improve the country's prospects for economic growth. The evidence on income distribution patterns in small and large countries is inconclusive. Small countries such as Ireland, Canada and the Netherlands, appear to have less equal post-tax income distribution than Japan and the UK. Moreover, from an equality of opportunity point of view, ease of transference from one income group to another in the course of an individual's lifetime — in technical jargon, his relative earnings mobility — may be vastly more important than the distribution of income between groups of people at any fixed moment in time.[4] Evidence on another possible indicator of social cohesiveness — a country's industrial disputes record — yields no less inconclusive results. Within the British Isles, for example, Ireland and Scotland have both exhibited a greater strike propensity than the UK average during the last decade.[5]

Policy instruments available to an independent government are conventionally classified into macro-economic and micro-economic.[6] This distinction will not be used here. Rather we propose an alternative distinction between stabilisation policies and development policies. The former include demand-management, monetary and exchange rate policies, whose primary function is to moderate cyclical swings. Most of the recent theoretical literature on small open economies is concerned with stabilisation policies and the related issues mentioned in the preceding paragraph. Development policies, on the other hand, refer to industrial policy agricultural policy and all other policies designed to reallocate resources in a manner favourable to faster economic growth. Some policies contain both a stabilisation and a developmental component. Commercial policy, for example, can be used for stabilisation purposes (as a short-term corrective to a balance of payments deficit) or it may be part of a strategy for overall economic development. All these policies, however classified, confer extra 'degrees of freedom' on the independent nation. The extent to which this extra degree of manoeuvrability can be translated into improvements in Scotland's standard of living will be the subject of discussion in the following sections.

PART I

STABILISATION POLICIES

Fiscal policy
In a unitary state, a conflict of interest often arises between the prosperous central region operating at full employment and the peripheral region suffering from an apparent insufficiency of aggregate demand. Rarely, if ever, are possibilities of conflict envisaged in the converse sense. In these circumstances, restrictions on demand may be imposed through fiscal or monetary policy which are appropriate for the nation as a whole but contrary to the interests of the peripheral region. The region may or may not be compensated by a circular flow of special regional inducements designed to stimulate local demand. Political independence, in theory, offers the

peripheral region freedom to manage aggregate demand in whatever manner it chooses. Decisions taken at the centre will still affect it sharply through their influence on export demand and the influx of foreign investment. But the nation alone decides on the level of *public* expenditure.

Experience of demand management policy elsewhere justifies many of the reservations economists express about the difficulty of implementing effective stabilisation measures in a small open economy. For example, studies of Irish government show that budgetary policy has tended to operate in a pro-cyclical rather than in an anti-cyclical manner.[7] This has occurred because of preoccupation with the current revenue and expenditure account (the current budget 'deficit' or 'surplus') to the exclusion of concern over the balance of total payments and revenue (the net borrowing requirement). As a result, the borrowing requirement has tended to fall in years of slow growth and to increase in years of rapid growth.

The unsatisfactory performance of demand management policy must be viewed in the context of the contraints on economic policy-makers in a small open economy. First, exposure to foreign trade fluctuations makes forecasting a very difficult exercise, a difficulty which is often compounded by the lack of an up-to-date quarterly GNP series. Secondly, in a small open economy, large expenditure changes are required to effect small real output changes because of high import propensities. Third, substantial short-run changes in real government expenditure are difficult to implement for political and administrative reasons. At issue here is not alone the existence of textbook 'policy lags' — recognition lags, decision lags and effect lags — but also the delicate balancing of the interests of various power groups within society which will require modification of government action.

The use of monetary policy as a means of bolstering (or even substituting for) fiscal policy is subject to much the same set of constraints as the latter. The formulation of an independent monetary policy would, in any event, require either a readiness on the part of the authorities to alter the sterling parity (as Canada broke from the US dollar) or else an administratively cumbersome set of exchange rate controls. These are just prior conditions for establishing the *possibility* of an effective monetary policy. The Scottish Government would then have the difficult task of converting potential into actual achievement.

Irish experience with monetary policy may, once again, prove instructive. Given fixity of exchange rates and free capital movements between the UK and the Republic, standard economic models would predict that the rate of interest in Britain effectively determines the rate of interest in Ireland. Reality conforms reasonably closely to theory in this respect although some 'spread' either way between Irish government bonds and British government bonds exists (up to two percentage points). Supply of money in these circumstances, therefore, responds passively to changes in demand at the predetermined interest rate. The Central Bank of Ireland's monetary policy, as such, influences the composition of money supply, as between its foreign and domestic components (in which case one is talking of official reserves policy and/or policy towards foreign borrowing by the public sector) and, more tentatively, between credit for consumption purposes *vs.* credit for investment purposes. Central Bank directives designed to influence the direction of commercial banks' credit could be significant in a micro-sense, for to circumvent them involves inconvenience and time, but we suspect that this factor is, in practice, of second-order importance. Continued adherence to a fixed exchange rate with sterling and free movement of capital funds implies, therefore, that the broad outline of monetary developments in the Republic is predetermined by British monetary and credit policies, in the formulation of which it (the Republic) has no say whatsoever.

In the course of a thought-provoking review of stabilisation policies in small open economies, Lindbeck[8] makes a number of points which deserve special attention. He stresses that a successful stabilisation policy in open economies cannot rely only on aggregate demand management — and the more open the economy, the less effective aggregate demand policy will be. What other measures are required? Lindbeck[9] suggests that more consideration be given to the possibility of introducing (a) temporary changes in indirect taxes on consumption and investment expenditure to stimulate or dampen aggregate demand (these measures have been adopted with some success in Norway, Sweden and Denmark), (b) encouragement of greater occupational and geographical mobility to avoid bottlenecks and dampen the inflationary effect often associated with economic recovery (some progress in this respect appears to be badly needed in Scotland for other reasons too), (c) selective demand management, *i.e.* careful choice of ways by which aggregate demand can be increased, with particular attention being devoted to each method's sectoral effects, and (d) supply management, improved training facilities and extra provision of capital in low demand areas. For a small country like Scotland, therefore, selectivity would have to be a major priority in the formulation of stabilisation policies.

An important constraint on stabilisation policy, not often mentioned in economic discussion of the subject, arises from possible conflicts of interest between political expediency and economic necessity. Because governments may be more interested in stabilising votes in the short-run than the economy in a somewhat longer perspective, the implementation of differentiated and sophisticated policy tools would create severe risks of macro-economic disturbances being accentuated by the dictates of political expediency. Pre-election budgets always tend to be 'generous' budgets, regardless of the state of the economy. Of course, the importance of this factor in Scotland would very much depend on the political framework which would emerge in an autonomous state. The expected high level of Scottish oil revenue would certainly make it difficult to justify restrictive policies, designed to moderate excessive wage increases, in terms of balance of payments constraints or IMF insistence, along the lines so skilfully exploited by Mr Healey in Britain in 1975–76. Independent Scotland would, for this reason, be more than usually vulnerable to internal inflationary pressures.

Exchange rate policy
Exchange rate policy can be used as an anti-inflationary instrument (*i.e.* as a method of insulating a small country from externally induced price inflation) or as a method of balance of payments adjustment. Both functions are important. Government action relative to the exchange rate should primarily be regarded as part of stabilisation policy, but the determination of the exchange rate is also a matter of considerable importance for long run development.

Use of changes in the exchange rate to prevent the transmission of inflation from England to Scotland would involve no change in the effective parity (*i.e.* after allowing for relative price changes in the two countries). Thus, imagine a situation where the Scottish pound equals one pound sterling. Then England inflates at an annual rate of 20%. If parity is maintained this means that the price of English imports into Scotland increases by 20% and likewise the price of Scottish exports to England will be bid up by 20%. If the pound sterling devalues, the inflationary impulse in Scotland will be greater still. The only way for Scotland to escape this transmission effect is to revalue the Scottish pound *pari passu* with British inflation (*e.g.* at end of year one, a Scottish pound will equal £1·20 sterling, etc.). If England inflates by 20% per annum and the Scottish pound is revalued by 20% per annum the sterling price of Scottish exports to England remains unchanged. Nothing 'real' happens; exchange rate changes simply insulate Scotland from the inflationary impulses emanating from elsewhere in the UK. Breaking the link does not, in this scenario, involve a change in the (inflation-corrected) parity with sterling.

If the effective parity remained constant, this implies that the effects on employment and real incomes would be zero, except to the extent that reduced inflation rates would *per se* encourage a larger volume of foreign and domestic investment, strengthen consumer confidence and/or change the real wage through incomplete adjustment of wage demands to the new set of domestic prices.

The abatement of inflation in the UK has removed this anti-inflation aspect of exchange rate policy from the centre of debate for the present. It remains to be seen whether this will be long-lasting. The point may be made, however, that Scotland's large prospective external reserves will place her in a strong position to insulate the economy from external price rises, should world inflation recur, through successive revaluations of the Scottish pound.[10]

Changes in a currency's effective parity are required if the economy concerned shows evidence of a systematic tendency to accumulate or de-cumulate reserves. Most Scottish economists, sensitive to the employ-ment-inhibiting effects of an effective revaluation, suggest that, through judicious investment of oil revenue abroad and/or through a diminished rate of oil extraction, accumulation of reserves should be avoided. Given the high level of unemployment in Scotland, there is much to be said for such an approach. It is interesting, in fact, to see how the focus of discus-sion has changed in recent years from the desirability of devaluation to avoidance of revaluation of an independent Scottish pound.

This last point requires elaboration, for it lies at the heart of much confusion over the usefulness of the exchange rate as an instrument of regional development. Many regional economists emphasise the role of the exchange rate as an adjustment mechanism between aggregate demand and aggregate supply. Imagine, for example, that a region runs into trouble because of a declining major industry. If money wages are inflexible down-wards, this leads to unemployment — the region has no way of improving competitiveness and expanding aggregate demand. While the decline in aggregate demand will be partly compensated by the inflow of social secur-ity funds and through the workings of other automatic stabiliser effects, these will not be sufficient to restore equilibrium. The major equilibrating instrument in such circumstances, so the argument goes, would be a change in the exchange rate.[11]

The key assumption underlying this argument is that real wages are flexible. The devaluation of the region's currency solves the unemploy-ment problem through a reduction in the real wage or, in the more realistic context of a growing economy, some moderation in its rate of growth. Scotland has been faced with a problem of endemic unemployment for many years, a level of unemployment, furthermore, which has been shown to be moderately responsive to chages in aggregate demand. In this respect, conditions should be 'right' for an exchange rate change. The main factors inhibiting such a move, in the absence of oil, would have been (a) a lack of confidence on the part of the government in its ability to persuade unions to accept the principle of real wage flexibility, (b) fear that one devaluation might give way to another, thus undermining confidence in the currency, and (c) realisation that, because of low import demand elasticities and the high import content of Scottish output, it would require a large devaluation to achieve a small increase in employment. With oil, factor (b) becomes irrelevant and has to be replaced by another consideration namely, that a country with a large balance of payments surplus on current account may find it practically impossible to maintain a deliberately overvalued ex-change rate for any sustained period of time.

The sterling link has been the subject of sporadic but heated debate in Ireland ever since independence in 1922. Immediately after independence, fears were expressed about the deflationary effects on the Irish economy of sterling's prospective return to the gold standard, the implication being that this might leave the Irish pound overvalued. Later, in 1931, when Britain left the gold standard, a collapse of sterling was feared. The Minister for Finance at that time, Mr Ernest Blythe, made it quite clear that should such a collapse occur, Ireland would have to break the sterling parity. Again, in 1949, there was some debate over the wisdom of letting the Irish pound devalue in line with the British pound. Reaction to the 1967 devaluation was more muted, but in recent years intense misgivings have been expressed over the fact that maintenance of parity with sterling has 'tied' the Irish economy to the British rate of inflation. In each case, however, the balance of advantage has always been judged to rest with adherence to the *status quo*.[12] The Republic came very close to revaluing, however, in 1976 and, had oil been discovered in Ireland equal to even a fraction of North Sea supplies, there is no doubt whatever that the break would have been made. Of course, in a way, this should occasion no surprise. The scale of UK inflation in the seventies caused a drastic fall in the number of currencies pegged to sterling. At mid-1977, only five countries — Ireland, Gambia, Bangladesh, Seychelles and Sierra Leone — remained pegged to sterling.

The experience of other small countries which have 'broken' the sterling link warns against the facile conclusion that this automatically guarantees a lower inflation rate. Over the years, for example, the Israeli pound declined from par with sterling to 18·40 Israeli pounds. A further substantial fall to 27 Israeli pounds has been reported since October 1977 when Israel decided to remove all foreign currency restrictions and float the pound. Associated with these successive devaluations was an extremely high internal rate of inflation. Iceland's experience with an independent exchange rate also underlines the point that exchange rate policy cannot substitute for active domestic anti-inflationary policies (Iceland has suffered from much greater inflation rates than the UK during the last decade). Indeed, exchange rate policy can only operate as an effective insulator against world inflation if economic forces inherent in the economy (more inflation-averse institutions as in Germany and Switzerland, for example, or the discovery of oil deposits in Norway) create confidence in the economy's capacity to make the revaluation of its exchange rate 'stick'. It is salutary to remember that, even with oil *and* an independent exchange rate policy, Norway was unable to escape completely the ravages of inflation over the last decade. The scale of an independent Scotland's oil reserves would, however, make the prognosis for a successful and sufficient revaluation much greater in its case than in Norway's.

We conclude that initially an independent Scotland would maintain parity with sterling, but that the option of breaking the link would be kept open as a means of insulating the Scottish economy against external sources of inflation. A break with sterling, however, would be unlikely to be associated with a freely floating Scottish pound. Like most small countries, Scotland would most likely seek some other standard to tie its currency to, whether it be the SDR, the 'Snake', the dollar or some trade-weighted basket of currencies.

PART II

DEVELOPMENT POLICIES

Trade relations
The thrust of our argument so far has been twofold: first that Scotland shares many of the same constraints on economic policy-making as other small open economies but that, second, access to North Sea oil has significantly eased some of these constraints, in particular, Scotland's capacity to spend her way out of a recession and to insulate the economy from externally sourced inflationary pressures. At the same time, we suggested that an independent Scotland might have rather more difficulty in curbing domestically induced inflation through restrictive demand management policies than a less well-endowed country. However, of much greater potential importance than stabilisation measures is the role to be played by oil revenues in financing a development strategy for the Scottish economy. In this section, we consider a selected number of issues bearing on the theme of development policy.

A distinctive feature of the debate on Scottish autonomy, in comparison with analogous discussions in say, pre-independence Ireland or, more recently, in the less developed countries prior to achieving independent status, is the lack of attention paid to commercial policy as an instrument of economic development. Elsewhere, protection has been viewed as a prerequisite for industrial growth and the denial of the power to build up local manufacturing industry through import-stabilisation has been regarded as imposing a major economic cost on underdeveloped regions of a unitary state. Practical experience with import-substitution policies, however, has led to some disillusionment with the efficacy of protection as a method of promoting development. While the case for supporting infant industries by protective measures is doubtless a strong one, small countries soon discover that only through exports and specialisation can the dynamic for a prosperous and growing industrial sector be achieved. This explains why small countries — such as the Scandinavian economies — tend to be the most enthusiastic supporters of trade liberalisation. In any event, Scotland's problem is not that of building up an industrial sector from scratch (as was the case with most import-substitution practitioners) but rather it concerns the reform and improvement of an existing industrial structure.

For Scotland, therefore, independence would most likely involve continued adherence to free trade. Such a policy stance is necessitated by the small size of the economy and the existing high export ratios of Scottish industry. Commercial policy, moreover, would have to be directed to obtaining not alone free access but also security of access to external markets. This particular objective could perhaps best be achieved in the context of membership of the EEC, where Community regulations protect the smaller and economically weaker member states from arbitrarily imposed barriers to the markets of larger member countries, and Community trade treaties at the same time help to ensure that non-member countries will treat the interests of even the smallest EEC member with more respect than would be the case if it remained unaligned. The high degree of openness of the Scottish economy implies vulnerability; vulnerability in the sense of exposure to the risk of larger countries taking action against Scottish exports which would inflict far greater damage on the Scottish economy than on the economy imposing protective barriers, and also in the sense of restricting the power of the Scottish authorities to impose selective trade restrictions of its own without provoking retaliation abroad. Scotland's exposed position would best be diminished through membership of the EEC — or failing that, but less effectively, through a more loosely tied grouping like EFTA. However, as Stephen Maxwell shows in *Politics*, there are other factors at work (the EEC energy and fishery policies, for instance) which would tend to diminish the attractiveness of EEC membership relative to alternative trading arrangements.

Thus trade dependence limits manoeuvrability in a general sense. Trade dependence on the English economy *per se* further restricts the scope for independent action.[13] It does this in two separate ways. First, the close economic ties between Scotland and England, which are even more extensive than the figures on trade flows would suggest, will closely bind the Scottish G.N.P. growth rate to that of England. Thus, slow growth in the English economy means, *ceteris paribus*, an unfavourable climate for Scottish export expansion and, no less important, for new investment into the Scottish economy from the rest of the UK. This particular form of dependence may, of course, be reduced through diversification into overseas markets, but this takes time to accomplish. The experience with export promotion policies in Ireland is that they stimulate Irish entrepreneurs to develop the traditional (UK) market and overseas investors to exploit the continental European and US markets. Efforts to persuade Irish manufacturers to diversify further afield — through language courses, export promotion subsidies, trade fairs, etc. — have met with little success.[14] If Irish experience is anything to go by, therefore, Scotland will reduce its dependence on the English market only through increasing its dependence on overseas manufacturing enterprises to carry out this task.

Close economic relations with the rest of the UK will also set limits to the degree to which Scottish economic policy can diverge from that of her neighbour. The English labour market, for example, will continue to attract Scottish workers, if it grows — and, if it fails to grow, pressure will be increased on the Scottish Government to create more jobs at home. In either case, events in the English market will continue to exert a powerful impact on Scotland's economy. Similarly the level of the real wage in Scotland will be determined largely by that obtaining in England. Political independence will not succeed in driving a substantial wedge between the two wage levels unless it be in Scotland's favour — and there is evidence that the Scottish real wage is at present too high relative to the economy's needs. A similar asymmetry probably applies to taxation policy. Scottish income taxes could be lower than English taxes, but it would be difficult for an independent government to impose higher taxes without incurring substantial real costs, through adverse effects on tourism, migration of skilled workers, discouragement of enterprise, etc. While most economists contributing to the debate on Scottish autonomy appreciate this point and, in fact, advocate substantial cuts in income taxation, one has reservations about the political feasibility of some of their suggestions.

Ideas regarding standards of government services are also heavily influenced by those prevailing in England. It will be difficult to dissuade people from equating the 'normal' or 'appropriate' level of public services — be they universities, social welfare or housing — with the English level. Unfavourable comparisons will attract even more attention in an independent Scotland than is the case at present — and few governments will be able to resist electoral pressure for parity with unpalatable arguments about the economic inappropriateness of parity to Scotland. This is a vitally important point, in my view, for a major problem faced by all peripheral regions of the British Isles (including the independent Republic) is their swift 'inheritance' of norms in the fields of social legislation, public expenditure and real wage levels which, however desirable in themselves and however appropriate to the more prosperous English economy, fail utterly to accord with the needs of their own economies at their particular stage of development. In this subtle, almost well-meaning way, the less developed regions' comparative backwardness is reinforced as a direct result of the better-off region's increased prosperity.[15]

The accumulation of oil revenues will, of course, greatly improve Scotland's chances of escaping from this dilemma. First, these revenues will more than compensate for the loss of the 'regional transfer' from Westminster to Scotland. (For less resource-rich regions, such as Northern Ireland, the possible loss of Westminster's subvention proves a decisive economic argument against autonomy — and, indeed, against union with the Republic, even if a majority were ever found to favour such a course on political grounds.) Second, oil revenues create the possibility of increases in the Scottish real wage being conceded, without creating a concomitant worsening of competitiveness, through across-the-board reductions in the level of taxation. Although Scottish economists have warned both of the dangers of frittering away the oil revenues in this manner (*i.e.* through raising the real wage and encouraging consumption) and also of its potentially inflationary consequences, there is much to be said for allocating a certain proportion of oil revenues for tax reductions. In this way, real disposable (*i.e.* after tax) income can be increased without raising wage costs to industry, since pre-tax wages is what matters to the employer. Such a policy would also result in a mild boost to aggregate demand which would generate additional jobs in the services sector and in that part of Scottish industry catering for the home market.

External investment

As is now well known, only 41% of manufacturing employees in Scotland are employed in Scottish-controlled firms, *i.e.* firms with headquarters located in Scotland. Many are inclined to regard this as a reason for the relatively unimpressive performance of Scotland's manufacturing sector since the War. Among the alleged disadvantages of possessing a large external sector are the following: (a) external subsidiaries rarely develop independent powers of investment, (b) the low level of R & D undertaken in these subsidiaries militates against growth, (c) the low ratio of senior managers to total employees emphasises the inferior status of the subsidiary and reduces managerial 'spin-off' effects on the rest of the economy, (d) control of marketing policies of the Scottish subsidiary by the parent company discourages export growth, (e) overseas firms have low linkages with the rest of the Scottish economy, *i.e.* they purchase most of their inputs abroad, and (f) these firms are more exposed to cyclical fluctuations emanating from abroad.[16] It has also been argued that extensive control of the Scottish economy by external interests means that the majority of important economic decisions affecting manufacturing in Scotland are made neither within Scotland nor with Scottish interests predominantly in mind. Although this last argument possesses considerable emotional appeal, it begs a number of important questions. For example, it relies on the dubious assumption that the indigenous firms afford more priority to Scottish (and not selfish) interests than external industry.

The above criticisms of certain characteristics of external firms and their role in the Scottish economy should be treated with the utmost caution. For one thing, a considerable volume of two-way traffic in direct foreign investment flows has been observed between the advanced Western economies over the last two decades. Thus, even a country as economically powerful as West Germany has 25% of its manufacturing sector controlled by foreign interests, without noticeably curbing either its capacity for growth or its standard of living (OECD, 1977). Moreover, despite all the heated debate on this question, the 50% share of foreigners in its manufacturing industry has not prevented the Canadian economy from registering a 30% increase in manufacturing employment between 1963 and 1974 (from 1504 to 1986 thousand). Besides, now that there is a net outflow of direct investment from Canada, attitudes towards capital inflows have mollified considerably.

A second point to stress is the actual employment record of external industry in the Scottish economy. The *a priori* reasoning of its critics would suggest that externally owned firms contributed little towards expanding job opportunities in Scotland. Yet the facts indicate the contrary. During the period 1955–71, Forsyth[17] shows that employment in US-owned firms rose from 20,200 to 91,810. The same study emphasises the fact that a considerable proportion of this employment growth originated in expansions of existing US plants beyond their initial size rather than from recurrent injections of new projects from abroad.[18] The growth in employment in US subsidiaries, moreover, took place in the context of a net decline of 6000 jobs annually in Scotland's manufacturing sector. Of course, US firms constitute only part of the externally owned sector, but there is no strong reason to believe that other subsidiaries fared any worse than the American. Research into the employment-creating record of overseas subsidiaries in Ireland shows that they accounted for virtually the entire increase in manufacturing employment during the period 1960–73. Furthermore, comparison on the basis of surveys carried out in 1966 and 1975 show that the size of the work-force in the pre-1966 cohort rose by 50% between 1966 and 1974. Evidence of the capacity of overseas subsidiaries to grow from within is not lacking.

Third, one must guard against the danger of comparing externally owned enterprises with some highly idealised form of indigenous enterprise rather than with indigenous enterprise as it actually is or could feasibly become. Most indigenous entrepreneurs in a small open economy have to survive in a highly competitive world. They are unlikely to develop linkages with the Scottish economy, undertake R & D and remain insulated from cyclical trends elsewhere merely because they are indigenous and it would be good for the Scottish economy!

These points are stressed because one detects a note of disapprobation in contemporary Scottish attitudes towards external investment. Given the shortage of indigenous entrepreneurs, Scotland is likely to depend on external investors to fill this gap for some years to come. Indeed, the only really serious problem that foreign investment is likely to create for the Scottish economy is that there will not be enough of it. For this reason, insistence by an independent Scottish Government on the provision of more information by external firms than is already required for Scottish firms (taking into account future disclosure obligations under EEC Company law), on the implementation of elaborate screening devices on new investors or on the obligatory participation of Scottish investors with foreigners in joint ventures, would have seriously adverse consequences for the growth of the manufacturing sector.

Political autonomy would give Scotland an opportunity of developing its own industrial policies towards external and indigenous investors. In view of the country's high rate of unemployment a strongly positive attitude towards both sources of entrepreneurship would be desirable. In the case of new foreign investors, this will mean adherence to the broad outline of current regional policy. Given the intense competition within the Brit-

ish Isles for a limited supply of industrial projects, it would be impossible
for Scotland to hope for substantial inflows of projects in response to an
industrial incentive package which offered less than that available in other
regions. However, an open-door policy with respect to export-oriented
manufacturing investment would not preclude measures designed to limit
the degree of external control exercised over the 'commanding heights' of
the Scottish economy, including Scottish land and the services sector. For
a long time, countries like Sweden and Norway have restricted foreign
investment in natural resources, arms manufacture and banking, without
detriment to a substantial inflow of foreign investment into activities outside these restricted areas. A pragmatic and balanced approach to existing external investment by an autonomous Scottish Government would
minimise the danger of frightening off the type of foreign enterprises
which Scotland needs to attract. It would be inappropriate for a country
seeking outlets for its oil revenues in investments abroad to opt for a policy
of severe curtailment of non-nationals' ability to invest in Scotland.

As far as existing industry is concerned, no distinction should, in my
view, be drawn between external and indigenous from the point of view of
policy. Encouraging the expansion of such domestic industry will involve,
in Schumpeter's words, 'difficult manoeuvring at an indefinite number of
points'. As a first step, material incentives for enterprises should be increased, through introduction of a less progressive tax structure. After that,
a system of supplementary aids and incentives could be devised which are
specially tailored to the needs of Scottish industry: financial aids to new
projects, management development programmes, R & D grants, etc. Special attention would also have to be devoted to public enterprise with the
aim of placing it on a sound economic basis and also encouraging public
enterprises to diversify into profit-making activities on their own initiative.
A number of specific measures have been suggested in previous studies of
the Scottish economy and there is no need to repeat them here.

In common with all peripheral regions of the UK, Scotland suffers from
an inadequate supply of native entrepreneurs to manufacturing industry. It
is shortage of ideas and enterprise that holds these regions back rather than
shortage of capital; and inadequate enterprise of a specific type. Thus the
Scots have not lacked enterprise in the areas of banking and insurance; nor
have they lagged behind in volunteering for duty overseas in the colonial
administration and in the British armed services. The Irish have suffered
no lack of artists and actors — two highly risky professions; no lack of
initiative in Catholic missionary activity; and no lack of supply of entrepreneurs in the building and construction industry. The problem is to
channel more entrepreneurial resources in these regions into manufacturing activity where society's need for them is most acute.

After a decade or more of reliance on external sources of entrepreneurship, experience suggests that more emphasis will have to be placed on
securing greater supplies of indigenous entrepreneurs. As already noted,

this conclusion follows not because of deficiencies in external investment *per se* but rather because of its inadequate supply, even in response to the most extravagant financial inducements. A topical example is the competition between Ireland, Germany and Britain for the Ford motor engine plant, now scheduled for location at Bridgend, at a cost to the British Government in excess of £30,000 per job.[19]

It is difficult to know exactly how much action is required to elicit an adequate supply of native entrepreneurs. There has been general recognition of the need to get market signals correct (even at a cost of a less equal distribution of income), which, in effect means lower marginal tax on high income earners and more government subsidies to manufacturing. No doubt, these measures point in the right direction. However, material incentives of this type will require a number of years for their effects to be realised, and an autonomous Scottish Government might also have to think in terms of fundamental changes in other areas of activity, *e.g.* the educational system, if sufficient progress is to be made.[20] We know uncomfortably little about the determinants of entrepreneurship, apart from acknowledging its paramount importance in the process of economic development. Furthermore, shortage of entrepreneurship is not a feature of small open economies in general, as the Scandinavian economies demonstrate, while being a recognisable feature of backward regions of (formally or informally) integrated areas.

Economic planning

A recurrent theme in the debate over Scottish autonomy relates to the benefits which would flow from the formulation of a coherent policy for economic growth, articulated within the context of a Scottish development plan, and to which an independent Scottish Government would be committed. Some would argue that the formulation of a national economic plan is an essential prerequisite if the Scottish economy is to be revitalised.[21]

It is certainly true that Scotland, no less than the UK as a whole, has suffered from the lack of consistency in British economic policy during the last two decades. Perhaps most damaging from Scotland's point of view has been the way in which successive British governments have changed track on the matter of regional incentives, investment grants and industrial policy generally.[22] This inconsistency, however, derives less from the absence of a British economic plan than from the different idiological biases of the Conservative and Labour parties. A precondition for an independent democratic Scotland evolving a consistent set of policies is either that a fair measure of accord exists between government and opposition or, alternatively, that one party stays in government for an extended period of time.[23]

Although a small open economy is more exposed than other countries to the vicissitudes of external events over which it has no control, there is

much to be said in favour of some sort of planning even in these circumstances. The psychological value of setting targets for national en-
deavour can easily be appreciated, provided they are reasonable and mutually consistent. Such targets in turn can provide a focus for constructive
and consistent policy-making.

Ireland's experience with economic planning has been mixed. By far
the most successful was the First Programme for Economic Expansion
which covered the period 1959–63. Ironically, and perhaps significantly, it
was the least ambitious of Ireland's plans. Only a few key targets were
specified — annual G.N.P. growth, employment, industrial and agricultural output — and no sophisticated tools of analysis were used to check for
consistency such as would be regarded as normal practice nowadays. Compared with a targeted 2% G.N.P. growth, a rate of 4% was actually achieved
due mainly to a rapid expansion in industrial exports and output and to the
co-ordination of policies which facilitated this expansion. Evaluating the
First Programme in retrospect, three main points must be emphasised: (1)
the setting of targets for growth in the context of a dispirited and declining
economy, gave a tremendous psychological boost to the country, (2) the
fact that these modest targets were exceeded reinforced (1), and (3) the
success of the first plan encouraged the belief that a more sophisticated
plan, embracing more ambitious targets, would result in even greater success than that achieved in the period to 1963.

Experience with the Second Programme (1963–70) showed this last
belief to have been erroneous. This plan had to be abandoned in 1968 when
it became obvious to the Government that the targets would not be
achieved. The Second Programme, it is now generally accepted, placed too
much weight on establishing consistent targets and not enough on the
policies needed to ensure their achievement. Examination of actual performance against targeted performance during this period led to another dis-
turbing conclusion. It was that the public sector was the one to deviate
most conspicuously from its planned course of development. Critics were
not slow to point out that the Government's failure to control its own
expenditure would hardly inspire confidence in its capacity to direct the
allocation of private sector activity.

A certain disillusionment with plans set in after 1968. A Third
Economic Programme (1969–72) was prepared and published but received
minimal commitment from the Government and generated little popular
interest. The Coalition Government (1973–77) refused to become involved
in planning, justifying this stance in terms of the uncertainty of the world
economic climate. A new Fianna Fail Government came to power in 1977.
Included in its manifesto was the promise to reintroduce planning and
work on the preparation of such a plan is now well under way.

What are the lessons to be drawn from Irish experience for Scotland?
One could argue that, first, it underlines the importance of government
commitment to a plan without which success cannot be achieved. This

means that government must accept the necessity of self-imposed constraints on the deployment of public funds. Second, it illustrates the fact
that, whatever the weight of *a priori* economic arguments in favour of
planning, politicians see many disadvantages in committing themselves to
fixed targets. If the targets are low, they will be criticised for being insuffi-
ciently ambitious; if the targets are high and are not attained, the plan will
be branded as a failure. Some form of 'rolling' plan would diminish these
criticisms — and it should be tried — without eliminating the problem
altogether.

An autonomous Scotland would not, of course, necessarily adopt the
same planning procedures as the Irish Government — and, even if it did, it
might well operate them more efficiently. Irish plans have tended to focus
more on the medium-term than on the short-term. In this respect they
compare more easily with the French and Spanish development plans
rather than with those of the Nordic countries and the Netherlands. The
French plan, however, is a complex instrument of economic policy,
worked out in considerable detail. It is indicative, in the sense of being
binding on the public sector but persuasive as regards the private sector.
Successive Spanish plans during the period 1964–75 have copied the
French model in nomenclature and organisation. Although both the
French and Spanish plans have coincided with periods of rapid economic
growth, no consensus exists as to how decisive they have been as a causal
factor in this growth. Wright[24] shows that the Spanish economy has
evolved along its distinctive path almost independently of the plans — not
atypically, the public secor deviated as much from the planned targets as
the private sector despite the formally binding character of these targets on
public expenditure. In France, too, the plan has run into problems and had
to be shelved on a number of occasions (1958, 1963 and 1973). Nevertheless, one can say that the plans have had a favourable (if unquantifiable),
impact on the economic climate, have helped to make investment decisions
consistent and have served the politically valuable purpose of providing a
basis for agreement between rival interest groups.

Planning in the Nordic countries, by contrast, focuses more on the
short-run than on the medium-term. Thus, in Sweden, five-year reports are
published regularly on the long-term tendencies of the economy but the
government does not as a rule adopt them as official policy. The reports are
regarded as a method of transmitting information about activities in various sectors of the economy. Government concern, in Sweden and Norway,
is concentrated on short-run stabilisation measures. Much the same is true
of the Netherlands, where the annual economic plan of the Central Planning Bureau serves as a co-ordination device for short-run counter-cyclical
policy.

Thus, to summarise, planning means different things to different countries. Like all mixed economies, a Scottish plan would have to be indicative
in approach. The value of the planning exercise consists in the assistance it

gives to ensuring consistent policy-making. To expect it to substantially reduce uncertainty — as was the intention of the French planners — is to expect the impossible in a small trade-dependent economy.

CONCLUSIONS

Notwithstanding any change in its political status, Scotland will continue to be closely integrated into the economic and social life of the United Kingdom. The ties between the two communities will remain very strong, a fact which limits the degree of divergence between Scottish economic policy and UK economic policy.

Experience in the field of stabilisation policies suggests that autonomous control over these instruments is not of much practical importance. In large part, this is a natural consequence of small size, openness and close integration with the UK economy. Oil revenues, however, should considerably enhance the degree of discretion available to an independent Scotland.

Development policies can be used with much greater effect. An autonomous Scotland could evolve a consistent and flexible industrial policy which would greatly improve on past performance. This presupposes, however, that Scotland's governments either do not change often or else that government and opposition agree on the broad outline of policy. A new industrial policy would have to focus strongly on building up domestic enterprise (defined as existing external plus indigenous) in addition to attracting projects from abroad. This necessity arises because of inadequate supplies of new external projects rather than because of anything inherently undesirable about them.

Irish experience was referred to on a number of occasions. We pointed out that political autonomy, and the limited powers of independent economic policy formation which accompany it, has not solved the deep-seated structural problems of the Irish economy. Unemployment remains at an intolerably high level; agricultural growth remains sluggish; a high dependency ratio persists reflecting the distortion of population structure created by emigration and large family size. Political independence has not made the Irish economy any less dependent on the outside world — it has merely changed the form of its dependence. Ireland still remains the least prosperous region of the British Isles, although, counterbalancing this, it has been one of its fastest growing regions also. Scottish oil revenues make comparison with Irish experience less sombre than this evaluation would suggest. Nevertheless, our conclusion is that political independence offers no easy solution to fundamental economic problems.

6
Money

John Purvis

PART I

SMALL, SURPLUS, DEVELOPED, OPEN ECONOMIES

In this book we are considering the type of country which we might call 'the non-self-sufficient industrialised primary producer'. It is probably of small to medium population size (under 10 million inhabitants), it has one or two very dominant primary products which are surplus to its own requirements and it has a developed industrial and service sector. The population therefore includes (whether native or expatriate) a considerable element of managerial, technical and professional people and the average standard of living is well in advance of subsistence levels. It follows that there is a major element of external trade with a tendency to a trade imbalance — probably positive. Governmental, social, educational and financial institutions are well developed, as is the physical infrastructure of transport (road, rail, air and sea), power transmission, telecommunications, schools and hospitals, housing, etc.

As monetary policy effectively reflects the politico-economic complexion and objectives of the policy makers in a country, we might well impose on our model various political regimes and see what scope they might have for independent action. Archetypal categories might be identified as interventionist and non-interventionist.

Interventionist

This may be a left-wing government desirous of directing funds into socially desirable areas or a right wing regime bent on elevating the country's status by strong-arm measures. There is an inbuilt tendency, especially in the former case, to protect struggling industries against external competition and to subsidise them by milking the earnings of the more successful and profitable industries (and individuals). This can be partially avoided (and the resulting electoral disaster!) by permitting expansion of the money supply. This avoids the phenomenon of the 'successful' producer crowding out the less successful in the competition for funds. There is enough for all.

Conscious measures must be taken in a deficit balance of payments position. The deficit is naturally diminishing the supply of money in the country unless conscious efforts are made to counteract its effect. This can be by borrowing from abroad to bring overall payments towards balance; it can be by artificially restricting outflows (*e.g.* controls on overseas invest-

ment, imports of goods, overseas travel, etc.); it can be by artificially boost-
ing inflows (*e.g.* subsidising exports, investment from abroad, realising
overseas assets, etc.); or it can be by printing money and either letting the
exchange rate reflect the diminishing value of the currency or imposing
exchange control procedures in order to maintain an otherwise unjustified
exchange rate. In the United Kingdom we have grown accustomed to some
or all of these various techniques.

The only difference in the case of our 'surplus' country is that it is
possible for the surplus to be absorbed first before 'unnatural' action need
be taken. Using such a notional surplus entails an increase in the money
supply in the same way that someone who receives a salary increase goes
out and spends it. He has that much more to spend before calling on the
bank again. If he saves it he effectively only defers spending it. However,
the financial institution, where he deposits it, will use his deposit to support loans to other people or companies (or even the government) who are
prone to spend. This spending could be for consumption or for capital
investment in productive equipment. Thus the argument goes that the
interventionist but orthodox manager of the economy will have to take
steps to withdraw such surplus funds from circulation. It would be misleading to brand the 'left-wing' interventionist with the tendency to take
the easy option all the time — the evidence of the Soviet Union and Eastern
Europe would indicate that such regimes are quite prepared to (and in fact
can justify the totalitarian aspects of their governments by the ability to)
ensure that such surpluses are employed in investments for the future
rather than consumer satisfaction for the present. It would seem to be more
a feature of the democratic socialist or middle ground regime to try to
satisfy social ambitions and at the same time mitigate the corresponding
unpleasant fiscal and monetary repercussions. This inevitably results in
the evil-day postponing with which we have become familiar.

Presuming that we are looking to the longer term benefits for our 'small
surplus country', is it necessarily so that only a totalitarian regime can
bring the requisite discipline to bear to ensure that the surplus is usefully
deployed for the future rather than frittered away on the present? Economic
discipline in general (and monetary discipline in particular) is just as important in the long term interests of the nation whether it is fundamentally
surplus or deficit. When someone spends a period of his life working in the
Gulf on a short-term contract earning large amounts of money, he can
either spend it on riotous living or put it by for the future. The latter course
requires a degree of self-discipline in his way of life. The former course
effectively puts him in the same *financial* position in the end as if he was at
home on the dole, where financial discipline becomes a categorical impera-
tive. In his prosperous condition it is difficult to resist the temptations of
the physical perquisites of such a life or to resist others' claims on his
generosity. Thus the political pressures on the economic managers of
a country in this position are very strong. You have the wherewithal

— it takes a strong will not to take the easy and immediately popular way.

It therefore behoves the interventionist government to look to the long-term benefits, especially if the cause of its present prosperity is due to a wasting natural resource with a limited life. What are they going to do when the milk runs dry? Some commentators (for example Alan A. Tait in *Scotland 1980*)[1] bemoan the monetary effect of large trade surpluses. If the profligate approach is followed, they are not for long going to be surpluses and the profligacy, in so far as it absorbs the surpluses, will not be increasing money supply beyond the levels which the economy is able to absorb. If the spending proceeds further to the extent of deficit financing, an inflation of money supply does occur with the familiar results. On the other hand, the prudent approach will have the effect of squirrelling away the surpluses into stores of value of some kind which can then be tapped for income at a later date. The significant point is that the money supply effect of using the surpluses to invest in, say, American shares or great works of art (being stores of value), or, say Japanese colour TV sets or Russian caviar (being consumption) is, in the present time-frame, the same. The international payments situation is balanced and, although the amounts on revenue and expenditure are bigger, the net result is the same. There is in fact no increase in the money in the hands (or bank accounts) of inhabitants. Obviously the flow may not be so clearly in one step — perhaps the 'squirrelling away' may be in the form of infrastructure investment such as a motorway network, improved education facilities or a modern telecommunications system. These will all improve the country's future earning power. But even though the expenditure is within the country and there is no primary expenditure abroad (for telephone exchange equipment perhaps), there will undoubtedly be a tendency for these funds to find their way by secondary or tertiary means into investment or consumption outwith the country. The motorway construction worker takes a holiday in Spain where he spends his high earnings, his employer buys Japanese bulldozers or buys out a foreign contractor to expand his business overseas.

The interventionist government may therefore have two possible aims by intervening — to make sure its supporters get the main advantage from the 'surplus' and thus enhance its own future prospects with short-term circuses, or, to ensure the long-term well-being of its supporters (and the country at large) by squirrelling away all or some of the surplus into stores of value. It may have difficulty resisting the begging bowls and blandishments. The chances are it will try to aim somewhere in between. But it will be the main agent of whatever policy is adopted. It cannot trust the people to decide their own fate — it will do it for them. Thus the left wing interventionist will absorb money out of the system by selling government stocks or by taxation in order to make sure the funds are diverted to where it wants it — social welfare, hospitals, lame ducks, subsidies for food prices and housing, etc. The right wing interventionist may well absorb money out of private and corporate hands to divert it into areas such as defence, overseas investment, prestige buildings, etc. But these are both merely transfers of money from one pocket to the other. Furthermore, the number of domestic loops before the funds leave the country in exchange for consumer goods or assets is monetarily irrelevant.

What matters fundamentally is the net asset base of either the country, or the individual within the country, and the triangle of credit that can be supported by it. As the base expands, the larger geometrically is the potential triangle above:

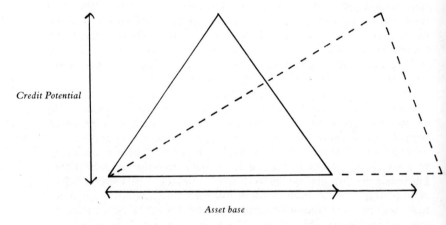

It is when we move into the triangle and start creating credit supported by our real assets, that matters of money supply become pertinent. On the triangle theory it is quite possible that a country's external credit potential is being contracted while it is expanding its credit domestically to fill its inhabitants' domestic credit potential. External liabilities (*e.g.* borrowings from foreigners) can be, and often are, converted into domestic assets. This is classic profligacy, even though the quality of these domestic assets can vary from wasting consumer goods to productive plant. We borrow abroad to support domestic comforts. The contrary would also be possible for a strong or very rich government — deny domestic comforts in order to build up external assets. By restricting the domestic asset base, we restrict also the credit potential. Meantime we are increasing the external asset base and its credit potential if and when required.

The mechanism of intervention starts with a central bank dominated heavily by the government machine. It is not provided with a strong objective charter (such as the US Federal Reserve Bank or the German Bundesbank) but is 'responsive to the wish of parliament'. The government may be weak and obsequious to a creature-comfort-demanding electorate or it may be a strong, even totalitarian, regime which knows what its long-term objectives are and is quite prepared to sacrifice short-term comforts in their pursuit. Either way, the central bank is merely the tool of the Treasury and only has the function of carrying out the technical implementation of a policy dictated elsewhere. Certainly this function could just as well be carried out by a department of the Treasury. The only advantage is perhaps that the private sector (if there is one) is kept at one remove from the government itself and the Central Bank fulfils a semi-official/semi-commercial buffer or bridge role. Having a central bank seems also to have something to do with a nation's virility — like an airline, a flag and a national anthem. From the point of view of managing an economy, and particularly one where the government is interventionist, there is no need for a central bank. The bank notes can either be 'Government of Ruritania' notes or 'Currency Commission of Ruritania' notes, or note issue could be left exclusively to the commercial banks supported by recognised liquid reserves held with the Treasury or in their own vaults (*e.g.* treasury bills, credit balances, bullion, etc.).

The interventionist monetary system does require a close linked mechanism for the government to control domestic money supply. The totalitarian regime may do this by edict, strictly controlling the note issue and credit creation by the banks. It may go so far as to immobilise bank credit balances by forced saving mechanisms. The non-totalitarian but interventionist government will have to develop methods of achieving the same with the apparent free consent of the inhabitants. Thus tempting national savings offers or government stocks will be dangled before them. The funds thus gathered can either be sterilised in the government's hands (to reduce supply of money) or switched out again via routes which satisfy their politico-economic aims (no net effect on money supply) or this 'public spending' can be greater than is supported by the country's wealth creation ability and requires the inflow of funds from abroad to finance it — *i.e.* overseas loans, or the sale of overseas assets, or domestic inflation of prices as the currency devalues and provides the equilibrating mechanism with other currencies.

The interventionist system almost certainly requires strict controls therefore on the movement of funds in and out of the country. Perhaps it could be avoided with what we might call 'orthodox interventionist' economic management. With even and firm control on the tiller, a satisfied population (when it compares its lot with others) and an ability to maintain this relative position, it is possible that no control need be kept on international money flows. The people will be happy to keep their funds in the country without coercion or at least any minor movement outwards will be compensated with movements inwards. The interventionist government will maintain a light touch on the rudder to obviate any significant lurching, pitching or rolling and a fair sail will be had by all. But if any dissatisfaction were to arise — *e.g.* falling behind other countries in apparent or perceived standards of living, unemployment, lack of consumer goods, inequality of opportunity, poor health, education or social facilities, restricted democratic freedoms — a tendency will arise among the people to switch resources abroad, even to emigrate themselves. This can occur on either side of the happy mean — conservative or liberal. In such circumstances the government will commonly resort to artificial restrictions on such movements — exit visas, Berlin Walls and barbed wire to control the movement of people, exchange control to restrict the movement of money, customs and tariff barriers and rationing to control the movement of goods. Money, like water, tends to find its own level and artificial barriers, which attempt to stem this tendency, will invite attempts to find ways around, under or over, to escape.

To be stable, an interventionist monetary policy requires management by a government of Platonic wisdom and omniscience. It requires a wise and forward-looking population to accept the short-term self-denial for longer-term benefits. It requires an economy which is not at any significant disadvantage economically compared to its more obvious neighbours. A small oil rich country may well qualify under the last of these headings. Can it produce the government to manage itself wisely?

Non-interventionist
In this context the government of our 'small surplus' country is of the hands-off type. Its economic involvement is one of attempting to smooth the peaks and troughs of cyclical variations and to mitigate real and, particularly, undeserved hardship amongst the population. This does not preclude the government from creating conditions that are conducive, say, to investment or consumption. It would have a responsibility to establish such broad policy aims and, even if it took no conscious position either way, this would represent a policy decision in itself with certain predictable and measurable implications. If, in the monetary sphere, it determined to allow the exchange rate to float and money supply to be a neutral self-equilibrating force, it would have decided, by our definition, on a non-interventionist course. This decision, though, may not have been an easy one and it certainly may not be the electorally most popular one in the short-term. But just such a decision for conservative economic policies would be more conducive to saving than consumption, because of the implied low levels of inflation for example. There is little point in discussing the anarchical extreme of complete non-intervention and this is not the subject of our paper.

We can also postulate a body of commercial law which regulates contracts, accounting standards, fraud and false pretences, and even goes so far as placing limits on imprudent financing. For example, prudent liquidity ratios of banks and capital ratios of insurance companies, the disclosure of financial information to shareholders and creditors, and other basic parameters, may well be legally imposed and policed by some suitable body. The objective is to protect the innocent from the wolf to the extent that fairness in commercial transactions is assured.

Having set the legal environment, the economy is then left largely to its own devices. The prosperity and well-being of the inhabitants will thereafter depend on (a) the natural attributes of the country (natural resources, geographical location, terrain, etc.), (b) the peoples' aptitude to work and/or innovate, and/or organise themselves efficiently, and (c) their propensity to consume, squirrel away (*i.e.* save passively) or to invest productively. Assuredly we can instance countries where disadvantages in one of these areas is compensated by advantages in others. Probably we can instance cases where advantages in one or even two such areas are compromised in the third. In the interventionist state these features could be counteracted by the government. In the non-interventionist state there is no such regulating body (even if it did work). A country which has considerable natural resources (or a single natural resource which is highly prized), but is lacking in an industrious, innovative or skilled native population, can counteract this deficiency by allowing expatriate expertise into the country. It can probably counteract the lack of a sophisticated financial sense by imposing restrictions or incentives (if interventionist) or permitting foreign economic domination (if non-interventionist). Good examples of this type of situation are the newly wealthy Gulf oil states. If properly managed the 'expatriate' phase can be kept relatively short-term. This period can be used to encourage the native population to achieve the skills and outlook necessary to manage their own affairs as well as the expatriates can. The non-interventionist state will probably find the expatriates become more and more successfully ensconced and the natives more and more subservient. Is it possible that anthropologically certain peoples are more suited to such environments and that, no matter how much training and cajoling is involved, the others just cannot match them? We think of the overseas Chinese, the Indian, the Jew, the Armenian and the Anglo-Saxon as peoples who have tended to dominate trade and finance as expatriates in countries where the native peoples have not been a match in these particular aspects of life.

So, of the small oil-rich states, the majority come into the category of being deficient in sophisticated financial skills (and probably deficient in other skills as well — scientific, engineering, medical, agricultural, etc). They are therefore liable to buy in, or encourage in, expatriates who will provide these skills for the short term and impart them to the natives for the longer term. Some may well have an established infrastructure of such human skills, including a sophisticated financial sector, and into this category could probably be placed an independent Scotland. But there is then the question as to whether there is a native tendency to consume, squirrel away or invest productively (while restraining consumption). We have all been looking on in amazement at what seems like ostentatious consumption by citizens of the newly rich oil states in the Middle East. This may be the buying of 100 suits or Rolls Royces by wealthy individuals or of airlines and defence equipment by governments. Before decrying these apparently unproductive examples of consumption, however, we should appreciate that they play their part in redressing the payments imbalances between the oil producing and the industrial countries. Expenditure on defence equipment can even be justified on higher priority criteria in the case of a small rich country on which envious foreign eyes are likely to be focussed. Investment policy regarding such surpluses may not be a monetary matter in itself but its monetary implications are significant enough that some consideration at this point is amply justified.

The first priority should then be towards investment in the future wellbeing of the country. Once the infrastructure is established, it becomes important to be selective, to consider what will be in the longer-term interests of the country and possibly to defer consumption or even investment of surpluses by 'squirrelling' them away in stores of value.

On current calculations it is expected that the government will be responsible directly for deploying two-thirds of the nation's oil reserves and the private sector only one-third.[2] We would see considerable attraction in the government handing over the investment decisions to the people of the country to a far greater extent. Probably they would use the fiscal system to reduce gross taxation by the requistite sum while at the same time constructing a fiscal and monetary environment which is conducive, say, to saving and investment of these funds for the future rather than consumption today. Such a policy might be called 'fiscal non-intervention'. Let the people decide what to do with what they earn.[3]

Whether it is the government or the people themselves who choose, the 'stores of value' may be overseas portfolio or direct investments or even, as suggested by Professor Donald MacKay, works of art.[4] A social conscience (or perhaps enlightened self-interest) may direct such investments to less fortunate countries. These can be as outright aid or as redeemable loans or as direct investments. From the international point of view, the worst that can happen is sterilisation of such surpluses thus reducing the world fund of liquidity. But even the hoarding of gold involves the movement of funds into the hands of either holders or producers of the metal and thus into the world's financial system. Is there any difference from buying a work of art (existing or newly commissioned)?

Perhaps we may hope that the IMF can operate rather more commercially as a central banker's bank — by attracting short- and longer-term liquidity from surplus countries to an extent much greater than the required quotas and then investing it in loans to international agencies (IBRD, etc.) for medium-term infrastructure lending or directly to its *temporarily* deficit customers. As it is, this function is, to a large extent, fulfilled by the large multinational commercial banks and the mechanism of the offshore currency markets. They can claim to be playing a significant role in assisting the development of the least developed countries while the interventionist will claim that, being subject exclusively to commercial considerations, they are unable to deal with the most vital and difficult situations. These can only be helped by government to government aid. This, however, tends to have political implications as the recipient of such aid can readily become resentful of his beholden position. The practical solution seems to be the international agency financed by surplus countries for the benefit of deficit countries and whereby the identities of both sides are muted and the criteria can be more objectively assessed.

At one extreme of our 'small rich countries' spectrum we might therefore place the pathetic example of Ocean Island. Here is an island of almost solid phosphates with a very simple unskilled and financially unsophisticated population. They were so simple that they let the British Government exploit their natural resources in exchange for a very meagre (though to them at the time seemingly attractive) consideration. For this they even accepted wholesale removal from their homeland. Only now have they realised what they have given away and are trying to obtain some degree of redress. They will be compensated in millions (realising a 'store of value') but not in any way equivalent to the resources mined out. At the other extreme we could hold up Hong Kong with no obvious natural resources (a harbour? or geographical location?) but a very industrious, innovative and financially sophisticated population. Both these are non-interventionist situations and, even in the 'success' story of Hong Kong, there may be drawbacks (corruption, poverty, slums) to set against advantages for the people (achieving potential, opportunity to accumulate wealth, stimulating environment, high standard of service, etc.). In Ocean Island the 'skilled expatriate' walked in, exploited the resources, dominated the natives and would have left them inadequately compensated. The resource has gone, the island is a mess and the inhabitants have £6½ million from here on out. If nothing else they have learnt a lesson but no investment in the future has taken place.

A heavily interventionist regime imposed on the above situation could have ensured a more controlled exploitation of Ocean Island's natural resources, more adequate payment and more useful investment of the proceeds. In Hong Kong it might cure some of the social evils but in the process would probably kill off the stimulating commercial environment which provides the prosperity and personal stimulation which attracts the inhabitants.

Scottish Economy

If we analyse Scotland against these criteria, we find that, as an independent country, there will be substantial natural resources. These would be sufficient to assure, at current import levels, a substantial balance of trade surplus. The people are industrious and skilled in a wide variety of industrial, professional and financial skills, and there is a marked propensity to save. On this last aspect, there has been a tendency to invest outwith Scotland in 'stores of value' (*i.e.* squirrel away) rather than in productive development within the country. And regarding the natives' skill level, it is perhaps significant that the high esteem in which these skills are held throughout the world is not necessarily repeated inside Scotland itself. There would appear to be a lack of self-esteem which is compensated for by a parochial brandishing of the tartan 'och aye' trappings of a subordinated culture. An environment that would be more conducive to the development of initiative, the maximisation of skills and the promotion of useful investment would be well rewarded in Scotland. The Scot has responded to such stimulation in many other corners of the world.

PART II

COMPARATIVE ECONOMIES

The closest parallels to the likely Scottish condition are probably Norway and Holland. Their experiences are useful guides to be heeded. As we have seen, the parallels with rich small undeveloped countries are only in the size and natural resource structure. These countries still have to provide a native infrastructure of skills and attitudes that are already well developed in countries like Norway, Holland and Scotland. It is interesting to note the, apparently, very different approaches Norway and Holland have taken to the 'problem' of equilibrating surpluses generated by exploitation of a wasting natural asset.

Norway has adopted what we might call an interventionist approach. Its powers-that-be have attempted to look into their crystal balls, assess what will be good for their country and then conscientiously steer a course in that direction. Uppermost in their minds seems to have been protection for traditional industries such as fishing, shipbuilding and shipping which might otherwise have been hurt by foreign competition as the currency strengthened and the burgeoning oil industry pre-empted labour and finance. These aims they reconciled with that of 'prudence' by strictly restricting the rate of depletion of the oil, either by formal regulations or by severe national participation requirements. Even so the strength of the currency would, by traditional economic theory, have had serious effects on traditional industries, if these had not been able to continue competing internationally by a combination of factors. Although subsidies of various sorts may play their part, there must also be improvements in productivity and the development of techniques, technology, quality (of product and service) and products which make the product less generic and therefore more price inelastic. This last point is of critical importance in a high cost economy. The Swiss and the Germans have achieved remarkable advances which have compensated for the adverse effects of an appreciating currency while permitting them to take full benefit of the advantages. Either we produce products for which the demand is not price elastic (*e.g.* Swiss high technology armaments, specialised pharmaceuticals, secure banking services, investment advice, alpine scenery) or employ the newest and most modern technology to produce products that are technologically ahead of all competition and/or cheaper (because of high labour productivity levels) (*e.g.* German cars, machine tools, computer controlled machinery, etc.).

Any interventionist Scottish government would have to consider seriously where the long-term future interests of the country lay. It will be a high-cost country and it will be of little avail if the whole emphasis of government policy were to be directed to conserving jobs without permitting the fundamental adjustments to take place which would occur, albeit harshly, in a non-interventionist regime. Undoubtedly, encouragement should be given to investment in high technology, research and development, innovation, quality services (*e.g.* financial, engineering and other advisory and functional services). If Scotland is to continue producing traditional products like ships, cars, textile products and generic engineering products, they must be better and/or cheaper than the competition. Their makers will be on a treadmill as they must get at least one step ahead of the competition and stay there. And surely the trend for lower technology industry to develop in low-cost Third World countries will make the treadmill all the more demanding. Would it not be better to *design* the new car factory in, say, Korea and be paid a price inelastic fee for the 'unique' design expertise? We have to face the inevitable fact that there will be a decreasing requirement for unskilled manual type labour in this type of country and an increasing demand for skills of many types (manual, professional, technical, scientific, managerial and intellectual).

The other principal plank of Norwegian policy is that, having limited requirements for oil domestically and having produced enough to provide a satisfactory trade surplus, it is prudent to hold oil in the oil fields for future generations to exploit as and when they need it. This is no more than the 'squirrelling away' that prudent economists are advocating widely for the United Kingdom's oil revenue surpluses. The choice of whether to invest such surpluses in oil reserves (*i.e.* by conserving them) or in a diversity of resources (*i.e.* by exploiting the oil and investing the proceeds in other things) is an investment decision. What will appreciate in value more by the year AD 2100 — a barrel of oil, a Rembrandt portrait, or a portfolio of stocks and shares? Sound investment advice would probably suggest diversifying our interests and the Norwegian policy of conserving its oil as a long-term investment smacks of many eggs in one basket. Commodity prices go up and down and oil is no more than a commodity. It may seem essential now; so did coal in 1850. By 2100 it may be quite different again.

Meanwhile, the Dutch are taking a much less interventionist approach to the exploitation of their natural gas reserves and to the employment of the proceeds. The result has been a very cold wind blowing through domestic industry as it tries to compete from a high cost base, which results largely from the high value of the Dutch guilder. The fundamental adjustments are being allowed to take their course. Undoubtedly the industries that survive this shake-out will be the ones most likely to succeed in the future and the longer term industrial future of the country will be assured at the expense, we might say, of some considerable hardship in the short term. Another significant aspect is the high level of overseas investment by the Dutch — both corporations and individuals.

Apart from the very high level of portfolio and industrial investment abroad Dutchmen are prominent among the overseas purchasers of Scottish, Irish and American farming properties. This is the natural way in which a strong current account payments surplus will, in the normal course, be compensated. Even if much goes on consumption of imports, a significant proportion is going into long-term stores of value abroad — it is being 'squirrelled away' for the rainy day when it will be needed by future generations. We will, however, hear the criticism that these investment funds should be used to boost domestic industry. In fact the capital movements outwards are helping to reduce the extent of appreciation of its currency and thus helping domestic industry's price competition problems. Also, domestic industry is being forced to compete not only in sales of its products but also for the available finance. It has to compete for the investor's guilder against the attractions of IBM or Scottish land. It therefore has to be profitable and efficient. Admittedly the adjustment is tough but the result will be a highly tuned industrial and service sector which will come into its prime in the next few years and be a fine source of employment and national revenue when revenue from the natural gas reserves starts running down.[5] At the same time income from the assets purchased overseas will also be available to help maintain the high standard of living to which the Dutch people will have grown accustomed. The British experience in 1914 and 1940 is ample evidence of how investments, into which many years' current account surpluses had been squirrelled away, can even mean the difference between retaining and losing cherished freedoms. As in Holland now, much of the British overseas investment was by individuals or their close surrogates (*e.g.* investment trusts and insurance companies). It is not necessary to have the government directing things in every detail or taking it upon itself to do it all itself.

Thus we have two contemporary cases where *different* approaches to a *similar* situation are by design or default likely to achieve *similar* results. The Norwegians may have got their investment medium wrong by putting all their eggs in the oil barrel. Unless they are very perceptive they may be propping up domestic industries that are not potentially viable for the long term or else, just because of excessive propping up, will not undertake the adjustments necessary for them to have a long-term future. Their strong stance against the fishermen's demands for subsidy are perhaps indicative.[6] The Dutch might find they have killed industries that with greater assistance might have adapted, survived and even prospered. They may have become too reliant on cheap, plentiful energy in the form of natural gas and have difficulty adjusting to its running out. Their inhabitants may have got very used to a high material standard of living with cheap imported consumer goods and liberal social welfare services, so that too little of the current surplus revenue will have found its way into long-term stores of value. However, the indications are that the monetary non-interventionist approach of the Dutch when combined with national characteristics which are inclined towards thrift and industry, and a politico-economic environment conducive to the same, will result in something approaching the optimum mix of consumption, social welfare, domestic productive investment and overseas (store of value) investment. The Norwegians may also achieve it and certainly their policy in this regard is much admired by, among others, the Scottish National Party. It is, however, evident that the Norwegian route requires a strong, wise and enlightened standard of government which can not always be guaranteed. There is more chance of 'getting it wrong' and getting it wrong will adversely affect the standard of living of the country for generations to come.

The interventionist democratic government has to face grave temptations not to take the short-term populist alternative when faced with a difficult choice. The non-interventionist can fall back on blaming 'external forces over which we have no control' if the present and immediate future looks rough and wait for nature to do its task of fundamental adjustment. However it must be admitted that sometimes nature gets so rough that political pressures demand intervention. The Canadian Government in 1962 faced this situation and gave in by abandoning the floating exchange rate regime. Samuel Brittan[7] opined: '. . . a floating rate cannot itself ensure sensible domestic policies. It can merely provide an opportunity for such policies to be followed, by removing the conflict between internal and external objectives likely to exist under a fixed rate. No system is proof against a failure to take advantage of it.'

Canada at this time had a central bank which was 'independent' of the government in its control of monetary policy. Once the directors were appointed (by the government) and they had appointed the Governor, they determined all aspects. They would have regard to the Bank's constitution which enjoined a responsibility 'to regulate credit and currency in the best interests of the economic life of the nation, to control and protect the external value of the national monetary unit and to mitigate by its influence fluctuations in the general level of production, trade, prices and employment, so far as may be possible within the scope of monetary action, and generally to promote the economic and financial welfare of the Dominion'.[8]

As the Governor and senior officials were appointed for seven year terms 'during good behaviour', it would have required joint action by the House of Commons and Senate to remove them.

In 1958 the Bank of Canada facilitated a significant government borrowing (the Conversion Loan) by fostering a rapid expansion of the money supply. Having achieved this immediate object it then reverted to its cus-

tomary conservative stance. The resulting monetary squeeze frustrated
recovery from a recession with 7·4% unemployment. Its 1959 annual report showed much greater concern with the levels of inflation and foreign
debt than with unemployment.[9]

We cannot, however, blame non-interventionism for this situation and
the traumas that followed. It was in fact the contrary. In an attempt to
accommodate the government's heavy borrowing requirements, the Bank
had departed from its usually non-interventionist *modus operandi*, and had
distorted the normal equilibrating forces (such as interest rates and exchange rates) by expansion of the money supply and encouraging borrowing from abroad. Having achieved the immediate objective (*i.e.* floating the
Conversion Loan), the abrupt return to normal caused monetary effects
whose implications were unacceptable politically. Thus we must agree
with Samuel Brittan that it was not the non-interventionist or floating
exchange rate policy that was wrong but the temporary aberration away
from it and the unrealistically abrupt return.

Even if it were not a matter of principle to have free movement of funds
between Canada and the USA, it would in any case be practically difficult
to impose effective exchange controls. With a tied exchange rate[10] which
cannot move under any circumstances, monetary policy in each of the
countries will be determined in proportion to the dominance of the other
over its economy. Thus Canada would be effectively 'tied' to monetary
policy in the USA. If the exchange rate is on a 'pegged parity' basis such as
existed under the Bretton Woods regime (*i.e.* with defined and protected top
and bottom limits) this would be the extent of any possible movement. This
influences the forward exchange rates and the relationship of the forward
and spot exchange rates determines the difference in interest rates between
the two currencies. Only in the event of severe speculation as to a devaluation or revaluation beyond the limits of the pegs, would we see the natural
results of pursuing a monetary policy out of line with that of the dominant
neighbour (or neighbours, because it can also be against a *group* of significant 'neighbours' such as exists with the European snake). Only with a free
floating exchange rate is the adjusting mechanism able to operate continuously and, therefore, probably more gradually. Monetary policies will be
reflected in the exchange rate as the measure of those policies against the
monetary policies of other countries.

Certainly an overhang can build up (cf. Canada late 1977) and the
actual break-away be postponed, probably due to psychological lags on the
part of currency holders and dealers, but the adjustment must follow. This
adjustment will itself help to redress the balance (*e.g.* a falling exchange
rate would, in the absence of expectations that further falls are coming,
tend to encourage exports, discourage imports, encourage inflows of investment capital and discourage outflows).

Thus a neutral monetary policy, which we can define as aligning the
growth in money supply with the growth of the economy or specifically

gross national product, would tend to bring the exchange rate back towards its starting point in this particular cycle. The mechanism is self-equilibrating. Thus, if we expand the money supply more or less than is justified by growth of G.N.P., the exchange rate will move up or down accordingly. This is the nub of our argument — a floating exchange rate and a monetary policy which aims at money supply growth aligned to growth of G.N.P. will provide a stable environment for trade and industry to flourish. It necessitates the matching of money inflows by outflows to the extent these are not absorbed by growth of G.N.P. In a deficit country, such as Canada, it has necessitated arranging inflows to support the inflated money supply required to support the predetermined rate of growth of G.N.P. This is the foreign debt with which the Bank of Canada was so concerned. In surplus Scotland we anticipate it will be outward foreign investment. If this were not done the excess or shortfall of money would correspond to the rate of inflation or deflation in the economy.[11]

Thus the Bank of Canada's reversion in 1958 to the 'neutral' type of monetary policy, which we have described, dampened out any incipient recovery in the economy. It prevented the government from undertaking growth oriented fiscal measures because of the inevitable monetary results that the Bank of Canada's stance dictated — high interest rates, for example, which would have made government and commercial borrowing very expensive and so unattractive. Ultimately the government decided this domination of their whole economic policy by the Bank of Canada was unacceptable. The stage was set for the confrontation which we keep expecting to happen in the United States as well. In this case Mr James Coyne resigned as Governor in July 1961 and was replaced by Mr Louis Rasminsky.

Mr Rasminsky declared that Parliament was, in his view, ultimately responsible for monetary policy. Certainly there has to be a high degree of co-ordination between the government and central bank because of the interdependence of monetary policy, fiscal policy and debt management policy. It is important to arrive at the right blend of these items in the interests of attaining over-all economic objectives.[12] This declaration was subsequently translated into a directive incorporated in the Bank of Canada Act 1966. As a constitutional check on the Minister of Finance, any instructions he makes to the Governor as the result of an insoluble difference of opinion, must be published immediately and set before Parliament within 15 days.

The Canadian compromise could be appropriate in Scotland and the constitution of a Central Bank of this type is discussed later. Also Canada's monetary experiences have useful lessons for the similar circumstances that will probably exist in Scotland's relationship with England.

If Canada asserts the maximum monetary independence possible from the United States, Ireland, in over 50 years has not yet, as Dermot McAleese points out in *Trade*, loosened these ties with its dominant neighbour. Its exchange controls, interest rates, credit restrictions and many other aspects of economic life are still firmly tied to those in the United Kingdom. Perhaps just now we are beginning to see signs of the fledgling testing its own wings even if this is while standing on the EEC branch. The degree of domination of Ireland by the United Kingdom is, in terms of trade, less than that of the USA over Canada. Less than half of Ireland's exports and imports are with the UK, while two-thirds of Canada's are with the United States.

The strains between Ireland and Britain are beginning to show in such areas as agricultural prices within the EEC's Common Agricultural Policy. If the Green Pound is different in the two countries, why not the Brown Pound? It is becoming plain that the economic problems of Ireland are not always necessarily the same as those of Britain. In fact it is beginning to find affinities it did not suspect existed with countries in continental Europe — particularly as regards its heavy dependence on agriculture and fishing while in Britain these can be sacrificed in the interests of cheap food prices for the consumer. To some extent the same arguments — *i.e.* that there is a different emphasis of interests — apply to Scotland when compared to England or the United Kingdom as a whole. For example, the farming, fishing, distilling and, yes, oil industries are much more significant in the Scottish context than the United Kingdom context. Furthermore, Scotland, like Ireland, has peculiar or more heavily accentuated problems such as geographical remoteness (communication problems), shortage of managerial and entrepreneurial skills, etc. Economic measures that may be appropriate for the large unit may not be appropriate for the particular parts of that larger unit. On the other hand, exclusion from that larger unit could be detrimental to the smaller unit's well-being. Evidently there must be some form of compromise.

It would seem that the inexorable force of economic nature is moving us in the right direction. This can be summed up as large and enlarging self-sufficient free-trading blocs which permit the optimisation of specialist production skills and economies of scale among the naturally cohesive constituent parts. Although the large bloc is potentially self-sufficient, this by no means signifies that it is closed to trade with other large blocs — in fact there will be all the more trade because of their efficiency based on economies of scale and specialist division of labour and capital. The internal monetary arrangements could be anything from monolithic to highly fractured between the constituent parts. We do not see that it matters greatly as, if there is little artificial interference, the most appropriate arrangements will evolve.

If several local currency units develop for regional monetary purposes, perhaps also an 'umbrella' basic currency unit will evolve in parallel — the Europa for instance. Perhaps the local currencies will wither away, perhaps the Europa will wither away, perhaps they will continue in parallel for many years. Basically currency must be a *useful* thing. Often European monetary union is equated with having a single common currency throughout Europe. Although this could be so, it is not essential. What is essential is that money can move freely throughout the area of monetary union. It could be that national and regional currencies continue to exist and that their relationships to each other and the Europa adjust in accordance with variations in economic fortunes and monetary policies.

The Irish have not yet felt courageous enough to cast adrift or, perhaps realistically, still feel there is economic advantage in tying their currency to the dominant neighbour. The time must be very close when this break should be made. Even if the United Kingdom relaxes its exchange controls and other interventionist manipulations of the international and domestic money markets, there is a case for Ireland to stand monetarily independent within the European framework and make its own monetary policy and decisions. We might hope that this will be an open door policy as this would ensure that the Irish economy specialises in the products to whose production it is most suited. Productivity and efficiency will be encouraged and rewarded and therefore the highest living standards possible in Ireland will be naturally achieved. Adjustments in the product mix of the country will be made gradually after an initial possible upheaval — mostly concerned with adjusting away from the largely artificial dependence on the United Kingdom for markets. Scotland would be every bit as able as Ireland to undergo this transition because it is a more diversified economy with a substantial industrial base as well as agriculture and natural resources. On the other hand, there will probably be some traumatic adjustments in certain of the less competitive industrial areas.

These adjustments are in fact being engineered now by the current interventionist United Kingdom Government. Even if we wanted to, the cost of stemming the tide is too much for the rest of the economy to support without unmerited damage. So overdue rationalisations of the motor car, steel and shipbuilding industries are being nodded through.

Chile could serve as an extreme example of an economy where intervention had distorted its structure to the point where it was simply no longer viable without a major adjustment of some sort. As it happens the coup of 1973 imposed on this scene a regime which was ruthlessly determined to restore Chile to 'economic reality' with an economic policy diametrically contrary to that of its predecessor. The regime's aim is to get the Chilean economy market oriented and, first of all, they have concentrated on stabilising the balance of payments and inflation. Fiscal measures were used exclusively to achieve these aims. The government's deficit was reduced to nil almost overnight, they insisted upon realistic pricing of government services and interest rates were allowed to reach 'real levels'. In order to gain control of the trade deficit, a crawling peg mechanism is being used to adjust the exchange rate frequently but with a gradual easing of the rate of decline — a sort of managed float. Meantime trade barriers are being dismantled with average tariff levels dropping from 94% in December 1973 to 21% in August 1977.

The cost of this policy has been extreme hardship, at least in the short term, for the large numbers of unemployed paying the new high prices, and the loss of democratic freedoms. In the regime's view the ends justify the means as they expect the reward to be a prosperous market-oriented economy set fair for the longer term future. Certainly it is quite likely that, in terms of G.N.P. and other overall measures, this will transpire. But the lot of each Chilean within this environment could vary considerably and protection of the disadvantaged elements in a society is certainly an example of where government intervention (through the fiscal mechanism) is amply justified. This is the difference between 'non-intervention', as we have defined it, with a human or an inhuman face.

After one of the most difficult situations where free market forces were brought to bear, we might spare a glance for one of the 'strongest' economies and how far the discipline of free market forces exerts itself on Switzerland.

We are all aware of the inexorable upward pressure that has pushed the Swiss Franc's exchange rate against the US dollar from SF4.37 in 1971 to under SF2 at the beginning of 1978. Conventional theory would have dictated that, as the currency strengthened, international competitiveness would have been reduced until a point of equilibrium was reached. Undoubtedly there are certain very special features of the Swiss environment which have continually postponed this interaction. Above all must be the character of the Swiss and the politico-economic system, commercial environment and attitude to life he has constructed. He shares some of the Scottish features of thrift, money consciousness, upright stolidness, reliability, industry and enterprise. He is perhaps more insular than the Scot — being more selfishly concerned with his own interests than those of anyone else — and, perhaps because of the long standing independence he has achieved and maintained, does not suffer from the anger and resentment against his imagined despoilers (*i.e.* the English) that exercises the Scottish breast. He is self-sufficient, he relies on only himself for his well-being and his success in exploiting the meagre resources of an unlikely piece of mountainous real estate bolsters his self-confidence.

And it is this Swiss character that has assured the adaptation of the economy to the exigencies of adverse monetary forces. Certainly it is conscious policy to discourage excessive inflows of hot capital from abroad both because of their potentially disruptive effects as they flow in and out unpredictably, and also because of the money supply effects such funds can have unless neutralised. The authorities have been insistent not to let the Swiss Franc become internationalised — *i.e.* effectively a reserve currency or one in which surplus liquid resources are deposited. Thus they impose artificial reserve requirements and penal charges to the extent that negative interest rates are paid on non-resident Swiss Franc deposits at times of heavy inflow. Otherwise there would have to be even heavier official sales of Swiss Francs against foreign currencies to keep the exchange rate down. It is difficult to tell if such palliatives are in fact attempts to influence fundamental trends rather than merely pragmatic efforts to smooth the volatile shorter-term movements that could unnecessarily disrupt Swiss trade patterns. Looking backwards it would appear from the empirical evidence that the fundamental trends have been permitted to fulfil themselves, whether intentional or unintentional. The Central Bank is authorised to 'protect' the currency. Long-sighted protection of the currency would dictate permitting free market forces to exert pressure on industry and commerce to be efficient, productive and concerned with selling, internationally, products and services that meet and continue to meet the demands of the market place. Thus we discern the high productivity levels of Swiss labour and the emphasis on products and services which compete on aspects other than price alone.

With the rate of inflation around 1% per annum and money supply growth at about 5% per annum, the object is to provide a stable environment. This is important both to the customers of Switzerland's large and sophisticated financial sector and to the ability to plan ahead in industry and commerce. The attitude of the Swiss authorities is pragmatic and this pragmatism extends to the point of realising that, while we can top and tail volatile short-term fluctuations, it is vital to let fundamental trends follow their course and force necessary adjustments gradually as they develop. Otherwise we risk periodic major upheavals and the much more concentrated social and other hardships these can entail — as we have seen in the case of Chile.

PART III

SCOTTISH CONTEXT

At some length we have set out the economic, political and social options that confront anyone considering possible monetary structures in a country like Scotland. We have considered the differing extents of intervention in such matters that a government might contemplate. We postulate that, given the characteristics of the Scottish people, and the environment in which they live and work, there is a case for a stimulating economic/financial/industrial/fiscal and therefore monetary framework. Given also that the Scot has a propensity to social conscience (evidence being a long tradition of free public education, health care, co-operative movements, trades unions, etc.) it would be unacceptable to have hardship pockets resulting from free-for-all economic policies. This leads us to conclude that Scotland needs a largely free monetary system, tempered by direction of sufficient resources into areas of hardship, deprivation and of *temporary* inability to meet competition. But it is essential that any 'featherbedding' be not too all embracing and that competition be strong enough to ensure the economy adjusts to changing fundamental circumstances as it progresses.

How important is monetary policy? If we want it to play an important part, what scope is there for any significant direction of monetary policy that will not be heavily dominated by a much larger neighbour's monetary (not to say whole economic) policy? And how do we reconcile domestic monetary policy with international obligations, legal or moral? Having built the frame we can then turn to the detailed picture inside it and consider what, if any, formal structure of institutions is required and how the money market might operate. We can consider the part a country structured in this way can play in supranational institutions.

The prime objective of monetary policy, and, in fact, overall economic and fiscal policy as well, will be to provide a stable growing and stimulating environment within which enterprise, inventiveness, industriousness and thrift will be encouraged and rewarded, within which the alleviation of social, financial and physical hardship can be afforded and by which a requisite contribution can be made to the well-being of the world at large. The country which is rich in natural resources can, as we have seen earlier, adopt the option of profligacy and achieve most of the secondary aims; but, the growth pattern is probably going to be one of boom followed by a longer term jading and finally bust. Monetary management can have a significant part to play in achieving stability in the growth pattern. This monetary management is comprised of a relatively light touch on the brake as speed gathers and on the accelerator as it slackens. But, how much scope is there for independent action to stimulate or suppress growth in an economy which is relatively small and heavily dominated by much larger neighbours, one of which, in particular, dominates most trade patterns?

This question was dominant in Professor Tait's essay on Scottish monetary management in *Scotland 1980*.[13] He suggested that the only solution was a barricade around Scotland constituted largely of heavy-handed border guards, voluminous exchange control forms and all the paraphernalia of xenophobia. In the 1950's there was scope for geniune discussion as to whether the West German open economy was going to have greater long-term success than the closed East German one. The East German theory was that the people didn't know what was good for them, and that intervention by government could assure long-term prosperity for all; whereas West Germany would achieve only a flash in the pan for a lucky portion of the population. To give time for this to happen, physical and financial barriers must isolate the materially less fortunate East Germans from the bright lights of the West. But even now men are risking their lives to get out. It is apparently not only for the material attractions but because of the human spirit's wish to be free to realise its potential and make its own decisions. This spirit is just as strong in the Scots, and we see artificial barriers as only resulting in an exodus of precisely those elements (the young, the enterprising, the talented, the hard working and the thrifty) which we so badly want to encourage to stay, to come back and even to immigrate. We would, therefore, opt for an open door policy and the substantial trade surpluses resulting from abundance of a scarce and valuable natural resource make this eminently feasible. We cannot see the disadvantages that Professor Tait does in such a strong positive balance of trade. Not only does it make it possible to maintain and improve standards of living, but also provides the wherewithal to fulfil a role in the wider world and, in fact, to *lessen* dependence on the dominant neighbour. The main concern of economic policy must, therefore, be the extent to which such surpluses should accrue to immediate and continuing improvements in material living standards, and how much to their longer term assurability. Unlike the poor country, our rich one can afford to err on the side of generosity and still achieve its long-term aims.

The first thing a country like Scotland will have to do after independence is to loosen the monetary apron strings to any one country or bloc and widen its scope. This, in itself, will help to reduce reliance on that country or bloc where it is over-dominant. We do not necessarily advocate a completely isolated position immediately, although this is not impracticable if we are quite confident that the self-interested advantages of being completely on our own, with no other birds in the nest to share warmth, outweigh those of mutual help (cf. Norway). But certainly we would rather move up to a grouping in which the balance of advantage and disadvantage was closer, where we would not be dominated by our very heavy partner but have scope for making our point felt. After all, even the world is 'an economic grouping' and you can hardly stop that and get off. We might well consider here how the stature in European and world affairs of the Republic of Ireland has changed since its shift from being an appendage of the United Kingdom into a member, even a small one, of the EEC.

In this regard, therefore, Scotland should go for direct membership of the EEC. It may have to compromise some of the immediate income potential of its oil; but, in effect, this is being invested in a warm nest for the years much further ahead when circumstances may have changed to its economic disadvantage. On purely economic grounds an argument could be raised for complete independence; but probably the best argument against this is that the country would suffer, particularly in its important agricultural and non-oil-related industries, as these struggle to compete in the open world markets against much stronger competitors. So, on the basis of crawling before we can walk, it would be as well not to go the whole way in one step but to become (or remain) a member of the EEC. The Community itself is expanding in the number of member countries, and probably will continue to do so — therefore the scope for any one member within it is ever-increasing. There are certain monetary obligations in the EEC to not all of which has it been possible for the United Kingdom to adhere so far. Above all, there should be no impediments to the free movement of people or money between member states. The longer term objective is full monetary union, and this has got as far as certain of the more able countries tying their currencies within tighter 'pegs' to each other, but freely floating en bloc against other currencies (*i.e.* the 'snake'). Sterling is still protected by exchange control which prevents many significant movements of capital to fellow member states while it has been unable to keep within or anywhere close to the snake. The Scotland which we envisage should be able to achieve both these steps quite readily, if it wished, or it could be a free floater.

We presume that, in spite of the international law of succession discussed in Chapter Two, the spinning-off component part of a member state of the EEC would be likely to have the right of immediate accession to the Community. It is already operating within it and will, with the passage of years, be more and more integrated into it. Unless the break-away has been characterised by unpleasantness or worse, there would seem to be no reason why any of the members should object. Furthermore, the country most likely to object on 'hurt pride' principles is also the most likely to support the application on economic grounds. Scotland would sign the Treaty of Rome in its own right; and we will assume that it would not expect to renegotiate its monetary obligations, but may, in fact, take on some that were previously set aside.

Meantime, the newly 'independent' country is deliberating over policy in many respects — near the top of the list will undoubtedly be economic policy and at what point a break is made with the United Kingdom monetary regime. If, by then, the United Kingdom is fully merged with the EEC, Scottish monetary policy would also be in line so there would be no problem to solve. But, if the United Kingdom is still following an independent monetary line within the EEC, there would be a strong case for Scotland to use its economic strength to break at least as far as adhering fully or much more closely to the EEC monetary regime and its objectives.

So Scotland will dismantle all restrictions on the movement of funds in and out of the country, to and from fellow member states of the EEC. If it is going to do this, it may as well fall in line with whatever may be the then current EEC 'exchange controls' on movement of funds in and out of the EEC. If these are non-existent, so be it. We now have full convertibility and transferability of the Scottish currency by residents and non-residents alike. By now Scotland will be a member of the IMF with its quota paid up and/or its share of any debts it has taken over from the United Kingdom. This will provide it with something of a buffer (*i.e.* a 'friendly bank manager') to manage an orderly adjustment of the exchange rate in this new environment. England may, if it is still beset by external economic pressures, have to continue its regime of foreign exchange controls against the outside world and Scotland would now fall into this category. Otherwise there would be a back door way in and out of England and the controls would be ineffective. Therefore the Bank of England would remove Scotland (probably Ireland will have gone by then too) from its list of the Scheduled Territories (*i.e.* Sterling Area).

The relationship between England and Scotland would then be similar to that between the United Kingdom and Holland today. The Dutch can move money into the United Kingdom at will and out again, if they fill in all the right forms, but their borrowings of domestic sterling are subject to control. Meanwhile, the English may still be restricted on what they can take to Holland, whether for a holiday, or as direct investment or portfolio investment. These restrictions apply unless they go through special complicated procedures with the UK exchange control authorities and/or pay a premium for the special investment currency they have to use. On the other hand the Dutch do not restrict how much they borrow or take out.[14] So the English would find these kinds of restriction on the movement of their funds in and out of Scotland. Much debate can then ensue as to whether this will be detrimental to the capital structure and investment levels in Scotland. Probably it will be an inhibiting factor from the English viewpoint — but if looking for 'foreign' investment, the English investor would not have been considering Scotland anyway. Perhaps some Englishmen will sell their Scottish investments to get the windfall of the investment currency premium on holdings they had bought with domestic currency. Perhaps English investors will tend to borrow Scottish currency in Scotland to finance their Scottish investments rather than effectively introducing capital from England. Perhaps free-spending English tourists will see no particular advantage in having their holidays in Scotland in so far as the travel currency limit would inhibit their enjoyment when compared to the Lake District. Experience of United Kingdom overseas investment during the current regime of exchange control (*i.e.* since 1940) would indicate that even if it does restrict the extent of this investment, there still appears to be plenty of urge to invest abroad. We could argue that the foreign exchange restrictions, and the bureaucratic procedures and premiums that go with them, are an inducement to increase overseas investment wherever we can, to maintain them wherever we can ('as a hedge') and a disincentive to outsiders to bring funds into the country. They have certainly been detrimental to the efficient management of such overseas assets.

Although technically illegal, how many United Kingdom citizens have a few marks, francs or dollars lying in a dressing-table drawer that were left over from the last holiday? Many probably have clandestine foreign accounts. Many probably take more than their strict entitlement of funds abroad. If it were free anytime — why bother? It can hardly be proved conclusively in advance that the removal of exchange controls by Scotland, and the imposition of controls by England, would have any marked detrimental effect on the funds available for investment in Scotland; it is much more likely that they would be stimulated, and anyway a shortage of capital in the Scotland we postulate is a problem we are not anticipating.[15] If there was a diminution of English investment in Scotland, this would at least contribute to achieving one basic objective of any likely Scottish Government. The Government will want to reduce the dependence on England and, even if this were not forced upon it, it would be trying to replace English ownership of Scottish productive resources by either native Scottish ownership, or, at least, ownership by nationals of other countries. If the problem is of Canadian proportions, it may, in any case, be politically necessary to control foreign ownership by formal restrictions. This could be achieved in blanket fashion by monetary policy (*i.e.* through the exchange rate), but, quite probably, foreign investment in manufacturing industry will be a 'good thing' while foreign investment in Highland sporting estates will be 'a bad thing'. Although we may deprecate such value judgements, as inevitably they result in undesirable distortions themselves, we must appreciate that any likely government of Scotland is going to be under such pressure as may possibly necessitate them. Thus the removal of exchange control restrictions would be a major step towards increasing the scope for monetary action by an 'independent' Scotland which is different from English monetary action. Critics might rejoinder that this 'independence of monetary action' could also be achieved by stricter — in fact just different — exchange control rules from England. This could be so, and, in fact, might be politically desirable if Scotland was becoming independent in a 'poor' economic state such as would have probably been the case prior to 1970. But, in the postulated circumstances of 'rich trade surplus country', there is just no such need politically and such restrictions would be in practice detrimental to the longer term well-being of the country.

So, Scotland is a full member of the EEC, adhering not only to the trade clauses of the Treaty of Rome but also the monetary ones. There is free movement of people and funds between it and other members (and in fact the rest of the world). Professor Tait[16] finds the monetary implications of this situation unacceptable. Being a rich surplus country, he argues, funds would be flowing into Scotland in such quantities on current and capital account that the money supply would become over extended to bloated proportions. There would be no way the central bank or Treasury could absorb this as they had no need for borrowing in such a wealthy state where budget surpluses were the easily achieved rule. His assumptions are blatantly false. The international money cycle is, as its name implies, a circle! What comes in will go out, even if in different form. We are postulating sizeable surpluses on current account in the first instance as large quantities of oil and petroleum products are exported from Scotland. We might even postulate large capital account inflows as foreigners invest in Scotland either because of the supply of hydro-carbon energy for their manufacturing processes, or because it looks like a growth point which will reward the investor with better than average returns; or it may just be due to speculation on the revaluation of the Scottish currency. Taking the various routes these funds could follow, let us consider their monetary implications.

Foreign currency flows

Foreign currency comes in, is held on deposit in foreign currency in Scottish bank. The bank probably pays the holder interest in that currency, deposits the counter money with either a bank in the country of the currency, or a euro-bank (which in turn, or after several turns, places in country of origin). In any case, the foreign currency is represented in the books of a bank domiciled in that country. That bank has, however, a liability now to a foreigner (*i.e.* a Scottish bank) counterbalanced by the Scottish bank's liability to the original depositor. The balance of payments implications are nil (or next to it — there will perhaps be minor commissions and interest rate margins accruing to the Scottish banks).

Capital account inflows

Foreign currency comes in, is exchanged for Scottish currency, and held on deposit in a Scottish bank (or as Euro-Scottish currency with a bank outside Scotland). The Scottish bank has an asset in foreign currency (deposited with a bank in that country, say), and a liability in Scottish currency. In the absence of any credit restrictions, and presuming its ratios and capital support it, it is now in a position to lend on funds to its borrowing customers. As these funds also end up back in the banks as deposits (or reduced borrowings) in one way or another, there is a multiplier effect on the credit expansion. This is what would tend to cause a money supply explosion with its resulting inflationary and other detrimental implications for the economy. But in a free monetary environment this cannot be so, given sufficient time for the secondary and tertiary cycles. And the smaller and more specialised the economy, the sooner will the funds spin out of the domestic orbit and into foreign hands either via the current or capital account. This naturally has the opposite effect to the original movement of funds and reduces the domestic credit levels correspondingly. The monetary authorities might have some concern to ensure such funds passing through the economy do not create too unstabilising an effect. This is, after all, the hot money route. The exchange rate and interest rate mechanism is the obvious one and, left to its own devices, it will take care of the *monetary* problems. As funds flow in, the spot and future exchange rates harden, making it more expensive to buy the Scottish currency, and more remunerative to sell it thereby making it less remunerative (in interest) to hold it, compared to returns on other currencies. Nevertheless, we must appreciate that considerable movements of this type can have grave implications in certain areas of the domestic economy — for example, on price sensitive exporting industries, their owners and their employees. Survival of the fittest will ensure the fundamental adjustments in the economy that are required; but the cost in human and social misery (even if it is only short term), is unlikely to be politically acceptable in the Scottish environment which we postulate. It is, however, a possible route for a strong right-wing non-interventionist regime and, under the influence of the arch-priest of non-interventionist monetarianism, Milton Friedman, is the policy currently being pursued in Chile. Milton Friedman[17] also advocates the tying of a small developing country's currency to that of a larger developed one. This will provide the objective discipline that will obviate opportunist or populist monetary management by the smaller country's government. Even in such a unified currency regime the moment may well arrive when an adjustment in currency values is inevitable; and this tends then to be all the more cataclysmic. As we saw, the Chileans are getting round this problem with a crawling peg system. In any case, our richer small state is likely to be having the opposite problems — *i.e.* of an increasing value of its currency *vis-à-vis* its larger neighbours — and we have already postulated membership of a major monetary unit (the EEC), and of the IMF as a banker of last resort. So, we do not wish to avoid the fundamental adjustments to the economy; we would welcome and advocate them. We do, however, profess concern for the hardship effects these may have in certain areas of the economy for the duration of that adjustment period. It is a problem that has beset many developing or adjusting economies. We would not advocate tampering with the monetary elements, as these have a blanket effect, except to make the adjustment as gradual as possible and, certainly, to avoid unjustifiably severe or frequent fluctuations — which could leave a trail of injured and killed who might have survived a more gradual and consistent adjustment. Furthermore an open door policy to outward investment (or consumption) would reduce upward pressure on the exchange rate that might have been caused, say, by a massive trade surplus.

A corollary to the blanket effect of using monetary techniques (such as rigging the exchange rate) in 'transition' situations might be a subsidy on bread prices — this aids the poor certainly, but also, quite unnecessarily, the rich. Would it not be better to aid the poor directly? Instead of 20p per week in bread subsidies perhaps we can afford 30p in family benefits. In the same way, for example, holding the exchange rate low will be only postponing the need to adjust in the inefficient or uncompetitive industry while not giving the efficient industry full reward. If it is felt essential to support the wilting industry (or company), it would be more effective to give it specific assistance. In this way more can be given, and furthermore, it will be seen to have been given. Meantime, the efficient industry will be more than compensated for the loss of exchange rate subsidy on its exports by the higher prices earned, the lower cost of raw materials, lower tax rates, etc.

Incidentally, the same arguments apply very well to all such blanket intervention whether it be subsidies on housing or legally binding pay, price and dividend restrictions. They all result in distortions, anomalies and, in the end, all the larger and more unpleasant fundamental adjustments. Sometimes hemlock will have to be applied and the hard facts of closure and redundancy faced. This can be eased by a humane and adequate welfare service providing financial, practical and training assistance. Because it is specific, it can be all the more generous, and, therefore,

effective in getting peoples' lives adjusted along with the country's industrial structure. In other cases it will be felt that for good reasons (*e.g.*
military strategy, short-term problems only, *gradual* phasing out, etc.), it is
necessary to support the industry itself. This again should be done by
specific subsidy and can then be adequate for the purpose. Meanwhile the
rest of the economy proceeds on orthodox monetary criteria. This in itself
will obviate many of the major traumas of industrial adjustment that are
usually attributable to putting off the minor adjustments earlier on.

Current account inflows

Foreign currency comes in as payment for added value on goods or services
exported or to purchase assets. The Scottish recipient exchanges it for
Scottish currency which he deposits in his bank. The credit base of the
bank is enhanced by the deposit balanced by the bank now holding a
foreign currency asset. The bank's credit can then be used to finance personal consumption, commercial working capital, investment in productive
plant or the purchase of stores of value. The long-sighted manager of the
economy will be concerned to see such surpluses either invested productively or 'squirrelled away'. There is no harm in substantial enhancement of
the people's standard of living; but, putting aside for a rainy day, or ensuring a *continuing* rise in the standard of living, comes as a priority over living
for today. We have seen that the interventionist can achieve this by rules
and regulations, or at least by sizeable manipulation of the money supply.
For example, he can take it upon himself to decide how such funds should
be utilised. He can draw funds out of the system fiscally (by over-taxing), or
monetarily (by over-borrowing), and invest these funds in the social programmes, industrial infra-structure, defence material, overseas aid and investments that he, in his wisdom, feels are advisable. Why not let the people
decide this for themselves? After all, the government is supposed to represent the people. If the people require agents to advise them on what to do,
they can be found around Charlotte Square. Certainly there will be some
items which the central or local government will probably have to organise
— priorities of strategic infra-structure such as telecommunications, road
and rail improvement programmes, defence. Even some of these can be
more directly related to the user (*e.g.* road users get the roads they can bear
to pay for directly in tolls or licence fees or petrol tax and the capital
borrowings are limited to what such sources of revenue can fully service).
For the 'great leap forward', that an underdeveloped country may need, any
loan from a banking syndicate or supra-national financial body should be
supported by projected cash flow in the same way, or else one is inviting
disaster. If it does not readily meet these criteria and yet still it must be
done, a specific and visible subsidy from some external body is essential.
The government can still greatly influence the way such surpluses in the
hands of its inhabitants go by the environment, both actual and psychological, that it imposes on the country. One which encourages and rewards

thrift will probably see a tendency for such funds to find their way into stores of value, either directly or via investment media such as insurance policies, unit trusts, stock exchanges, savings banks, etc. It is no accident that Scotland is so well endowed with just such institutions, and a further fillip would be given by an encouraging environment in the home market. Of course, with free movement of money from country to country, they will have to be sure they are competitive with similar institutions abroad; and this, in turn, will enhance their international 'sales'. A government that encourages and rewards (or at least does not penalise), those who are successful innovators, inventors, entrepreneurs or just high-earning hard-working workers, will find not only response amongst its own people, but others will be attracted from abroad to invest and work in this stimulating environment. A government that encourages consumption will also see results and very quickly, as we have noted all too often in the past. But who is not in favour of motherhood? All the above will be shouted from the hustings as broad brush ambitions — when we can afford it, after the next spell of 'austerity' or 'free-for-all boom' or 'election'. How is it possible to achieve what we all know is desirable? At least our small surplus country is in a better position than most to achieve such a paradise — but also it is all the easier to be diverted for short-term expediency into the popular or easy palliative.

Conclusion

We must conclude that because monetary manipulation does not have as close and immediate a linkage to the individual as fiscal measures, it is better left alone by government. We would advocate that the money supply not be regulated consciously by open market transactions, exchange rate and interest rate management. This should be left to natural forces and an essential prerequisite is that the economy as a whole and the monetary regime in particular should be free and open to international influences. The management of the economy, in so far as the effects of such an open monetary policy have to be mitigated, should be left to fiscal tools. These have the great merit of being either immediately linked to the individual, or almost immediately if imposed on his employer. Similarly, on the supportive side of the the fiscal account there will be specific subsidies to ailing industries or unfortunate people. Thus the citizen (whether individual or corporate), can see readily where the money is coming from, and where it is going. Manipulation of exchange rates and public sector borrowing requirements are too far removed from the individual, which probably explains why hard up governments have been finding them so attractive — spend today and pay tomorrow!

It should be stressed that a passive monetary policy which permits natural forces to determine the equilibrium is not an easy hands-off option. Nature will exert strict monetary discipline on the managers of the economy. Nor will such a regime deny the possibility of inflationary or deflationary fiscal measures — but it will translate such measures into their monetary implications with, one hopes, the result that such measures are taken only with due and considered circumspection.

PART IV

A MONETARY SYSTEM FOR SCOTLAND

Because the monetary system of the country is free and open, a minimum of formal institutionalisation is required. Some bank notes will have to be printed and issued — though this can be left as heretofore to the Scottish banks. There would be a direct linkage to reserves held with the Central Bank or Central Bank 'notes' in their vaults. In order to even out seasonal exchequer cash flows it will be necessary to have short-term government bills (*i.e.* Treasury Bills) and longer term gilt edged government securities will be required (a) to absorb Scotland's share of the United Kingdom National Debt and (b) to provide for borrowings to finance long-term development projects which will be serviced from fiscal revenue and not further borrowings. What it comes to is cash flow management as exercised by most modern corporations. The country will thus play its full part in the international monetary environment, as it will neither hoard international liquidity as a creditor nation nor fuel international inflation as a debtor. Its overseas commitments whether in aid to needy countries, defence expenditure or general trade, will be fulfilled as needful but through the fiscal mechanism, the monetary system automatically compensating any net outflows or inflows of foreign currency.

If Scotland is to be monetarily managed on basically non-interventionist lines, it would probably be most appropriate for this function to be delegated to a monetary management board or, as is the current fashion, a Central Bank. It would be eminently desirable that this organisation be set up under a written constitution or charter whose amendment would require the full and normal legislative processes.

This in itself will assure the monetary authorities of a reasonable degree of freedom from interference. Nevertheless we have seen in our study of the Bank of Canada that conflicts can arise whereby the monetary policies of the Central Bank can negate or render impractical the fiscal policies which the government feels necessary. In Germany and the United States this state of affairs is accepted as a reasonable constraint on the executive's freedom of action. In Britain we have, for better or worse, become used to the omnipotence of the executive branch of government. If Scotland is to have a single chamber Parliament, there is a good argument for this extreme degree of independence in the Central Bank. We suspect that we will be lucky to have the degree of independence granted to the Governor and directors of the Bank of Canada. So we would expect the directors of the

Central Bank to be appointed by the Minister of Finance. Perhaps the term of appointment could be longer than the three years in Canada — say five years. The directors would be responsible for appointing a governor and deputy governor whose terms of office would be seven years. If the Minister is represented on the board (even without a vote), a channel of communication is available and there is less chance of unnecessary misunderstandings and disagreements developing to crisis proportions. Not only should the Central Bank be, in its own interests, conscious of its communication channels with the government but also with the public at large. The mobilisation of public opinion in its support should be considered a legitimate manoeuvre in its dealings with the Minister. On the other hand we will probably have to defer ultimate responsibility for the economy to the government and therefore to parliament's overriding control over the Bank's policies. The Canadian safeguard that such instructions should be laid before parliament within 15 days[18] seems eminently reasonable.

The constitution of the Central Bank should include a section of 'Guiding Principles' for the directors. In particular this will charge them with 'safeguarding' of the national currency, maintaining orderliness in the money markets consistent with a free market economy and assisting the government in its borrowing programme. They will manage the resulting market in its debt instruments, foster, supervise and control, where necessary, an efficient, dynamic and diversified banking industry, and all this with a long-term view of the interests of the economy and the nation. In particular the Bank should play its part in encouraging the accumulation of wealth in the nation and providing the monetary and banking framework to facilitate this.

Having got the constitution through Parliament, the Governor, board of directors and senior officials then have to get the Bank set up and launch forth into the cold, swift-flowing stream. No doubt advice from Mother (the Bank of England) and other experts will be readily available. Even before vesting day they will have to draw up the rules under which the banking sector will operate, and they will be recruiting, training and indoctrinating their senior staff who will translate policy into day-by-day decisions.

Once activity commences, the most difficult problem on a policy level that they will have is in differentiating short-run from long-run trends. This will seldom be obvious and, even if it is superficially so, short-run can readily become fundamental because of the greater psychological impact of the closest events. We might suggest the use of a gradualist or cushioning technique — *i.e.* to do not all that appears to be needed but to do some of it.

For instance, there may be a positive overall balance of payments profile with increasing reserves and/or an appreciating currency, and/or falling interest rates and/or eager buyers of securities. It is difficult to tell if this is fundamental and due to, say, a favourable change in the terms of trade or more to an inflow of short-term financial funds (*i.e.* hot money) which are exaggerating the extent of any fundamental flow.

Such exaggerations are almost bound to accompany any fundamental flow; in fact they may well continue after the fundamental trend has already changed to the contrary posture and thus be misleading as to the corrective action or the extent of the corrective action that is required. The money manager's function is to try and reduce, perhaps even eliminate, if we are very optimistic, the disruptive or 'exaggerated' element without affecting the fundamental element which has the seeds of its own correction already within it. The motor-car driver who gets into a skid has an automatic reaction to jerk the wheel away rather than taking the safer, but not so obvious action of steering into the skid.

Thus the classic response to such a situation is to lend to debtor nations (to reduce your and increase their 'reserves'), to sell your currency and buy theirs (to keep the exchange rate stable), to let interest rates fall (to discourage inflow of funds) and to keep on issuing government securities (to satisfy demand, mop up inflowing liquidity and so stabilise money supply).

This is all very well for the fundamental element but the 'exaggerated' froth is going to swing back quite soon and hit the money manager in the face. The skid will be the harder and more uncontrollable as a result of the reflexive jerk he took in response to the first movement. For example, foreigners will buy gilts for (a) the capital profit as interest rates fall and prices rise, compounded by (b) the essentially concomitant improvement in the currency's value *vis-à-vis* alternative currencies. If they buy a gilt yielding 10% per annum, hold it for six months to show a 10% improvement in capital value and a 10% improvement in the currency, the yield on their investment is 50% per annum for the six months offset only by the cost of the funds in the original currency. The international hot money investor is looking at the likely future movement of these various items and not at their current level. Thus offering 15% per annum on gilts will not in itself attract money unless the likely next movement is downwards. A $7\frac{1}{2}$% rate with a likely next movement down will attract more than 15% with a likely next movement up.

With gilts selling easily as interest rates fall, there will be no apparent increase in the domestic money supply even though foreign funds are flowing into the country. They are being absorbed but building up an overhang which a turn around or bottoming out of interest rates — *i.e.* an expectation that the next movement will be upwards — will unleash. The holder sells his gilts to realise his gain and the foreign holder will also sell the currency for another he sees as potentially more stable or liable to appreciate. Unless we then support our currency (*i.e.* buying Scots pounds and selling other currencies) there will be an increase in money supply. In fact the position was built up in the 'good times' of easy gilt selling but comes home to roost just at the most inappropriate moment. This of course will only add impetus to the pendular swing back as you frantically prop up your currency (thus losing reserves but reducing money in circulation) and increase interest rates (supposedly to attract the hot money back in but in fact scaring it off even more).

So it is advisable to steer into the skid during good times, forego as much as possible the temptation to sell gilts and thus avoid building up an over-hang which will only hit you the next time you are vulnerable. This will mean interest rates coming down much faster as bulls scramble to buy what stock is available. More of the foreign funds coming in will end up in bank balances and therefore directly increase money supply statistics. But at least this will occur at a point in time when we are better placed to sustain it. Also capital gains made on gilts are not available on unmarketable bank balances[19] so there is less incentive for foreigners to rush in. You will not reward foreigners with absurdly large capital gains as they bet on a sure thing against your unavailing resistance.

It may seem paradoxical, but it is best to let happen what the hot money holders expect to happen. If this looks like advocating 'precipitate gradual-ism' it is surely true that once expectations are fulfilled speculative interest will wane and, in the end, the fluctuations will not be so violent. If we try to stem the flood against world-wide pressure we will only end up exaggerat-ing the movements as the pendulum is pushed further and further and more opportunities are offered to speculators for windfall profits at your expense. The same philosophy applies to the contrary situation of a weakening currency and increasing interest rates. Let it go to the point where the next move must be better and the bulls will rush in to make their profits.

Thus the speculator will in fact help achieve a stable situation if we get him moving contrary to the roll of the ship. At first the ride will be rough and there could well be a place for a little intervention so as to smooth the fluctuations. But in the end of the day, a low degree of intervention will be a better stabiliser than the contrary. Apart from anything else the speculator will not have sure things to bet on and will feel so vulnerable as to limit his exposure to such potential, if in fact unrealised, risks.

It is to be hoped that those chosen to fill the positions of Governor, Deputy Governor and Directors will be people not only of technical com-petence but, much more importantly, of fearless and upright character. They will have to follow policies which they feel to be in the best interests of the country as defined in their constitution. Probably this will mean their being in an exposed political situation from time to time. It may necessitate their threatened or actual resignation. But their single-mindedness could also be very useful to a government which knows what it should do but has to satisfy various political streams and currents. Even if they are just there to take the blame, they will be giving strength to the political spine. *In extremis* the government can override them but, up to that point, they are in charge of the country's monetary policy.

There should be a relatively formal system of licences or approvals for institutions that are permitted to operate in the banking sector and money markets. The procurement of such licences would be dependent on the attainment of certain qualitative criteria (*e.g.* qualifications of key personnel, past history of principles) as well as quantitative (ratios, capital, etc.). Otherwise the banking sector should be flexible and competitive with freedom for new domestic and foreign organisations to enter the market. In this way it will be kept dynamic and new financial services will be developed for the good of Scottish business and industry. A protectionist attitude to the financial sector will only result in poor service for the Scottish customer and ultimately domination of even the domestic banking market by foreigners as the local banks become stultified. Furthermore a broad-minded attitude to the structure and components of the money market as a whole will encourage innovation and new adaptable institutions to develop (*e.g.* securities dealers, Foreign exchange and money brokers, merchant banks and acceptance houses, *et al.*). A completely free regime might encourage the cowboys, but a fair, strict and broad-minded regulatory authority should achieve the optimal mix of stability with dynamic financial services.

Scotland is going to be a prosperous country as its oil wealth is exploited. The picture beyond is uncertain. One of the 'guiding principles' is to consider future generations before taking all the honey today. The Scot has a natural inclination to look to the future and this tendency has only been eroded by the apparently poor rewards earned by the thrifty when compared with the security afforded to the profligate. The Central Bank will be in a position to look after the interests of the saver and investor — that he should be able to enjoy full value of and a reasonable real return on his savings. This involves a responsibility for protecting the purchasing power of the currency and for encouraging a broad range of institutions geared to the competent management of such savings. In this way future reliance on social security transfer payments will be reduced as people become self-sufficient and capital will be formed by individuals and companies out of current incomes in order to provide investment in infrastructure and productive assets at home and abroad, whose returns will prolong the windfall of North Sea oil long past the last drop.

PART V

CONCLUSION

The conclusion therefore of this chapter is that the best interests of Scotland and its inhabitants would be served by a liberal non-interventionist monetary system. The principal monetary authority (probably a Central Bank) would operate under a charter and only at the Treasury's behest in the last resort. The government's principal control of the economy of the country would be through the taxation system. The monetary system would provide an objective mechanism for equilibrating any short-term imbalances and exert a gentle discipline against undue fiscal profligacy or stringency. This would be supported by the discipline of exposure to external forces with the dismantling of foreign exchange controls and commitment to the relevant supra-national agencies.

It is felt that the character of the Scot would respond to the stimulating environment that would, in this way, be provided. The fiscal regime would be one that encouraged the native traits of inventiveness, self-reliance, personal application, hard work, energy and thrift, while mitigating severe cases of hardship and ensuring a fair degree of social justice. It must be admitted, however, that achieving the necessary political climate to make this possible will require a degree of enlightenment on the part of a majority of Scotsmen that may be difficult to achieve in the face of sectarian interests. This is probably the reason many less developed countries end up with totalitarian regimes of left or right, and we can only hope that Scotland can maintain its democratic and liberal traditions.

Thus the lucky chance of oil can be transferred into long-term fundamental assets for the country or be frittered away in short-term profligacy. It is, as in all such cases, up to the Scots themselves to decide which it will be and to insist on the political and economic system that will achieve it.

References

Introduction
1. Mayo, *Roots of identity: three national movements in contemporary European politics*, London (1974)
2. Seton-Watson, *Nations and states*, London (1977)
3. Nairn, *The break-up of Britain*, London (1977)
4. Hechter, *Internal colonialism: the Celtic fringe in British national development*, London (1975)
5. MacKay, *Scotland 1980*, Edinburgh (1977)

1   *Politics*
1. McGilvray, 'Economic policy and management' in MacKay ed. *Scotland 1980*, Edinburgh (1977), p. 48
2. Firn, 'External control and regional policy: the case for Scotland' in Brown ed. *The red paper on Scotland*, Edinburgh (1975), p. 158
3. Scottish Council (Development and Industry), *Export Survey*, Edinburgh (1973)
4. Estimate based on information from EEC Commission, Abstract of Scottish Statistics 1977, and evidence to Trade and Industry Sub-committee of House of Commons Public Expenditure Committee, 19th June, 1977
5. *Forestry Industry in Scotland*, Scottish Council (Development and Industry), Edinburgh (1978)
6. *Scotland's foreign policy, pt. 2: Europe and North America*, Scottish National Party, Edinburgh, n.d.
7. Simpson, 'Scotland, England and North Sea Oil' in Kennedy ed. *The Radical Approach: papers on an independent Scotland*, Edinburgh (1976), p. 60
8. McGrath, 'Scotland up against it' in *The red paper on Scotland*, op. cit., p. 137
9. Nairn, 'Scotland the misfit' 13 *Question* (1976)
10. Jeremy Thorpe, *Edinburgh Evening News*, 26th September, 1974
11. 1976 World Bank, *World Tables*
12. Discussed in Snout 'The Scottish identity' in Underwood ed. *The future of Scotland*, London (1977) and in McRae, *Norway: a model for Scotland's future?*, Andrew Fletcher Society, paper no. 6, Edinburgh (1977)

2   *Self-determination and state succession*
1. *Saturday Evening Post*, 9th April, 1921
2. The departure in the Scotland Bill of 1977 from the simple majority requirement for the Scottish referendum has been interpreted as a limitation on the principle that Scotland has the ultimate right to determine its own political or constitutional future
3. Pomerance, 'The United States and self-determination', 70 *American Journal of International Law* (1976), p. 1
4. Sureda, *The evolution of the right of self-determination*, Leiden (1973)
5. UNCIO Docs. 6 (1945), p. 296
6. Kamanu, 'Secession and the right of self-determination: an O.A.U. dilemma', 12 *Journal of Modern African Studies* (1974), p. 355
7. Connor, 'Self-determination, the new phase', 20 *World Politics* (1967), p. 30. A less pessimistic view of the prospects of multinational states is taken by Cobban: 'The multinational state must re-enter the political canon from which, as Acton many years ago declared, it should never have been expelled'. *The nation state and national self-determination*, London (1969), p, 127

8. At p. 48 *infra*

9. League of Nations, Council Document B.7. 21/68/106

10. 7 *U.N. Monthly Chronicle*, February 1970, p. 36

11. ibid., p. 39

12 G. A. Res. 2625 (XXV)

13 Emerson, 'Self-determination', 1966 *Proceedings of the American Society of International Lawyers*, pp. 135, 136

14. For example, Nayer, 'Self-determination — the Bangladesh experience', 7 *Revue des droits de l'homme* (1974) p. 231

15. Kamanu, op. cit., p. 359

16 Ijalaye, 'Was Biafra ever a State in international law?', 65 *American Journal of International Law* (1972), p. 321.

17. Nanda, 'Self-determination in international law', 66 *American Journal of International Law* (1972), p. 321

18. Brossard, 'L'accession a la souveraineté et le cas du Quebec', Montreal (1976)

19. Chowdhury, 'The status and norms of self-determination in contemporary international law', 24 *Netherlands International Law Review* (1977), p. 72, at p. 76

20. See, for example, Agrawala, 'Attitudes of the Asian-African States towards certain problems of international law'. 15 *International and Comparative Law Quarterly* (1966), p. 55

21. Falk, 'The new States and international legal order', Académie de droit international, *Rec. des Cours* (1966) (II), p. 1, at p. 10

22. The Norway-Sweden Union provides an example of a union in which much of the autonomy of the partner states was retained. See Lindgren, *Norway-Sweden*, Princeton (1959), p. 27

23. Harvie, 'Scotland and nationalism', London (1977), p. 29

24. Smith, *The United Kingdom; the development of its laws and constitution*, London (1956), p. 646. Cf. views of Mitchell in *Public Law* (1956), p. 295

25. Middleton, 'New thoughts on the Union', 66 *Juridical Review* (1954), p. 37 at p. 59

26. On the question of identity in general, see Marek, *Identity and continuity of States in Public International Law*, Geneva (1934). It should be noted that the Union did not change England's international identity in the view of other states: Cansacchi, 'Identité et continuité des états', Académie de droit international, *Rec. des Cours* (1970) (II), p. 37

27. O'Connell, *State Succession in Municipal Law and International Law*, Cambridge (1967), Vol. 2, pp. 1–24

28. Udokang, *Succession of New States to international treaties*, New York (1972)

29. O'Connell, op. cit., Vol. 2, p. 88 et seq.

30. Ireland, *Parliamentary Debates, Official Report*, Vol. 48, cols 2058–59

31. *Yearbook of the International Law Commission* (1974) II, p. 265

32. Criticism by Stewart, *Harvard International Law Journal* (1975), p. 643

33. Jenks, 'State succession in respect of law-making treaties', 29 *British Yearbook of International Law* (1952), p. 105

34. Zemanek, 'State succession after decolonisation', Académie de droit international, *Rec. des Cours* (1965) (III), p. 181, at p. 187

35. The possibilities are discussed by Birnie, 'The unquiet limits of Britain', *Question*, July, 1976, pp. 4–5

36. Aufricht, 'State succession under the law and practice of the International Monetary Fund', 11 *International and Comparative Law Quarterly* (1962), p. 154

37. Zemanek, op. cit.

38. For support of the view that dispositive contracts are succeeded to, see Vali, *Servitudes of International Law*, London, 2nd ed. (1958), p. 319 et seq.

39. Udokang, op. cit., pp. 400–2

40. O'Connell, op. cit., Vol. 1, p. 204

41. O'Connell, op. cit., Vol. 1, p. 220 et seq.

42. *Yearbook of the International Law Commission* (1974) II, p. 114

43. United Kingdom Treasury, Press Office Report, April, 1977

44. O'Connell, 'Public debts and state succession', 28 *British Yearbook of International Law* (1951), p. 204. Doubts have been expressed as to the whole concept of the validity of security for debts in international law: Wolff, 'Les principes generaux du droit applicable dans les rapports internationaux', Académie de droit international, *Rec. des Cours* (1931), p. 547

45. *Yearbook of the International Law Commission* (1969) II, p. 69

46. O'Connell, Vol. I, p. 404 et seq.

47. P.C.I.J. 1934 A/B. 62, p. 20

48. Friedmann, *The changing structure of international law*, London (1964), p. 201

49. Mitchell, *The contracts of public authorities*, London (1954)

50. Delson, 'Succession to concessions and administrative contracts', *Proceedings of the American Society of International Lawyers* (1966), p. 111

51. O'Connell, 'Economic concessions in the law of state succession', 27 *British Yearbook of International Law* (1950), p. 93, at p. 95

52. For example, Hyde, *International Law* (1922), p. 228

53. P.C.I.J. A.5. 1925. 27

54. 1956 I.L.R. 81

55. See, for example, the decision of the Supreme Court of Israel reptd. 1955 I.L.R. 113

56. Heirs of Mohamed Selim *v.* The Govt. of Palestine, *Annual Digest*, 1935–37, no. 39

57. O'Connell, 'Independence and problems of state succession', in O'Brien ed. *The new nations in international law and diplomacy*, London (1965), p. 29

58. Udokang, op. cit., at p. 476

59. Zemanek, op. cit., p. 288

60. Kaekenbeeck, 'The protection of vested rights in international law', *British Yearbook of International Law* (1936), p. 1, at p. 13; Sik, 'The concept of acquired rights in international law', 24 *Netherlands International Law Review* (1977), p. 120, at p. 129

3 Land

1. *Glasgow Herald, Who Owns Scotland,* 7th, 9th and 23rd February and 8th June, 1977; *The Scotsman,* 7th, 25th and 28th October, 1977; SNP discussion paper on Land Ownership and Use in Scotland, Edinburgh 1977; Highlands and Islands Development Board, Occasional Paper, Inverness, May 1977

2. For reasons of consistency the date of sale has been taken as the date of registration in the Register of Sasines

3. Denman, 'Who owns Britain', *The Countryman,* 1977–78, pp. 23–32

4. Bryden and Houston, *Agrarian Change in the Scottish Highlands,* London (1976); Highland Regioal Council, Regional Report, part II, Inverness, 1977, p. 30; White Paper: The Scottish Economy 1965 to 1970, Edinburgh (1966), pp. 139–43

5. *Glasgow Herald,* 7th February, 1977

6. ibid., 11th March, 1977

7. ibid., 8th February, 1977

8. One Perthshire estate has recently concluded a deal with an Arab syndicate who will be paying £500 per head per day's stalking

9. *Daily Telegraph,* 7th November, 1973; *Financial Times,* 27th October, 1973; Estates Gazette, 17th November, 1973, Wood and Leisure Land, *An Investment in Woodland,* London (1973)

10. *An Investment in Woodland,* op. cit., p. 11

11. See n. 1 op. cit.

12. *Glasgow Herald,* 8th June, 1977

13. Canadian Foreign Investment Review Act, 1973 s. 3; Bundesbeschlüsse von 23 März 1961/23 März 1973 über den Erwerb von Grundstücken durch Personen in Ausland, art. 3

14. s. 45 (5)(b)

15. Irish Land Acts, 1923 s. 24(1); Land Act, 1933, s. 32(3) as amended by the land Act, 1965, s. 35(1)

16. Routon Simpson, *Land Law and Registration* esp. Appendices A and B on France and Germany, Cambridge (1976)

17. Finance Act, 1975, Schedule 4 s. 5
18. *Agrarian Law and Judicial Systems,* F.A.O. Legislative Study no. 5, Rome (1975), p. 24
19. Heimburger, *Land Policy in Sweden,* Stockholm (1976), pp. 13–16
20. *Structural Reform Measures in Agriculture,* O.E.C.D. Paris (1972), pp. 228–32
21. Congres Europeen de Droit Rural, 6th–8th November, 1975, Rapport General, Pikalo, esp. pp. 25, 29–31
22. Danish Agriculture Act 1973, s. 16 and 18; O.E.C.D. Agriculture Policy Report (Denmark), Paris (1974), pp. 45–6
23. Norwegian Koncession Act 1974, no. 19, 13th May s. 7, 14
24. *Structural Reform Measures,* op. cit., pp. 118, 122; la loi du 8 Août 1962, art. 7, modified by art. 3 of ordinance no. 67–824, 23rd September, 1967; art. 10 of decree of 14th June, 1961; the German attitude to companies is closer to Sweden's, Lange, Grundstückverkehrsgesetz, Munich, 1964, pp. 168–9
25. France, la loi du Août 1962, no. 62–933, Code Rural art. 188–1; West Germany, Grundstückverkehrsgesetz, 1961, s. 9(i), (ii), both discused in Pikalo op. cit., p. 30. See also Danish Agriculture Act, 1973, paras 9, 13, 16 and Norwegian Koncession Act, 1974, op. cit., s. 7
26. See esp. Lange, op. cit., pp. 161–2, 166–7; Grundstückverkehrsgesetz, 1961 op. cit., s. 9(1)/i, (2), (3); Norwegian Land Act Lov Av, 18th March, 1955 (translated F.A.O. Legislation Series, 1955, vol. 14) s. 1, 10, 14, 20; Danish Agriculture Act, 1973, para 18; for Ireland see op. cit. n. 14
27. Botschaft des Bundesrates an die Bundesversammlung über den Erwerb von Grundstücken durch Personen in Ausland, 25 October, 1972, 11405, pp. 9–13
28. Bundesbeschluss über den Erwerb von Grundstücken durch Personen in Ausland, Änderung vom 21st March, 1973 in force since 1st February, 1974; for the Swiss position, Dagon, Erwerb von Grundstücken durch Ausländer in der Schweiz, in A.W.D. des Betriebs-Beraters, August/September 1974, p. 453, at pp. 454, 457
29. Advice of the Irish Land Commission: Purchase of Land in Ireland by Non-Citizens. Leaflet currently distributed by Irish Land Commission
30. Morgan *v.* A-G for Prince Edward Island 55 D.L.R. (1975) S.C.C. 527 *re* s. 3 of the Real Property Act R.S.P.E.I. 1951, Ch. 138 as re-enacted by the R.P.A. 1970 c. 40.1; for a discussion, Spencer, 'The Alien Landowner in Canada', 51, *Canadian Bar Review,* p. 389, at pp. 396, 408
31. Interim Report, Dublin (May 1977) pp. 10–12
32. For a contrary view, see Kolbert, *Land Reform, land Settlement and Co-operatives,* F.A.O., Rome (1974), no. 1/2, at pp. 106, 110
33. Norway Act no. 16, 14th December, 1917 on the acquisition of waterfalls, mines and other real properties; Swedish Act of 30th May, 1916, amended by Government Bill 65, 1975; see Bogdan, 'Restrictions limiting the right of foreigners to acquire real estate property in Sweden', *Rabels Zeitscrift* (1977), p. 536
34. Morrison, 'Alien investment in Real Estate in the US' 1976. *Minnesota Law Review,* pp. 657–81, also pp. 625–6, 635–6. The writer participated in two US Government reports; Albuquerque, International Legal Practitioner, May 1977, p. 30. For West Germany see Weber, ibid., at p. 27
35. Kolbert, op. cit.
36. R *v.* Bouchereau (unreported) Case 30/77, see Usher, *European Law Review,* December 1977 pp. 449–53
37. Bogdan, op. cit., p. 536, at pp. 538, 543
38. The latter formula is much used in UK compulsory acquisition legislation, *e.g.* Land Clauses (Scotland) Act, 1845 and Land Compensation (Scotland) Acts of 1963 and 1973. Cf. Community Land Act, 1975, s. 24, 25 and Crofting Reform (Scotland) Act, 1976, s. 2, 3
39. Baden-Würtemberg, Landwirtschafts und Landeskulturgesetz 14th March, 1972, and explanatory Memorandum; see more generally Dolzer, *The Social Obligation of Property,* Basel (1976)
40. A formula of the Federal Supreme Court expressed in s. 48 of the Swiss Federal Planning Bill, 1974; Friedrich, 'Eigentumsguarantie und Landwirtschaftliches Bodenrecht', in *Blätter für Agrarrecht* (1967) p. 1
41. Karst, 'Land reform in international law', in *Essays in expropriation,* Miller and Stranger

(eds.), Chicago (1967) pp. 51, 65, 67; also Karst 'Latin American land reform: the uses of confiscation' 63 *Michigan Law Review* (1964/1965), p. 327, at pp. 349–55

42. Interim Report, op. cit., para 27; the Swedish Land Maintenance Act is under complete revision at present

43. Goldman, Pascam, 'Real Property Valuations in Argentine, Chile and Mexico', in R. Lilhch ed. *Valuation of Nationalised Property in International Law*, Virginia, 1976, p. 129, at p. 143; also Karst, op. cit., pp. 62–3

4 *Oil*

1. Grant, 'Oil and Gas' in Grant ed. *Independence and devolution*, Edinburgh (1976); Brown, 'It's Scotland's Oil', *Marine Policy* (1978), p. 3

2. A matter about which Scottish economists are not in full agreement. See MacKay, 'North Sea Oil and Gas', in MacKay ed. *Scotland 1980*, Edinburgh (1977), p. 133, and McRae, *North Sea Oil and the Scottish Economy*, Andrew Fletcher Society, paper no. 2, pp. 5–7, 12

3. In *The Brotherhood of Oil*, Chicago (1977), Enger estimates, pp. 153–61, that US oil companies are responsible for the speculative withholding of offshore production of oil potential of more than 100 billion barrels

4. Penrose, 'Equity participation and sovereignty', 1 *Arab Oil and Gas* (1971), p. 25, at p. 26

5. See for instance Cattan, *The Law of Oil Concessions in the Middle East and North Africa*, New York (1967), esp. p. 21, and Mughraby, *Permanent Sovereignty over Oil Resources*, Beirut (1966), pp. 48–53

6. 1963 *International Law Reports*, p. 117, at pp. 122–25, 142, 168, 176–77

7. Proceedings of the Commonwealth Law Conference held in Edinburgh, 1977 (to be published)

8. 1956 *International Law Reports*, p. 810, at pp. 816–19

9. See especially D. I. MacKay and G. A. Mackay, *The political economy of the North Sea Oil*, London (1975), p. 33

10. Hansard, 3rd July, 1975, cols. 1146–51, 1164–67, cited in Daintith, Oil and Gas Law, Teaching Materials, Dundee

11. *Petroleum Economist*, September 1974

12. *Guardian*, 15th June, 1975

13. *Financial Times*, 12th April, 1975

14. *Sunday Times*, 22nd October, 1974

15. *U.K. Offshore Oil and Gas Policy* (1974), (cmnd. 5696)

16. *Financial Times*, 20th September, 1974

17. H. C. Public Accounts Committee, evidence of the Dept. of Trade and Industry, 1973, para 96, and Minutes of evidence, Q. 293–305, 1973

18. *The Banker*, May 1977

19. *The Scotsman*, 21st December, 1977

20. Woodliffe, 'State participation in the development of U.K. offshore petroleum resourses', 1977, *Public Law*, p. 249, at p. 257

21. Balogh, H. L. (Deb.), 23rd July, 1975; Dam, *Oil resources*, Chicago (1977), pp. 106–7

22. Dam, op. cit., pp. 119–20

23. *Sunday Times*, 20th July, 1975

24. *Financial Times*, 6th January, 1975; Woodliffe, op. cit., p. 258

25. Woodliffe, op. cit., p. 260

26. ibid., p. 261

27. Dam, op. cit., p. 106

28. Cattan, op. cit., pp. 16–17 and Mughraby, op. cit., p. 53

29. Cattan, op. cit., pp. 23–30

30. D. I. Mackay, op. cit., p. 33

31. See, however, Kemp, *Taxation and profitibility of North Sea Oil*, Fraser of Allander Research Monograph no. 4, Glasgow (1976)

32. MacKay, op. cit., esp. p. 36

33. Oil Taxation Act 1975 (O.T.A.) s. 9(1); Dam, op. cit., pp. 125–6; Daintith and Willouby eds. *Oil and Gas Manual,* London (1977), p. 108

34. O.T.A., op. cit. s. 3(5); Dam, op. cit., p. 127

35. The author is indebted to Donald Bain for extensive discussion on this point

36. Stoerk, *Middle East Oil and the energy crisis,* New York (1975), pp. 8–16

37. Zabariya, 1 *Arab Oil and Gas,* September 1972; 4 *Petrol et le gaz Arabes* no. 73, 1st April, 1972

38. See United States, 93rd Congress, 2nd Session, Senate Committee on Foreign Relations, sub-committee on multinational corporations, Hearings on multinational corporations and foreign policy (1974), and 82nd Congress, 2nd Session, Senate Small Business Committee. *The International Petroleum Cartel,* Staff Report of the Federal Trade Commission (1952) discussed in Blair *The Control of Oil,* London (1977), pp. 29–76

39. Penrose, 'The development of the crisis', 104 *Daedalus* (1975), p. 39 at p. 55; also Stark, op. cit., pp. 174–6

40. See esp., 'Nationalisation by instalments' *Petroleum Press Service (P.P.S.),* April 1972

41. On the incompatability of participation with the concession system see for Aramco Habachy, Supplement to the *Middle East Economic Survey (M.E.E.S.),* 20th December, 1968. Texaco recently vindicated the oil company view against Libya in an arbitral award, *Journal de Droit International,* July 1977. The Libyan Government did not, however, participate in the proceedings

42. *P.P.S.,* November 1971; *M.E.E.S.,* 24th September, 1971

43. *M.E.E.S.,* 16th May, 1972

44. ibid., 13th October, 1972

45. ibid., 14th September, 1973

46. ibid., 11th September, 1970 and 16th October 1970

47. ibid., 23rd February, 1973

48. ibid., 15th November, 1974 and 20th December, 1974

49. Hartshorn, 'Oil diplomacy', *World Today,* July 1973

50. Blair, op. cit., pp. 289–92

51. Seymour, editor, *M.E.E.S.,* 20th December, 1974

52. Bedjaoui, *Year Book of the International Law Commission* (1969), 2, p. 73

53. See the *German Settlers* case, P.C.I.J., B.6. 1923; *Certain German Interests in Polish Upper Silesia,* P.C.I.J., A.7. 1926

54. Bedjaoui, op. cit., p. 73

55. O'Connell, *State Succession in Municipal Law and International Law,* 1, Cambridge (1967), p. 300

56. Cases mentioned by Bedjaoui, op. cit., pp. 97–8

57. For the releance of good faith see the Transvaal Report made after the Boer War, cited by O'Connell, op. cit., p. 351

58. A balancing of interests formula was used in the *Sopronköskeg Local Railway Company Arbitration,* Annual Digest of International Law Cases (1929–30), Case no. 34

59. Nore, *Norway and the multinational oil companies,* unpublished manuscript, p. 63

60. Norway Parliamentary Report no. 30, *Operations on the Continental Shelf,* p. 44 et seq.

61. Nore, op. cit., pp. 12–20

62. Norway Report, op. cit., pp. 35–6, 44; Nore, op. cit., p. 20

63. Norway Parliamentary Report no. 25, *Petroleum Industry in Norwegian Society*

64. Nore, op. cit., pp. 55–7. See also G. Mackay in *The Scotsman,* 17th January, 1978, attributing much of the £5500 million foreign debt to/financing of Ekofisk, Frigg and Stratfjord oil fields

65. Norway Royal Decree of 8th December, 1972 relating to exploration for, and exploitation of, petroleum

66. Hamilton, *The Observer,* 11th December, 1977

67. Nore, op. cit., pp. 35–7

68. Norway Royal Decree, op. cit., s. 38; Norway Report no. 30, op. cit., p. 65 et seq.

69. Norway Report no. 30, op. cit., p. 67 and Norway Parliamentary Report no. 25, p. 65 et seq.

70. Norway Parliamentary report no. 91, *Petroleum Exploration North of 62N,* p. 80

71. Norway Report no. 30, op. cit., p. 66. The UK now seems to be coming around to this view with its three stages of depletion control

72. Norway Act no. 3 of 11th June, 1965; Norway Act no. 33 of 9th June, 1972; Norway Report no. 30, op. cit., p. 52

73. Nore, op. cit., pp. 25–6; Norway Report no. 25, op. cit., p. 13 and Appendix p. 50

74. Norway Act no. 35 of 13th June, 1975, relating to the taxation of submarine petroleum resources; Ministry of Finance and Customs, O.T.P.R.P. no. 26 (1974–75), pp. 11–15, pp. 35–42

75. *M.E.E.S.*, 11th September, 1970

76. Cooper and Gaskell, *The adventure of North Sea Oil*, London (1976), Appendices 2 and 3, see also *North Sea Information Sheet*, Scottish Economic Planning Dept. (August 1977), Annex B, Commercial Fields

77. *Sunday Times*, 11th December, 1977

78. *Financial Times*, 23rd April, 1975

79. *Disclosure of Corporate Ownership*, prepared by the sub-committee on intergovernmental relations and budgeting management, 93rd Congress, 1st Session, Washington, 1973, pp. 30 and 370

80. Marine Engineer's Beneficial Association, *The American Oil Industry: a failure of Anti-Trust Policy*, New York (1973), pp. 78–85, 108–13

81. *Disclosure of Corporate Ownership*, op. cit., p. 1

82. See Bentham, *supra*, 7

83. Cited in Dam, op. cit., and generally on assignment, pp. 47–9

84. UK Offshore Oil and Gas Yearbook, 1975/1976, 1973 estimate, p. 158; *The Rose Mary* (1956), Ch. D323

85. Blair, op. cit., p. 29

86. 'The Oil Companies adapt to a new role', *The Banker*, March 1977

87. 1976 Annual Reports of B.P. Co. Ltd, Mobil Corporation, Texaco Inc., Royal Dutch Petroleum Company and Exxon

88. American Entreprise Institute for Public Policy Research, *Horizontal Divestiture* (1977), pp. 16–17; Enger, op. cit., pp. 220, 227; Blair, op. cit., pp. 12–19, 29, 131, et seq., 246–54

89. *M.E.E.S.*, 7th November, 1975; *The Banker*, March 1977

90. *M.E.E.S.*, 26th January, 1973; 6th December, 1974

91. Townsend, 'Growing acceptance of Arab financial management, the euro-market', *New York Herald Tribune*, December 1977; 'Middle East bankers spread their wings', *The Banker*, March 1977

5 Trade

1. These percentages substantially exceed those of independent economies of similar size (*e.g.* Iceland, Denmark, Norway and Finland). Scotland's extreme degree of openness relative to other countries may be due to a number of factors: (i) it is well established that trade between regions has advanced to a much greater degree of specialisation than trade between independent nations — hence the importance of trade with the rest of the UK in Scotland's trade figures, (ii) the above general tendency may be sharpened by the high degree of external control of Scottish industry, but the absence of comparative data on a regional basis makes this impossible to verify and (iii) there may be biases in the compilation of the input-output table which result in under-representation of the services sector and of small industrial firms, both of which are characterised by lower-than-average trade ratios

2. Kuznets, 'Economic growth of small nations' in Robinson ed. *Economic consequences of the size of nations*, London (1960)

3. ibid.

4. This point is stressed by Schiller, 'Relative earnings mobility in the United States', *American Economic Review*, December 1977

5. The correlation coefficient between size of country, as measured by total population, and (a) its degree of equality of income distribution (measured by the Gini coefficient) and (b) number of

man-days lost per 1000 employees through industrial disputes, yielded non-significant results in each case. Our correlation included all OECD countries for which data were available

6. For further details see Nevin, *The economics of devolution*, Birmingham (1978)

7. See Ryan 'Fiscal policy and demand management in Ireland 1960–70' in Tait and Bristow eds. *Ireland: some problems of a developing economy*, Dublin (1972)

8. Lindbeck, 'Stabilisation policy in open economies with endogenous politicians, *American Economic Review*, May 1976

9. ibid.

10. Revaluations could also be used to conceal and/or dampen internal inflationary pressures. But this would also involve a change in effective parity and not just nominal parity; the desirability of such a policy would depend on the persistence of the source of internal inflation and also on the considerations referred to in our discussion below of effective parity changes

11. This point is argued forcefully by McCrone in 'The determinants of regional growth rates' in Vaizey ed. *Economic sovereignty and regional policy*, Dublin (1975)

12. The history of the 'sterling debate' up to 1960 is detailed in Moynihan, *Currency and central banking in Ireland 1922–1960*, Dublin (1975). An excellent source on the more recent discussion is Whitaker 'Monetary integration: reflections on Irish experience' in *Central Bank of Ireland Quarterly Bulletin*, Winter 1973. The issue is also discussed in Gibson and Spencer eds. *Economic activity in Ireland: a study of two open economies*, Dublin (1977)

13. Roughly half of Scotland's exports are sold to the rest of the UK; the proportion of imports is not known. For purposes of comparison, we may note that over half of Irish foreign trade is conducted with the UK

14. An exception is the food industry, which shares some features in common with the Scottish distilling industry

15. To cite another example from Irish experience, the objective of raising Irish social welfare benefits to the British level has long been accepted as a desirable aim of economic policy. Substantial progress towards this objective was made by the last Coalition Government during the period 1973–77. Only a few economists — but no politicians — questioned the wisdom of such action. One important unfavourable consequence of the policy, identified in a study by Walsh, 'Unemployment compensation and the rake of unemployment: the Irish experience', paper read to conference on Unemployment Insurance and the rate of unemployment, Farmer Institute, Vancouver, 1st–4th September, 1976, was a shift in the migration function reflecting an increased propensity to stay at home, unemployed, rather than to seek work elsewhere

16. This list is compiled from Firn 'External control and regional policy: the case for Scotland' in Brown ed. *The red paper on Scotland*, Edinburgh (1975) and Firn 'Industrial policy' in MacKay ed. *Scotland 1980*, Edinburgh (1977)

17. Forsyth, *U.S. Investment in Scotland*, New York (1972)

18. As a recent Scottish Council Research Institute 'US investment in Scotland', Edinburgh, n.d., study has shown, US companies also experience job losses through closures, etc. The Institute's figures for the period 1968–72 show that gains in employment through expansions numbered 5500 as against job losses of 4700. Given the short period of the investigation — and the rapid spurt in employment in US subsidiaries in 1973 — it is not clear to what extent these results reflect the influence of exceptional cases

19. *The Economist*, 17th August, 1977 describes this lavish level of subsidisation as being 'on the generous side', which merits inclusion in the *Guinness Book of Records* for understatement

20. Given the large share of public enterprises in Scottish manufacturing, special policies might be devised to encourage entrepreneurial activity in these firms also. It is doubtful, however, if the reservoir of entrepreneurial talent in the public sector is any greater than in the private sector which makes suggestions to the effect that state enterprise should fill the gap left by private enterprise ring rather hollow

21. Although this view was firmly expressed by a number of contributors to *Scotland 1980*, op. cit., the book itself contains no chapter on planning

22. These inconsistencies are detailed in Denton, Ash and O'Cleireacain, *Trade effects of public subsidiaries to private enterprise*, London (1975)

23. Ireland may be cited as a case in point: the Fianna Fail Government stayed in power from

1958–73 and its successor, the National Coalition Government (1973–77) adhered closely to Fianna Fail industrial policy. This was a most important ingredient in the success of Ireland's strategy
24. Wright, *The Spanish economy 1959–1976*, London (1976)

6 *Money*
1. Tait 'Financial institutions and monetary policy' in MacKay ed. *Scotland 1980*, Edinburgh (1977), pp. 120–2
2. *Scotland 1980*, op. cit., p. 138
3. In fact the non-intervention aspect is far from idle doing nothing — it involves (a) making a conscious policy decision and (b) finely constructing the environment to achieve broad policy aims even if the agents for implementing that policy are the people themselves. In this respect fiscal non-interventionism is of the same category as the monetary non-interventionism we describe later and advocate in this paper
4. *Scotland 1980*, op. cit., p. 14
5. Imports and exports account for 50% of Holland's G.N.P. and most of this is within the EEC. The international recession of 1976–77 combined with a highly valued currency (because of gas export induced current account surpluses) has not surprisingly resulted in a low level of domestic industrial activity. Unemployment is historically high, but interest rates low and inflation moderate and falling. Levels of domestic industrial investment would have been even lower if it was not for a marked investment in labour-saving machinery. While accentuating the present unemployment levels, this should place Dutch industry in a competitive position for the future and the unemployment levels can be considered partly a symptom of this structural adjustment (cf. Abecor Country Report, *Netherlands*, 1st August, 1977)
6. *Financial Times*, 6th January, 1978
7. Brittan, *The Price of economic freedom*, London (1970)
8. Preamble to Bank of Canada Act 1934
9. Bank of Canada, Annual Report 1959, pp. 7–8
10. Compare the useful study of the close relationship between the Irish and UK interest rates in Gibson and Spencer eds. *Economic activity in Ireland*, Chapter 7, s. 4 : 1, Dublin (1977). In this a consistent interest rate advantage to Ireland is evident. This represents the premium required by Irish borrowers to overcome the 'sovereign risk' for lenders in the London Money market
11. See Milton Friedman, *The optimum quantity of money*, New York and London (1969)
12. Bank of Canada, Annual report 1961, pp. 3–5; Bank of Canada, Evidence of the Governor of the Bank of Canada before the Royal Commission on Banking and Finance, pp. 131–2
13. *Scotland 1980*, op. cit.
14. Currently (January 1978), there is pressure to relax or even eliminate UK exchange controls. Probably they are counter-productive and are a deterrent, especially to small businesses, to get involved in exports. There is a question as to what England's external position would be after Scotland is detached. Perhaps it will reimpose exchange controls although, with Chile's example, their use as a protectionist buffer for more than the short term would probably just aggravate the distortions by preventing the necessary fundamental adjustments in the country's economic structure
15. We are not anticipating a shortage of capital because the remit of this paper is confined to a surplus situation. It is however possible, if remote, that a major drop in the oil price (or even a grossly consumption-oriented economic policy) would result in Scotland being deficient in investment capital, in which case external resources of such capital could be critical
16. *Scotland 1980*, op. cit., p. 126
17. 'Money and economic development', The Horowitz Lectures, 1972, in Friedmann, *Special study in international economics and development*, New York (1973)
18. Bank of Canada Act 1966
19. Except certificates of deposit